# Contents

i

# Contents

Name _____

# Strategy Workshop

As you listen to the story "The Pumpkin Box," by Angela Johnson, you will stop from time to time to do some activities on these practice pages. These activities will help you think about different strategies that can help you read better. After completing each activity, you will discuss what you've written with your classmates and talk about how to use these strategies.

Remember, strategies can help you become a better reader. Good readers

- use strategies whenever they read

- use different strategies before, during, and after reading

- think about how strategies will help them

Name _____

**Strategy 1: Predict/Infer**

Use this strategy before and during reading to help make predictions about what happens next or what you're going to learn.

Here's how to use the Predict/Infer Strategy:

1. Think about the title, the illustrations, and what you have read so far.
2. Tell what you think will happen next—or what you will learn. Thinking about what you already know on the topic may help.
3. Try to figure out things the author does not say directly.

Listen as your teacher begins "The Pumpkin Box." When your teacher stops, complete the activity to show that you understand how to predict what the pumpkin box is.

Think about the story and respond to the question below.

What do you think the pumpkin box is?

_____

_____

_____

_____

As you continue listening to the story, think about whether your prediction was right. You might want to change your prediction or write a new one below.

_____

_____

_____

_____

_____

Name _____

**Strategy 2: Phonics/Decoding**

Use this strategy during reading when you come across a word you don't know.

Here's how to use the Phonics/Decoding Strategy:

1. Look carefully at the word.
2. Look for word parts you know and think about the sounds for the letters.
3. Blend the sounds to read the words.
4. Ask yourself: is this a word I know? Does it make sense in what I am reading?
5. If not, ask yourself: what else can I try? Should I look in a dictionary?

Listen as your teacher continues the story. When your teacher stops, use the Phonics/Decoding Strategy.

Now write down the steps you used to decode the word *munching*.

_____

_____

_____

_____

_____

_____

_____

_____

_____

_____

Remember to use this strategy whenever you are reading and come across a word that you don't know.

Name _____

**Strategy 3: Monitor/Clarify**

Use this strategy during reading whenever you're confused about what you are reading.

Here's how to use the Monitor/Clarify Strategy:
- Ask yourself if what you're reading makes sense—or if you are learning what you need to learn.
- If you don't understand something, reread, use the illustrations, or read ahead to see if that helps.

Listen as your teacher continues the story. When your teacher stops, complete the activity to show that you understand how to figure out how the pumpkin box got underground.

Think about the pumpkin box and respond below.

1. Describe the pumpkin box.

   _____

   _____

   _____

2. Can you tell from listening to the story how the pumpkin box got there? Why or why not?

   _____

   _____

   _____

3. How can you find out why the pumpkin box was buried in the ground?

   _____

   _____

   _____

   _____

Name _____

**Strategy 4: Question**

Use this strategy during and after reading to ask questions about important ideas in the story.

Here's how to use the Question Strategy:

- Ask yourself questions about important ideas in the story.
- Ask yourself if you can answer these questions.
- If you can't answer the questions, reread and look for answers in the text. Thinking about what you already know and what you've read in the story may help you.

Listen as your teacher continues the story. Then complete the activity to show that you understand how to ask yourself questions about important ideas in the story.

Think about the story and respond below.

Write a question you might ask yourself at this point in the story.

_____

_____

_____

_____

_____

_____

_____

_____

_____

If you can't answer your question now, think about it while you listen to the rest of the story.

Name _____

**Strategy 5: Evaluate**

Use this strategy during and after reading to help you form an opinion about what you read.

Here's how to use the Evaluate Strategy:

- Tell whether or not you think this story is entertaining and why.
- Is the writing clear and easy to understand?
- This is a realistic fiction story. Did the author make the characters believable and interesting?

Listen as your teacher continues the story. When your teacher stops, complete the activity to show that you are thinking of how you feel about what you are reading and why you feel that way.

Think about the story and respond below.

1. Tell whether or not you think this story is entertaining and why.

_____

_____

_____

_____

2. Is the writing clear and easy to understand?

_____

_____

_____

_____

3. This is a realistic fiction story. Did the author make the characters interesting and believable?

_____

_____

_____

_____

Name _____

**Strategy 6: Summarize**

Use this strategy after reading to summarize what you read.

Here's how to use the Summarize Strategy:

- Think about the characters.
- Think about where the story takes place.
- Think about the problem in the story and how the characters solve it.
- Think about what happens in the beginning, middle, and end of the story.

Think about the story you just listened to. Complete the activity to show that you understand how to identify important story parts that will help you summarize the story.

Think about the story and respond to the questions below:

1. Who is the main character?

_____

_____

_____

2. Where does the story take place?

_____

_____

_____

3. What is the problem and how is it resolved?

_____

_____

_____

Now use this information to summarize the story for a partner.

Name _____

# Nature's Fury

**After reading each selection, complete the chart below and on the next page to show what you discovered.** Sample answers shown.

|   | **What is the setting or settings for the action or descriptions in the selection?** | **What dangers do people face in the selection?** |
|---|---|---|
| **Earthquake Terror** | Magpie Island, in California **(2.5 Points)** | Jonathan and Abby are stranded on Magpie Island when an earthquake strikes, toppling trees all around them. **(2.5)** |
| **Eye of the Storm** | Tucson, Arizona and Tornado Alley (Amarillo, Texas and towns in Texas, Oklahoma and Kansas) **(2.5)** | Warren Faidley faces danger from lightning bolts and spiders while photographing from an underpass. He and Tom Willett face danger from tornadoes forming around them in Tornado Alley. **(2.5)** |
| **Volcanoes** | Hawaii, Washington state, Iceland, Guatemala, California, Oregon **(2.5)** | People face danger from the eruption of Mount St. Helens; people on the island of Heimaey, Iceland, face danger from a volcano; people in Hawaii face danger to their houses from quick-moving lava. **(2.5)** |

Assessment Tip: Total **10** Points per selection

Name _____

# Nature's Fury

**After reading each selection, complete the chart to show what you discovered.** Sample answers shown.

| | What warnings or events happen before nature's fury occurs in the selection? | What did you learn about an example of nature's fury in the selection? |
|---|---|---|
| **Earthquake Terror** | Moose, the dog, is nervous, barking and shaking. The air is still and there is a deep rumbling sound. **(2.5)** | Most earthquakes occur along the shores of the Pacific Ocean, many of them on the San Andreas fault. **(2.5)** |
| **Eye of the Storm** | Cool, moist air meets hot desert air to cause thunderstorms in Arizona. Cool, dry air collides with warm, moist air to cause tornadoes. **(2.5)** | Tornadoes form from funnel clouds. When a funnel cloud touches the ground, it becomes a tornado. **(2.5)** |
| **Volcanoes** | Before volcanoes erupt, magma pushes up through cracks in the earth's crust. Before Mount St. Helens erupted, there were thousands of small earthquakes. **(2.5)** | There are different kinds of volcanoes: shield, strato-volcanoes, cinder cone, and dome volcanoes. **(2.5)** |

What advice would you give others about the different kinds of nature's fury featured in this theme?

Student answers should reflect an understanding of the dangers and

settings of the different kinds of nature's fury in the theme. **(2)**

Assessment Tip: Total **10** Points per selection and **2** points for the final question

Name _____

# A Scientist's Report

**Use the words in the box to complete the scientist's report on the Magpie Island earthquake.**

### Vocabulary

shuddered
debris
undulating
fault
jolt

## Earthquake Report

Magpie Island lies near the San Andreas
<u>fault</u> **(2 points)**_____, so it was susceptible to
the recent earthquake. On a cloudless day, witnesses
reported hearing a sound like thunder and feeling a
<u>jolt</u> **(2)**_____ as the earth started to
shake. Next, the ground below their feet
<u>shuddered</u> **(2)**_____ and heaved. Trees began
to fall with a forceful impact. As the earthquake reached
its peak, the ground began <u>undulating</u> **(2)**_____
in a continuous motion.

After the shaking stopped, people examined the
devastation that the earthquake had caused.
<u>Debris</u> **(2)**_____ lay everywhere. The
upheaval had struck a great blow to the island.

Name _____

# Event Map

**Record in this Event Map the main story events in the order in which they occurred.**

**Page 30**

At first Moose listens.  Then he barks and paces back and forth as if he senses that something is wrong. **(2 points)**

**Pages 30–31**

After Jonathan puts the leash on Moose, they all slowly start to walk back to the camper. **(2)**

**Pages 32–33**

Jonathan and Abby hear a strange noise.  At first Jonathan thinks it is thunder or hunters.  Then suddenly he realizes they are _____ caught in an earthquake. **(2)**

**Page 35**

Abby screams and falls.  As Jonathan lunges forward, he tries to catch Abby.  Then he shouts, "Stay where you are, I'm coming." **(2)**

**Pages 36–37**

Jonathan sees the huge redwood tree sway back and forth.  Then he scrambles away from it as it falls. **(2)**

Assessment Tip: Total **10** Points

Name _____

# True or False?

**Read each sentence. Write T if the sentence is true, or F if the sentence is false. If a sentence is false, correct it to make it true.**

1. <u>F</u> Jonathan and Abby's parents had left the island to go grocery shopping. **(1 point)**

   Their parents had gone to get treatment for their mother's broken ankle.

2. <u>T</u> Moose became restless because he could feel the earthquake coming.

   **(1)** _____

3. <u>T</u> Jonathan thought the first rumblings of the earthquake were distant thunder.

   He had practiced earthquake drills in school. **(1)**

4. <u>F</u> Jonathan knew what to do because he had been in an earthquake before.

   He had practiced earthquake drills in school. **(1)**

5. <u>F</u> When the giant redwood began to fall, Moose dragged Jonathan to safety.

   When the giant redwood began to fall, Jonathan crawled out of the way. **(1)**

6. <u>F</u> Jonathan and Abby found shelter in a large ditch.

   Jonathan and Abby found shelter under the fallen redwood. **(1)**

7. <u>F</u> In a panic, Moose ran off and didn't come back.

   Jonathan held Moose under the tree with him and Abby. **(1)**

8. <u>T</u> As quickly as it had begun, the earthquake stopped and the woods were silent.

   **(1)** _____

Theme 1: **Nature's Fury**    5
**Assessment Tip: Total 8 Points**

Name _____

# Mapping the Sequence

**Read this passage. Then complete the activity on page 7.**

### Rapids Ahead!

Alison scanned the river nervously. She had already endured two sets of violent rapids. Each time, she had grasped the ropes of the raft so hard that her knuckles turned white. Luckily, the guide on her raft was strong and skilled. "Relax, Alison," Anushka had smiled when the trip had begun three hours earlier. "Rafting is a blast, once you get the hang of it."

During the first hour on the river, Anushka had taught Alison how to paddle on one side to make the raft go in the opposite direction. She had instructed Alison on what to do if the raft flipped or if she were tossed out. "Don't fight the current," Anushka had said. "Let it carry you downstream as you swim for the shore."

Six months earlier, when Alison's parents had proposed a whitewater rafting trip down the Snake River, Alison said "No way." Her brother Zack was thrilled, though, so Alison's parents signed all four of them up for a seven-day run. So far, the trip was as bad as Alison had expected.

"Rapids ahead. Hold on!" Anushka said. Alison's stomach knotted as the raft pitched forward with the current. "Paddle left!" Anushka shouted. As Alison's paddle hit the water, the bow of the raft hit a boulder and shot into the air. Alison shut her eyes as icy water drenched her.

When she opened her eyes, Anushka was gone. In a panic, Alison scanned the rapids. "Anushka!" she screamed. Then she saw her. Anushka was making her way to shore, feet first, letting the current do the work. "It's up to me now," Alison said to herself. She paddled left, then right, steering between the rocks. She was amazed that she could control it. Left. Right. Left again. Now Anushka was on the bank, shouting directions over the roar of the river. Alison managed to nose the raft into an eddy and a moment later, onto the shore.

"Great job, Alison!" Anushka grinned. "You really kept you head out there!" Alison beamed. Maybe this trip would be all right after all.

6   Theme 1: **Nature's Fury**

Name _____

# Mapping the Sequence continued

**Write each story event from page 6 in the sequence map below. Put the events in order.**

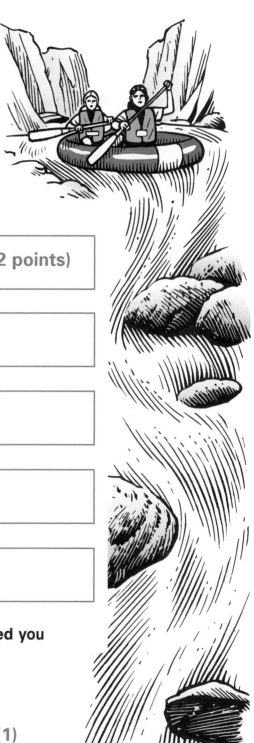

► Alison successfully guides the raft to shore.
► Anushka tells Alison to relax.
► The raft hits a boulder and Anushka falls overboard.
► Anushka teaches Alison how to steer the raft.
► Alison's parents suggest a raft trip on the Snake River.

| |
|---|
| Alison's parents suggest a raft trip on the Snake River. **(2 points)** |

| |
|---|
| Anushka tells Alison to relax. **(2)** |

| |
|---|
| Anushka teaches Alison how to steer the raft. **(2)** |

| |
|---|
| The raft hits a boulder and Anushka falls overboard. **(2)** |

| |
|---|
| Alison successfully guides the raft to shore. **(2)** |

**Now go back to the passage. Circle the words that helped you understand the following:**

► when the family plans the trip **(1 point)**
► when Anushka tells Alison that rafting is fun **(1)**
► when Anushka teaches Alison some basic rafting techniques **(1)**
► whether Anushka's spill occurs during the first, second, or third set of rapids that she and Alison encounter **(1)**

Name _____

# Getting to Base

**Read the sentences. For each underlined word, identify the base word. Write the base word and the ending.**

**Example:** shake + -ing

1. Magpie Island was a popular place for <u>hiking</u>. <u>hike + -ing **(1 point)**</u>

2. Jonathan was nervous about staying in such an <u>isolated</u> place.
<u>isolate + -ed **(1)**</u>

3. He thought it would be <u>safer</u> to go back to their trailer.
<u>safe + -er **(1)**</u>

4. Jonathan and Abby followed the trail past blackberry <u>bushes</u>.
<u>bush + -es **(1)**</u>

5. Neither of them had the <u>slightest</u> idea how the day would end.
<u>slight + -est **(1)**</u>

6. Moose cocked his head and began <u>sniffing</u>. the ground.
<u>sniff + -ing **(1)**</u>

7. At first the earthquake was a <u>thunderous</u> noise in the distance.
<u>thunder + -ous **(1)**</u>

8. Trees <u>swayed</u> all around Jonathan and Abby.
<u>sway + -ed **(1)**</u>

9. The ground began rising and falling like ocean <u>waves</u>.
<u>wave + -s **(1)**</u>

10. Abby <u>cried</u> for Jonathan to come help her. <u>cry + -ed **(1)**</u>

Assessment Tip: Total **10** Points

Name _____

# Short Vowels

Remember that a short vowel sound is usually spelled by one vowel and followed by a consonant sound. This is the **short vowel pattern.** These vowels usually spell short vowel sounds:

/ă/ *a*     /ĕ/ *e*     /ĭ/ *i*     /ŏ/ *o*     /ŭ/ *u*

► The short vowel sounds in the starred words do not have the usual short vowel spelling patterns. The /ĕ/ sound is spelled *ea* in *breath* and *deaf*. The /ŭ/ sound is spelled *ou* in *tough* and *rough*.

**Write each Spelling Word under its vowel sound.**
Order of answers for each category may vary.

**/ă/ Sound**
staff **(1 point)**
grasp **(1)**

**/ĕ/ Sound**
slept **(1)**
breath **(1)**
dwell **(1)**
swept **(1)**
deaf **(1)**

**/ĭ/ Sound**
mist **(1)**
ditch **(1)**
swift **(1)**
split **(1)**

**/ŏ/ Sound**
dock **(1)**
fond **(1)**

**/ŭ/ Sound**
bunk **(1)**
bunch **(1)**
stuck **(1)**
tough **(1)**
crush **(1)**
fund **(1)**
rough **(1)**

**Spelling Words**

1. bunk
2. staff
3. dock
4. slept
5. mist
6. bunch
7. swift
8. stuck
9. breath*
10. tough*
11. fond
12. crush
13. grasp
14. dwell
15. fund
16. ditch
17. split
18. swept
19. deaf*
20. rough*

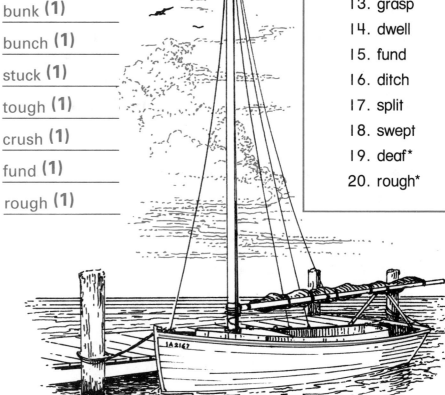

Theme 1: **Nature's Fury**   9
Assessment Tip: Total **20** Points

Name _____

# Spelling Spree

**Letter Math** **Add and subtract letters from the words below to make Spelling Words. Write the new words.**

1. b + dunk – d = _bunk_ **(1 point)**
2. sl + kept – k = _slept_ **(1)**
3. f + pond – p = _fond_ **(1)**
4. burn – r + ch = _bunch_ **(1)**
5. st + duck – d = _stuck_ **(1)**
6. dw + shell – sh = _dwell_ **(1)**
7. cr + mush – m = _crush_ **(1)**
8. d + rock – r = _dock_ **(1)**
9. m + wrist – wr = _mist_ **(1)**
10. sw + lift – l = _swift_ **(1)**
11. spl + bit – b = _split_ **(1)**
12. t + cough – c = _tough_ **(1)**
13. d + leaf – l = _deaf_ **(1)**
14. gr + clasp – cl = _grasp_ **(1)**

**Spelling Words**

1. bunk
2. staff
3. dock
4. slept
5. mist
6. bunch
7. swift
8. stuck
9. breath*
10. tough*
11. fond
12. crush
13. grasp
14. dwell
15. fund
16. ditch
17. split
18. swept
19. deaf*
20. rough*

**Phrase Fillers** **Write the Spelling Word that best completes each phrase.**

15. to take a deep _breath_ **(1)**
16. as _rough_ **(1)** as sandpaper
17. to put money into a _fund_ **(1)**
18. to dig a _ditch_ **(1)**
19. _swept_ **(1)** with a broom
20. to join a company's _staff_ **(1)**

Assessment Tip: Total **20** Points

Name _____

# Proofreading and Writing

**Proofreading** Circle the five misspelled Spelling Words in this newspaper article. Then write each word correctly.

MAGPIE ISLAND — An earthquake struck yesterday, and children are reported to be stranded in the island campground. No one on the campground's staf was there at the time. An early report said that "a bunch of kids" were stouk on the island. However, it turns out that only two children are there. Rescuers in a boat are reported to be nearing the island's dok. A heavy missed has slowed the rescue effort. One rescuer said, "It's been touph going so far, but we'll get them off the island safely."

1. staff **(1 point)**

2. stuck **(1)**

3. dock **(1)**

4. mist **(1)**

5. tough **(1)**

## Spelling Words

1. bunk
2. staff
3. dock
4. slept
5. mist
6. bunch
7. swift
8. stuck
9. breath*
10. tough*
11. fond
12. crush
13. grasp
14. dwell
15. fund
16. ditch
17. split
18. swept
19. deaf*
20. rough*

**Write a Description** If you were to go to the scene of an earthquake right after it happened, what do you think you would find? What would you see? Whom would you meet?

**On a separate piece of paper, write a description of the scene you might encounter. Use Spelling Words from the list.** Responses will vary. **(5 points)**

Name _____

# Synonym Shakeup

**Read the definition of each thesaurus word and its synonyms.  Then rewrite the
numbered sentences using a different synonym for each underlined word.**

> **shake** *verb* To move to and fro with short, quick movements.
> *The branch shook as the eagle flew off.*
>
> > **quake** To shake or vibrate, as from shock or lack of balance.
> > *With all the students stamping their feet, the gym floor quaked.*
> >
> > **shiver** To shake or tremble without control. *She was shivering
> > when she came out of the swimming pool.*
> >
> > **quiver** To shake with a slight vibrating motion. *I felt the horse
> > quiver as I patted its leg.*
>
> **noise** *noun* A sound that is loud, unpleasant, or unexpected. *I was
> awakened by a noise in the alley.*
>
> > **crash** A loud noise, as of a sudden impact or collapse. *They heard a
> > crash of thunder.*
> >
> > **racket** A loud, unpleasant noise. *The students made a racket while
> > tuning their instruments.*
> >
> > **thud** A heavy, dull sound. *Jeff dropped his books with a thud.*

1. Soon after the ground began to <u>shake</u>, the children heard the <u>noise</u> of
   a deer leaping from the bushes.

   Soon after the ground began to quake, the children heard the crash of

   a deer leaping from the bushes. **(4 points)**

2. Jonathan began to <u>shake</u> from cold and fear, listening to the <u>noise</u> of
   the crows.

   Jonathan began to shiver from cold and fear, listening to the racket of

   the crows. **(4)**

3. Abby's lip began to <u>shake</u> as she heard the <u>noise</u> of running footsteps.

   Abby's lip began to quiver as she heard the thud of running footsteps. **(4)**

12    Theme 1: **Nature's Fury**
Assessment Tip: Total **12** Points

Name _____

# Sensing Danger

**Kinds of Sentences**  There are four kinds of sentences:

1. A declarative sentence tells something and ends with a period.
   Earthquakes occur along fault lines in the earth.

2. An interrogative sentence asks a question and ends with a question mark.
   Can earthquakes be predicted?

3. An imperative sentence gives a request or an order and usually ends with a period.
   Protect your head in an earthquake.

4. An exclamatory sentence expresses strong feeling and ends with an exclamation mark.
   How frightening an earthquake is!

**Add the correct punctuation mark to each sentence below.**
**Then write what kind of sentence each one is.**

1. Why is the dog barking? **(1 point)**
   interrogative sentence **(1)**

2. Put him on his leash. **(1)**
   imperative sentence **(1)**

3. Some animals can sense a coming earthquake. **(1)**
   declarative sentence **(1)**

4. How frightened I am! **(1)**
   exclamatory sentence **(1)**

5. The earth has stopped shaking at last. **(1)**
   declarative sentence **(1)**

Name _____

# On Vacation

**Subjects and Predicates**  Every sentence has a subject.  It tells whom or what the sentence is about.  The complete subject includes all the words in the subject, and the simple subject is the main word or words in the complete subject.

Every sentence has a predicate too.  It tells what the subject is or does. The complete predicate includes all the words in the predicate, and the simple predicate is the main word or words in the complete predicate.

**Draw a slash mark (/) between the complete subject and the complete predicate in the sentences below.  Then circle the simple subject and underline the simple predicate. (3 points each sentence)**

1. The whole (family) / travels in our new camper.

2. (Everybody) / helps to pitch the tent under a tree.

3. (They) / will use a compass on their hike.

4. A good (fire) / is difficult to build.

5. The (smell) of cooking / is delicious to the hungry campers.

Assessment Tip: Total **15** Points

Name _____

# Sentence Combining

A **compound subject** is made up of two or more simple subjects that have the same predicate. Use a connecting word such as *and* or *or* to join the simple subjects.

**Jonathan** yelled. **Abby** yelled.   **Jonathan and Abby** yelled.

Combine two simple subjects into one compound subject, as shown above, to make your writing clearer and less choppy.

A **compound predicate** is made up of two or more simple predicates that have the same subject. Use a connecting word such as *and* or *or* to join the simple predicates.

Moose **barked**. Moose **howled**.   Moose **barked and howled**.

Combine simple predicates into compound predicates, as shown above, to make your writing smoother.

**Jonathan has written a draft of a letter to his aunt about his vacation. Revise his letter by combining sentences. Each new sentence will have either a compound subject or a compound predicate. Only Jonathan's first sentence will remain the same.**

*What an exciting vacation we had! Mom broke her ankle. Mom had to go to the hospital. Abby stayed on the island. I stayed on the island during an earthquake. Moose barked. Moose warned us. The ground shook. The ground rolled. Have you ever been in an earthquake? Has Uncle Adam ever been in an earthquake?*

What an exciting vacation we had!  Mom broke her ankle and had

to go to the hospital.  Abby and I stayed on the island during an

earthquake.  Moose barked and warned us. The ground shook and

rolled.  Have you or Uncle Adam ever been in an

earthquake?  (**2 points** for each combined sentence)

Name _____

# Writing a News Article

Jonathan and Abby Palmer experience firsthand an unforgettable event — the terror of an earthquake. Imagine you are a reporter for the *Daily Gazette*. Use the chart below to gather details for a news article about an interesting or unusual event at your school, in your neighborhood, or in your town. Answer these questions: What happened? Who was involved? When, where, and why did this event occur? How did it happen?

| Who? (2 points) |
| --- |
| What? (2) |
| When? (2) |
| Where? (2) |
| Why? (2) |
| How? (2) |

Now use the details you gathered to write your news article on a separate sheet of paper. Include a headline and a beginning that will capture your reader's attention. Present facts in order of importance, from most to least important. Try to use quotations from eyewitnesses to bring this news event to life. (3)

Assessment Tip: Total **15** Points

Name _____

# Adding Details

**A good reporter uses details to hold the reader's interest, to clearly explain what happened, and to bring an event to life. Read the following news article by a cub reporter with little experience. Then rewrite it on the lines below, adding details from the list to improve the article.**

(**1 point** per detail)

**Details**

twelve-year-old

in the woods

giant redwood

one-hundred-year-old

for several weeks

under a fallen redwood

afternoon

to the mainland

on Magpie Island

his six-year-old sister

---

**Quake Rocks Campground**

A powerful earthquake rocked an isolated campground in California yesterday. No serious injuries were reported. Some trees were uprooted, and a bridge was destroyed. Two members of the Palmer family, Jonathan and his sister Abby, were trapped during the quake.

"I was very scared," said Jonathan Palmer. "I'm just glad no one got hurt. My sister only had a minor cut."

The campground will be closed to visitors until the debris is cleared and the bridge is repaired.

---

A powerful earthquake rocked an isolated campground **on Magpie Island** in California yesterday **afternoon**. No serious injuries were reported. Some **one-hundred-year-old giant redwood** trees were uprooted, and a bridge **to the mainland** was destroyed. Two members of the Palmer family, **twelve-year-old** Jonathan and his **six-year-old** sister Abby, were trapped **in the woods under a fallen redwood** during the quake.

"I was very scared," said Jonathan Palmer. "I'm just glad no one got hurt. My sister only had a minor cut."

The campground will be closed to visitors **for several weeks** until the debris is cleared and the bridge is repaired.

Name _____

# Evaluating Your Description

**Reread your description.  What do you need to make it better?   Use this page to help you decide.  Put a checkmark in the box for each sentence that describes what you have written.**

### Rings the Bell!

☐ My description is well organized and easy to follow.

☐ All the details are important and in order.

☐ My description has a lively style.

☐ My description has a strong ending.

☐ There are almost no mistakes.

### Getting Stronger

☐ My description could be easier to follow.

☐ Some details are not important to the description.

☐ My word choices could be more lively.

☐ The ending doesn't make the description feel finished.

☐ There are a few mistakes.

### Try Harder

☐ My description is not easy to follow.

☐ Many details are not important.

☐ My word choices are not interesting.

☐ There are a lot of mistakes.

Name _____

# Writing Complete Sentences

**Make each incomplete sentence complete. Change words or add extra words if you need to.** Answers will vary. Sample answers given.

1. Being a photographer

   Being a photographer can be exiting. **(1 point)**

2. Photographing nature

   Photographing nature can be dangerous. **(1)**

3. Lightning flashing in the sky

   You can take pictures of lightning flashing in the sky. **(1)**

4. Chasing storms

   You could travel the world while chasing storms. **(1)**

5. Tornadoes in the distance

   You could take pictures of tornadoes in the distance. **(1)**

6. The black funnel is impressive, even far away.

   Complete. **(1)**

7. Planes in storms

   Planes can get tossed about in storms. **(1)**

8. A bumpy ride

   Turbulence can create a bumpy ride for passengers. **(1)**

9. Dangerous to be out in some storms.

   It's dangerous to be out in some storms. **(1)**

10. Don't stand under a tree when there's lightning.

    Complete. **(1)**

Name _____

# Spelling Words

**Words Often Misspelled** Look for familiar spelling patterns to help you remember how to spell the Spelling Words on this page. Think carefully about the parts that you find hard to spell in each word.

**Write the missing letters in the Spelling Words below.**

1. en o___ u___ g___ h___ **(1 point)**

2. c a___ u___ g___ h___ t **(1)**

3. br o___ u___ g___ h___ t **(1)**

4. th o___ u___ g___ h___ t **(1)**

5. ev e___ ry **(1)**

6. nin e___ ty **(1)**

7. th e___ i___ r **(1)**

8. th e___ y___ '___ re **(1)**

9. th e___ r e___ **(1)**

10. th e___ r___ e___ '___ s **(1)**

11. k___ n___ ow **(1)**

12. k___ n___ ew **(1)**

13. o___ '___ c___ lock **(1)**

14. w e___ '___ r___ e **(1)**

15. p e___ o___ ple **(1)**

**Study List** **On a separate piece of paper, write each Spelling Word. Check your spelling against the words on the list.**

Order of words may vary.

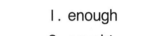

**Spelling Words**

1. enough
2. caught
3. brought
4. thought
5. every
6. ninety
7. their
8. they're
9. there
10. there's
11. know
12. knew
13. o'clock
14. we're
15. people

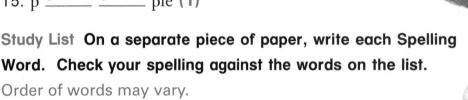

Name _____

# Spelling Spree

**Word Clues** Write the Spelling Word that best fits each clue.

1. the sum of eighty-nine and one
2. a contraction for describing what other people are doing
3. to be aware of a fact
4. a time-telling word
5. as much as is needed
6. a word for other people's belongings
7. took along
8. a contraction for "there is"

1. ninety **(1 point)**
2. they're **(1)**
3. know **(1)**
4. o'clock **(1)**

5. enough **(1)**
6. their **(1)**
7. brought **(1)**
8. there's **(1)**

**Word Addition** Write a Spelling Word by adding the beginning of the first word to the end of the second word.

9. caution + fight
10. we'll + more
11. knight + flew
12. peony + steeple
13. even + wary
14. them + cure
15. think + bought

9. caught **(1)**
10. we're **(1)**
11. knew **(1)**
12. people **(1)**
13. every **(1)**
14. there **(1)**
15. thought **(1)**

Name _____

# Proofreading and Writing

**Proofreading** Circle the five misspelled Spelling Words in this announcement. Then write each word correctly.

The staff of the Science Museum is pleased to announce that our new Natural Disasters Hall will open to the public next Monday at nine (oclock) in the morning. We've put a lot of (thaught) into this exhibit, and we're sure that you'll enjoy it. Just about (evry) form of nature's fury is represented, from lightning to earthquakes to volcanoes. Even if you already (kno) a lot about the topic, we think you'll learn something new. We hope to see you (their.)

1. enough
2. caught
3. brought
4. thought
5. every
6. ninety
7. their
8. they're
9. there
10. there's
11. know
12. knew
13. o'clock
14. we're
15. people

1. o'clock **(1 point)**
2. thought **(1)**
3. every **(1)**
4. know **(1)**
5. there **(1)**

✏️ **Write Song Titles** Pick five Spelling Words from the list. Then, for each one, make up a song title that includes the word and mentions some form of **Nature's Fury.** Responses will vary. **(5 points)**

Assessment Tip: Total **10** Points

Name _____

# Stormy Weather

**Use words from the box to complete the diary entry below.**

May 10, 2000

Dear Diary,

Today was by far the scariest day of my trip. Everything was fine as I crossed the border into Oklahoma. The highway stretched out over a ___prairie **(1 point)**___ that seemed to go on forever. As I looked into my rear-view mirror, I spotted some dense clouds forming behind me. "I hope they aren't ___funnel clouds **(1)**___," I thought. Then I spotted a flash of ___lightning **(1)**___. The clouds started to ___rotate **(1)**___, slowly at first, and then faster and faster. A couple of ___tornadoes **(1)**___ were forming right before my eyes! I realized that a ___severe **(1)**___ storm had formed behind me, and it was moving fast in my direction. The ___jagged **(1)**___ bolts of lightning were getting closer. One of the tornadoes lifted a tractor into the air, spun it around, and dropped it. I watched it ___collide **(1)**___ with a shed on the ground. Lightning struck a dry bush behind me. It turned into a ___sizzling **(1)**___ ball of flames.

## Vocabulary

- sizzling
- collide
- funnel clouds
- tornadoes
- lightning
- rotate
- jagged
- prairie
- severe

**Write a sentence to end the diary entry.**

Answers will vary. **(1)**

_____

Name _____

# Selection Map

**Fill in this selection map.**

## Pages 59–68

Page 59   Storm Chasing   how Warren chases a lightning storm

Page 60   Warren Faidley: Storm Chaser   how Warren was
interested in storms since he was a child

Page 64   What Happens to Warren's Photos After He Takes Them?
how Warren created a stock photo agency, where
people can go and buy his photos **(1)**

Page 65   Storm Seasons and Chasing   how tornadoes form and how storm
chasers follow weather patterns that form tornadoes **(1)**.

Page 67   Chasing Tornadoes   how Warren knows where to go to get the best
pictures of tornadoes **(1)**

## Pages 69–75

One Day in the Life of a Storm Chaser

Morning   Check the weather, get Shadow Chaser
ready for the day, test the equipment, pack supplies **(2)**

Afternoon   Get an update on the weather conditions, change the
oil in Shadow Chaser, check maps **(2)**

Evening   Look at the map, call the National Weather Service,
head north following the storm,  follow the tornadoes from
Texas into Oklahoma, shoot the photos **(2)**.

Assessment Tip: Total **15** Points

Name _____

# An Interview with Warren Faidley

The questions below can be used to interview Warren Faidley about his life and work. Write the answer Warren might give to each question.

**What is your occupation?**

I chase tornadoes, hurricanes, and lightning storms and try to photograph them. I sell my pictures through my stock photo agency. **(2 points)**

**When did you first become interested in storms? Describe one of your early experiences with storms.** I've been interested in storms since I was a boy. One time I rode my bike into the middle of a dust whirlwind. **(2)**

**What led you to become a professional storm chaser?** I was working for a newspaper. I had a hobby, which was taking photos of lightning from my balcony. During one particular storm, I chased a dark thundercloud and managed to get an astonishing picture of a lightning bolt hitting a pole. I realized I could sell photos of storms, so I started a stock photo agency. **(2)**

**How important is it for someone in your line of work to have a good knowledge of weather patterns? Why?** It's very important, because weather patterns cause storms, and the same patterns occur in the same places every year. Knowing about storm patterns tells a storm chaser where to go, and when. **(2 )**

**What advice would you give a young person who wants to become a storm chaser?** Possible response: Be patient. Be careful. **(2)**

Name _____

# Text Tracking

**Read the article below.  Then complete the activity on page 27.**

## Hurricane Basics

A hurricane is a powerful storm with swirling winds. Hurricanes form over water in tropical parts of the North Atlantic and North Pacific Oceans.  Most hurricanes in these regions occur between June and November.

### Rise of a Hurricane

A hurricane does not form all at once.  First, areas of low pressure develop in ocean winds.  These areas, called easterly waves, then grow into a tropical depression, where winds blow at up to 31 miles per hour.  As the winds pick up speed, they become a tropical storm.  Finally, when the winds reach 74 miles per hour or more, and the storm is 200 to 300 miles wide, it is considered a hurricane.

### Path of Destruction

The great speed of a hurricane's winds can cause severe damage. A hurricane can destroy buildings and other property when it reaches land.  The force of these winds can also create huge waves.  The waves along with the heavy rains may cause flooding in rivers and low-lying coastal lands.  Many hurricane deaths are the result of flooding. Because of the devastating power of hurricanes, meteorologists keep a close watch on the Pacific and Atlantic Oceans during hurricane season.

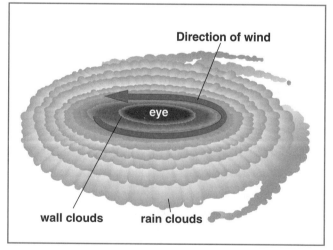

The winds of a hurricane rotate around the eye, which is an area of calm in the storm's center. Wall clouds surround the eye.

Name _____

# Text Tracking continued

**Write words from the box to indicate the order in which these parts
appear in the article on page 26. Then answer the questions.**

> caption    graphic aid    headings    introduction

1. introduction **(1 point)**

2. headings **(1)**

3. graphic aid **(1)**

4. caption **(1)**

5. What is each paragraph about?

    Paragraph 1: what hurricanes are; where and when they form **(2)**

    Paragraph 2: how hurricanes form **(2)**

    Paragraph 3: the damage hurricanes can cause **(2)**

6. Is the information in paragraph 2 organized by main idea and details, or by
   sequence of events? by sequence of events **(2)**

7. How is the information in paragraph 3 organized? by main idea
   and details **(2)**

Name _____

# Stormy Syllables

**Write the underlined word using slash marks (/) between its syllables.**
**Then write a new sentence that uses the underlined word.** Sample answers shown.

1. The photographer changed her position to get a better shot of the storm.
   po/si/tion **(1 point)** I moved the chair to a new position. **(2)**

2. A good photographer tries to capture the excitement of the moment.
   cap/ture **(1)** I tried to capture a butterfly in my net. **(2)**

3. Warren showed exciting videos of tornadoes. vi/de/os **(1)**
   We watched three videos over the weekend. **(2)**

4. I wonder how she was able to get so close to the lightning bolt.
   won/der **(1)** I wonder where we will go on our vacation. **(2)**

5. By rotating his body, he could follow the circular path of the tornado.
   ro/tat/ing **(1)** The moon is rotating around Earth. **(2)**

Assessment Tip: Total **15** Points

Name _____

# The /ā/, /ē/, and /ī/ Sounds

When you hear the /ā/ sound, think of the patterns
*a*-consonant-*e*, *ai*, and *ay*. When you hear the /ē/ sound, think of
the patterns *ea* and *ee*. When you hear the /ī/ sound, think of the
patterns i-consonant-*e*, *igh*, and *i*.

| | | | |
|---|---|---|---|
| /ā/ | **fade** | **claim** | **stray** |
| /ē/ | **leaf** | **speech** | |
| /ī/ | **strike** | **thigh** | **sign** |

► The long vowel sounds in the starred words have different
spelling patterns. The /ē/ sound in *thief* and in *niece* is spelled *ie*.
The /ī/ sound in *height* is spelled *eigh*.

**Write each Spelling Word under its vowel sound.**
Order of answers for each category may vary.

| /ā/ | /ē/ | /ī/ |
|---|---|---|
| claim **(1 point)** | speech **(1)** | strike **(1)** |
| stray **(1)** | leaf **(1)** | sign **(1)** |
| fade **(1)** | thief **(1)** | thigh **(1)** |
| waist **(1)** | beast **(1)** | height **(1)** |
| sway **(1)** | fleet **(1)** | mild **(1)** |
| stain **(1)** | niece **(1)** | stride **(1)** |
| praise **(1)** | | slight **(1)** |

### Spelling Words

1. speech
2. claim
3. strike
4. stray
5. fade
6. sign
7. leaf
8. thigh
9. thief*
10. height*
11. mild
12. waist
13. sway
14. beast
15. stain
16. fleet
17. stride
18. praise
19. slight
20. niece*

Raugust Library
6070 Jamestown College
Jamestown, ND 58405

Name _____

# Spelling Spree

**Find a Rhyme** For each sentence write a Spelling Word that rhymes with the underlined word and makes sense in the sentence.

1. On what <u>day</u> did you last see the <u>stray **(1 point)**</u> cat?

2. It looks like the <u>stain **(1)**</u> got washed out by the <u>rain</u>.

3. She liked to <u>stride **(1)**</u> down the beach at low <u>tide</u>.

4. They swam out to <u>meet</u> the <u>fleet **(1)**</u> of ships.

5. How <u>high</u> on the <u>thigh **(1)**</u> did the ball hit you?

6. His <u>niece **(1)**</u> asked for another <u>piece</u> of pie.

7. The police <u>chief</u> took credit for catching the <u>thief **(1)**</u>.

8. The young <u>child</u> liked <u>mild **(1)**</u> food better than spicy food.

**Crack the Code  Some Spelling Words have been written in the code below.  Use the code to figure out each word. Then write the word correctly. (1 point each)**

| **CODE:** | R | V | L | O | C | A | D | X | P | T | Y | Q | J | N | E | I | M |
|-----------|---|---|---|---|---|---|---|---|---|---|---|---|---|---|---|---|---|
| **LETTER:** | a | b | c | e | f | g | h | i | l | m | n | p | r | s | t | w | y |

9. LPRXT <u>claim</u>

10. IRXNE <u>waist</u>

11. VORNE <u>beast</u>

12. NQOOLD <u>speech</u>

13. NXAY <u>sign</u>

14. DOXADE <u>height</u>

15. NPXADE <u>slight</u>

16. NIRM <u>sway</u>

17. QJRXNO <u>praise</u>

18. PORC <u>leaf</u>

## Spelling Words

1. speech
2. claim
3. strike
4. stray
5. fade
6. sign
7. leaf
8. thigh
9. thief*
10. height*
11. mild
12. waist
13. sway
14. beast
15. stain
16. fleet
17. stride
18. praise
19. slight
20. niece*

Assessment Tip: Total **18** Points

Name _____

# Proofreading and Writing

**Proofreading** **Circle the five misspelled Spelling Words in this weather log entry. Then write each word correctly.**

May 20 — There was a report today of a lightning streik at the shopping mall outside town. The same storm passed over our house, with heavy winds. It made the trees sweigh so much that I was sure at least one would fall. The winds started to faide before that happened, though. On the news, the reporter said that the base of the storm clouds was actually at a hight of over 5,000 feet. The weather tomorrow is supposed to be mild, with a slite chance of rain.

1. strike **(1 point)**
2. sway **(1)**
3. fade **(1)**
4. height **(1)**
5. slight **(1)**

## Spelling Words

1. speech
2. claim
3. strike
4. stray
5. fade
6. sign
7. leaf
8. thigh
9. thief*
10. height*
11. mild
12. waist
13. sway
14. beast
15. stain
16. fleet
17. stride
18. praise
19. slight
20. niece*

✏️ **Write a Storm Warning** Storm chasers are able to provide firsthand, "you are there" reports of storms because they chase the storms.

**On a separate sheet of paper, write the script of a storm warning that a storm chaser might issue by radio. Use Spelling Words from the list.** Responses will vary. **(5 points)**

# Words in Their Places

Read each set of words, and decide which two could be the guide words and which one the entry word on a dictionary page. Then in the columns below, write the guide words under the correct heading, and the entry word beside them.

| trout | weather | prance | durable | chase |
| trust | wayward | practice | dust | charter |
| tropical | weave | prairie | dusky | chatterbox |

Name _____

| Guide Words | | Entry Word |
|---|---|---|
| tropical **(1)** | trust **(1)** | trout **(1)** |
| wayward **(1)** | weave **(1)** | weather **(1)** |
| practice **(1)** | prance **(1)** | prairie **(1)** |
| durable **(1)** | dust **(1)** | dusky **(1)** |
| charter **(1)** | chatterbox **(1)** | chase **(1)** |

Assessment Tip: Total **15** Points

Name _____

# It's a Twister!

**Conjunctions** The words *and*, *or*, and *but* are **conjunctions**. A conjunction may be used to join words in a sentence or to join sentences. Use *and* to add information. Use *or* to give a choice. Use *but* to show contrast.

■ Clouds **and** wind signal a coming storm.
  **This conjunction joins words.**
■ I saw lightning, **and** I heard thunder.
  **This conjunction joins sentences.**

**Write the conjunction *and*, *or*, or *but* to best complete each sentence. Then decide whether each conjunction you wrote joins words or joins sentences. Write W after a sentence in which words are joined. Write S after a sentence in which sentences are joined.**

1. Kansas __and__ Oklahoma have many tornadoes. _W_ **(2 points)**

2. Warren Faidley chases tornadoes __or/and__ thunderstorms. _W_ **(2)**

3. Warren has special equipment, __and__ he has a special vehicle to carry it. _S_ **(2)**

4. I have never seen a tornado, __but__ I have seen lightning many times. _S_ **(2)**

5. Go into a cellar __or__ another low place if you see a funnel cloud. _W_ **(2)**

Name _____

# In Focus

**Compound Sentences**  A **compound sentence** is made by joining two
closely related simple sentences with a comma and a conjunction.

I like to read.
You like to write. } I like to read, but you like to write.

**Draw a line from each simple sentence in column A to the most
closely related sentence in column B.  Read all the choices before
you decide.** Answers may vary. (**1 point** for each line.)

| A | B |
|---|---|
| 1. Zoe takes photos for the school paper | Zoe took pictures of the musicians. |
| 2. Should Zoe use color film | Tom writes stories for the paper. |
| 3. Color photos are nice | the photos in our newspaper are black and white. |
| 4. Tom wrote about the school concert | should she use black and white film? |

**Now, write the sentences above and join them by using
conjuctions instead of lines.  Don't forget to put a comma
before each conjunction!**

1. Zoe takes photos for the school paper, and Tom writes
   stories for the paper. **(1)**

2. Should Zoe use color film, or should she use black and
   white film? **(1)**

3. Color photos are nice, but the photos in our newspaper
   are black and white. **(1)**

4. Tom wrote about the school concert, and Zoe took
   pictures of the musicians. **(1)**

Assessment Tip: Total **8** Points

Name _____

# Lightning Strikes!

**Correcting Run-on Sentences** A **run-on sentence** occurs when a writer runs one simple sentence into another without using a comma and a conjunction between them. The sentence below is a run-on sentence.

Marco lives on a farm his cousin likes to visit him there.

Correct run-on sentences in your writing by inserting a comma and conjunction to make a compound sentence:

Marco lives on a farm $\overset{, and}{\underset{\wedge}{}}$ his cousin likes to visit him there.

**Marco is excited and has quickly typed an e-mail message to his cousin Jamie. Revise Marco's message by adding missing commas and conjunctions. (2 points each)**

Lightning struck near our farm $\overset{, and}{\underset{\wedge}{}}$ I saw it happen. The bolt hit an old tree on top of a hill $\overset{and}{\underset{\wedge}{}}$ the tree split in half. There was a loud boom $\overset{, and}{\underset{\wedge}{}}$ the air crackled. It was scary $\overset{, but}{\underset{\wedge}{}}$ I was safe in our house at the bottom of the hill. Should I send you a picture of the tree $\overset{, or}{\underset{\wedge}{}}$ do you want to visit to see it for yourself?

Name _____

# Responding to a Prompt

A **prompt** is a direction that asks for a written answer of one or more paragraphs. Read the following prompts.

**Prompt 1**

What job do you think is the most difficult or dangerous? Explain why you think it is difficult or dangerous.

**Prompt 2**

Think about how Warren Faidley customized Shadow Chaser for chasing tornadoes. Describe how you would customize a vehicle for a specific task.

**Choose one prompt and use the chart below to help you write a response. First, list key words in the prompt. Then jot down main ideas and details you might include. Finally, number your main ideas, beginning with *1*, from most to least important.**

| Key Words | Main Ideas | Details |
|---|---|---|
| Prompt 1: explain **(1 point)** Prompt 2: describe | **(2)** | **(2)** |

**Write your response on a separate sheet of paper. Start by restating the prompt. Then write your main ideas and supporting details in order of importance from most to least important, or from least to most important. (5)**

Assessment Tip: Total **10** Points

Name _____

# Capitalizing and Punctuating Sentences

A fifth-grade class was given this writing prompt: **Warren Faidley is a storm chaser.  Summarize what he does for a living.**  One fifth grader wrote the response below but forgot to check for capitalization and punctuation errors.

**Use these proofreading marks to add the necessary capital letters and end punctuation. (1 point each)**

⊙  Add a period.          ⌃! Add an exclamation point.
≡  Make a capital letter.  ⌃? Add a question mark.

what does Warren Faidley do for a living? He follows dangerous storms⊙
for example, he tracks down tornadoes and hurricanes⊙then he
photographs lightning striking the earth and funnel clouds whirling in
the sky.  if he has been successful, he can sell his dramatic photos to
magazines, newspapers, and other publications⊙What a risky but
exciting job storm chasers have !

Name _____

# Volcanic Activity

Write each word from the box under the correct category below.

**Vocabulary**

molten
lava
crater
crust
cinders
eruption
magma
summit

**Description of Hot Lava**

molten **(1 point)**

**Earth Layer**

crust **(1)**

**Materials in a Volcano**

lava **(1)**

magma **(1)**

cinders **(1)**

**Volcano Parts**

crater **(1)**

summit **(1)**

**Event**

eruption **(1)**

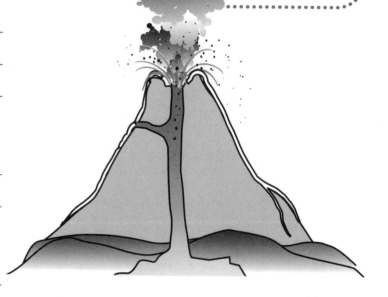

Now choose at least four words from the box. Use them to write a short paragraph describing an exploding volcano.

**(1 point for each word)** _____

_____

_____

_____

_____

Assessment Tip: Total **12** Points

Name ______________________________

# Category Chart

**Fill in the boxes in each category.**

### How Volcanoes Form

Magma pushes up through vents or cracks in the earth's crust. **(1 point)**

### Two Types of Volcanic Vents

a hole in the ground that lava flows from **(1)**

a mountain or hill that lava flows from **(1)**

### Where Volcanoes Form

Most volcanoes form where the plates of the earth come together. Hawaiian volcanoes are in the middle of the Pacific plate. **(1)**

### Types of Volcanoes

| shield volcanoes **(1)** | cinder cone volcanoes **(1)** | composite volcanoes **(1)** | dome volcanoes **(1)** |
|---|---|---|---|
| **examples** | **examples** | **examples** | **examples** |
| Mauna Loa<br>Kilauea **(1)** | some volcanoes in Guatemala **(1)** | Mount Shasta<br>Mount Hood **(1)** | Lassen Peak **(1)** |




Assessment Tip: Total **12** Points

Name _____

# Show What You Know!

**The following questions ask about volcanoes. Answer each question by writing the letter of the correct answer in the space provided.**

B **(1)** 1. Where does the word *volcano* come from?

A. the Hawaiian name for the goddess of fire, Pele

B. the name for the Roman god of fire, Vulcan

C. the scientific name for mountains that spout fire and ash

D. the name for a race of mythological creatures called Vulcans

A **(1)** 2. How are volcanoes formed?

A. Hot magma beneath the earth's crust pushes up through cracks or holes.

B. The earth's crust melts and forms rivers of hot lava.

C. Wood and other materials catch fire and cause explosions that melt mountaintops.

D. Glaciers melt, leaving craters through which magma can escape.

B **(1)** 3. What happened when Mt. St. Helens erupted in 1980?

A. The first of the Hawaiian islands was formed in the Pacific Ocean.

B. Homes, roads, and forests were destroyed, and 60 people were killed.

C. Ash spewed into the air, but no real damage was done.

D. A new volcanic island appeared in the North Atlantic Ocean.

D **(1)** 4. Where in the earth's crust do most volcanoes erupt?

A. in the weakest parts of the earth's plates, near the center

B. in the Atlantic Ocean

C. wherever mountains or mountain ranges are found

D. in places where two of the earth's plates meet

C **(1)** 5. How have volcanoes helped to create the Hawaiian Islands?

A. Eruptions destroyed much of the land area, leaving only islands.

B. Eruptions caught the attention of explorers, who settled there.

C. Eruptions built up the islands, and new eruptions add lava to the shoreline.

D. Ash and cinders from thousands of eruptions have mixed with seawater to help form new land.

Assessment Tip: Total **5** Points

Name _____

# Classifying Clouds

**Read the article. Then complete the activity on page 42.**

## Clouds

Clouds come in a variety of forms and colors. They occur at different heights. Some are made of water and some of ice. With all these differences, a good way to identify clouds is by their groups.

Clouds are grouped by how high above the earth they are found. Low clouds are usually not more than 6,000 feet above sea level. They include stratus and stratocumulus clouds. A stratus cloud looks like a smooth sheet, while stratocumulus clouds are lumpy. They look like fluffy gray piles of cotton.

Middle clouds form between 6,000 and 20,000 feet. They include altostratus, altocumulus, and nimbostratus clouds. An altostratus cloud forms a white or gray sheet. Altocumulus clouds appear as fluffy piles that may be separated or connected in a lumpy mass. Nimbostratus clouds look like a smooth, gray layer. Rain or snow often falls from them, making them hard to see.

High clouds form above 20,000 feet. Unlike other kinds of clouds, which are made of water droplets, these clouds consist of ice crystals. Cirrus, cirrostratus, and cirrocumulus are types of high clouds. Cirrus clouds are very high in the sky and have a feathery appearance. A cirrostratus cloud is a very thin cloud layer. Cirrocumulus clouds look like millions of bits of fluff high in the sky.

Name _____

# Classifying Clouds  continued

**Follow the directions or answer the questions based on the article.**

1. Add the names of any cloud types mentioned in the
   article that are missing from this chart.

| low | middle | high |
|---|---|---|
| stratus | altostratus | cirrus |
| stratocumulus **(1 point)** | altocumulus **(1)** | cirrostratus **(1)** |
| | nimbostratus **(1)** | cirrocumulus **(1)** |

2. How are the clouds in this chart classified? by shape or appearance **(2)**
   Write the correct category for each list of clouds in this chart.

| sheet or layer **(1)** | fluffy **(1)** |
|---|---|
| stratus | stratocumulus |
| altostratus | altocumulus |
| nimbostratus | cirrocumulus |
| cirrostratus | |

3. How are the clouds in this chart classified? by what they are made of **(2)**
   Add the names of cloud types not listed to the correct column.

| water | ice |
|---|---|
| stratus | cirrus |
| altostratus | cirrostratus |
| nimbostratus | cirrocumulus **(1)** |
| stratocumulus **(1)** | |
| altocumulus **(1)** | |

Assessment Tip: Total **14** Points

Name _____

# Construct a Word

**Read each sentence. Then, using two or three columns in the chart, build a word containing the root *-struct* or *-rupt* that completes the sentence. Write the word on the line.**

| de | rupt | ive |
|------|--------|-----|
| dis | struct | or |
| con | | ion |
| e | | ure |
| inter | | |
| in | | |

1. Sam's swimming <u>instructor **(1 point)**</u>
   taught him how to do the backstroke.

2. I watched the <u>eruption **(1)**</u> of the
   volcano from my window.

3. We helped our cousin <u>construct **(1)**</u> a tree house
   in the backyard.

4. The hurricane left a path of <u>destruction **(1)**</u>
   along the coast.

5. Please don't <u>interrupt **(1)**</u> me when
   I'm talking!

6. The noise in the hall was very <u>disruptive **(1)**</u>
   during our rehearsal.

7. The leak was caused by a <u>rupture **(1)**</u>
   in the pipeline.

8. The children sat on top of the climbing
   <u>structure **(1)**</u> in the playground.

Name _____

# The /ō/, /ōō/, and /yōō/ Sounds

**Spelling Words**

When you hear the /ō/ sound, think of the patterns *o*-consonant-*e*, *oa*, *ow*, and *o*. When you hear the /ōō/ and the /yōō/ sounds, think of the patterns *u*-consonant-*e*, *ue*, *ew*, *oo*, *ui*, and *ou*.    Order of answers for each category may vary.

| | |
|---|---|
| /ō/ | sl**o**pe, b**oa**st, thr**ow**n, str**o**ll |
| /ōō/ or /yōō/ | r**u**le, cl**ue**, d**ew**, ch**oo**se, cr**ui**se, r**ou**te |

**Write each Spelling Word under its vowel sound.**

### /ō/ Sound

thrown **(1` point)**          loaf **(1)**

stole **(1)**                  growth **(1)**

boast **(1)**                  slope **(1)**

stroll **(1)**                 flow **(1)**

### /ōō/ or /yōō/ Sounds

clue **(1)**                   mood **(1)**

dew **(1)**                    youth **(1)**

choose **(1)**                 bruise **(1)**

rule **(1)**                   loose **(1)**

cruise **(1)**                 rude **(1)**

route **(1)**                  flute **(1)**

1. thrown
2. stole
3. clue
4. dew
5. choose
6. rule
7. boast
8. cruise
9. stroll
10. route
11. mood
12. loaf
13. growth
14. youth
15. slope
16. bruise
17. loose
18. rude
19. flow
20. flute

44     Theme 1: **Nature's Fury**
Assessment Tip: Total **20** Points

Name _____

# Spelling Spree

**Letter Swap  Write a Spelling Word by changing the underlined letter to a different letter.**

1. st<u>a</u>le     stole **(1 point)**
2. lo<u>u</u>se     loose **(1)**
3. clu<u>b</u>     clue **(1)**
4. loa<u>d</u>     loaf **(1)**

5. r<u>o</u>le     rule **(1)**
6. <u>t</u>oast     boast **(1)**
7. moo<u>n</u>     mood **(1)**
8. de<u>n</u>     dew **(1)**

**Word Switch  Write a Spelling Word to replace each underlined definition in the sentences.  Write your words on the lines.**

9. My parents are taking a <u>sea voyage for pleasure</u> on that ship.
10. Which item did you <u>pick out</u> from the catalog?
11. Many people are active in sports in their <u>time of life before adulthood.</u>
12. You can use a ruler to measure the <u>increase in size</u> of the plant.
13. I play the <u>woodwind instrument shaped like a tube</u> in the band.
14. A clerk should never be <u>lacking in courtesy</u> to a shopper.
15. Would you care to <u>walk slowly</u> down the beach with me?

9. cruise **(1)**
10. choose **(1)**
11. youth **(1)**
12. growth **(1)**

13. flute **(1)**
14. rude **(1)**
15. stroll **(1)**

## Spelling Words

1. thrown
2. stole
3. clue
4. dew
5. choose
6. rule
7. boast
8. cruise
9. stroll
10. route
11. mood
12. loaf
13. growth
14. youth
15. slope
16. bruise
17. loose
18. rude
19. flow
20. flute

Assessment Tip: Total **15** Points

Name _____

# Proofreading and Writing

**Proofreading** Circle the five misspelled Spelling Words in this paragraph from a personal narrative. Then write each word correctly.

Our (roote) led us up the side of the volcano. We had just reached an old area of lava (flo) when we heard a rumbling noise from above. Hikers ahead of us on the trail had knocked some rocks loose! The avalanche was heading down the (sloap) of the mountain, straight for us. In the rush to reach safety, I tripped and was (thron) off the trail. Luckily, the mass of rocks passed me by, and all I got was a (briuse) on my leg.

1. route **(2 points)**
2. flow **(2)**
3. slope **(2)**
4. thrown **(2)**
5. bruise **(2)**

**Spelling Words**

1. thrown
2. stole
3. clue
4. dew
5. choose
6. rule
7. boast
8. cruise
9. stroll
10. route
11. mood
12. loaf
13. growth
14. youth
15. slope
16. bruise
17. loose
18. rude
19. flow
20. flute

**Write a List of Safety Tips** What safety tips would it be good to keep in mind when exploring a volcano?

**On a separate sheet of paper, list some tips for volcano explorers. Use Spelling Words from the list.** Responses will vary. **(5 points)**

Name _____

# Missing Definitions

**The dictionary entries below include an entry word and a sample sentence, but they are missing the definition. Read each sample sentence and use it to help you fill in the definition.**

Accept any reasonable answer. Sample answers shown.

1. ancient (**ān′** shənt) <u>Very old **(2 points)**</u>

   *The dinosaur tracks in the rocks show how ancient they are.*

2. astonishing (ə **stŏn′** ĭ shĭng) <u>Surprising **(2)**</u>

   *It was astonishing to see it snowing in the middle of July.*

3. awaken (ə **wā′** kən) <u>To wake up **(2)**</u>

   *The campers awaken at the first light of dawn.*

4. damage (**dăm′** ĭj) <u>To harm or hurt **(2)**</u>

   *Using too much water can damage the plants.*

5. extinct (ĭk **stĭngkt′**) <u>No longer active **(2)**</u>

   *Since its last eruption a thousand years ago, the volcano*

   *has been extinct.*

6. fiery (**fīr′** ē) <u>Like fire; made of fire **(2)**</u>

   *The flames made a fiery glow in the sky.*

7. spout (spout) <u>To gush or spurt out **(2)**</u>

   *Water from the fountain spouts into the air.*

8. summit (**sŭm′** ĭt) <u>The highest point; peak **(2)**</u>

   *After a long hard climb, we reached the summit of the mountain.*

Name _____

# Finding Your Way

**Singular and Plural Nouns** A **singular noun** names one person, one place, one thing, or one idea. A **plural noun** names more than one person, place, thing, or idea. To decide how to form a plural, look at the end of the singular noun. Here are four rules to study:

1. To most singular nouns, add -*s* to form the plural.
2. If a singular noun ends in *s*, *ss*, *x*, *ch*, or *sh*, add -*es* to form the plural.
3. For singular nouns ending with a vowel plus *y*, add -*s* to form the plural.
4. If a singular noun ends in a consonant plus *y*, change the *y* to *i* and add -*es*.

| |
|---|
| bench |
| table |
| tree |
| fox |
| fireplace |
| tent |
| daisy |
| bush |
| bus |
| pathway |

**Conrad and Carmen have drawn a map of a campground they are visiting. Label each landmark on the map with a plural noun. Use nouns from the list. (1 point each)**

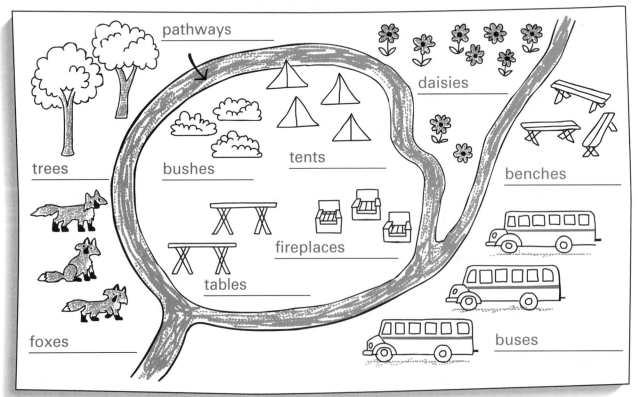

Assessment Tip: Total **10** Points

Name _____

# Science Fair

**More Plural Nouns** Here are a few more rules for forming plurals:

1. To form the plural of some nouns ending in *f* or *fe*, change the *f* to *v* and add *-es*. For others ending in *f*, simply add *-s*.
2. To form the plural of nouns ending with a vowel plus *o*, add *-s*.
3. To form the plural of nouns ending with a consonant plus *o*, add *-s* or *-es*.
4. Some nouns have special plural forms.
5. Some nouns are the same in the singular and the plural.

For the science fair, Jody made a model of the volcano Mount Saint Helens and wrote a report about it. Jody isn't sure how to form the plural of some words in her report. She made a list of these words.

**Write the plural next to each word on Jody's list. Check your dictionary if you are unsure of a plural.**

| | |
|---|---|
| leaf | leaves **(1 point)** |
| child | children **(1)** |
| volcano | volcanoes **(1)** |
| man | men **(1)** |
| ash | ashes **(1)** |
| home | homes **(1)** |
| deer | deer **(1)** |
| woman | women **(1)** |
| plant | plants **(1)** |
| mouse | mice **(1)** |

Name _____

# Roaming Through the Woods

**Using Exact Nouns** You can make your writing more lively and interesting by replacing general nouns with more specific ones. Here is an example of writing with a general noun:

> For my birthday, I received **several things**.

A reader does not know what the person received. Here is the same sentence revised to use more specific nouns:

> For my birthday, I received **a book about sports legends, a basketball, and basketball shoes**.

**Read the following paragraph. Revise the general nouns in bold type by replacing them with a more specific noun from the box. (1 point each)**

> a rabbit
> dragonfly
> maples and oaks
> Duck Pond
> minnows
> peanut butter
> sandwiches
> my ankles
> mint
> bark
> sneakers

Yesterday, Aunt Dorothy and I walked through the woods to the
Duck Pond
**pond**. My aunt knows much about nature. On our way, she
^    maples and oaks
pointed out **trees** and showed me how to recognize them by
^    bark
their leaves and **stuff**. She even taught me how to recognize
mint                  ^
**a plant** by its minty smell! When we arrived at the pond,
^    dragonfly
I saw a **bug** hovering low over the water. Because it was a warm
^    sneakers
day, I took off my **shoes** and waded in the pond. The water
^    minnows
                              my ankles
was so clear I could see **things** swimming around **me**. After that,
peanut butter sandwiches  ^           a rabbit   ^
we ate our **food**. On the way home, we saw **an animal** hop
^                              ^

across the path.

Assessment Tip: Total **10** Points

Name _____

# Writing a Paragraph of Information

**Read the following paragraph of information from page 87 of *Volcanoes*.**

Volcanoes are formed by cracks or holes that poke through the earth's crust. Magma pushes its way up through the cracks. This is called a volcanic eruption. When magma pours onto the surface it is called lava. . . . As lava cools, it hardens to form rock.

**Now get ready to write your own paragraph of information about volcanoes. Use the following graphic organizer to help you organize your paragraph. (5 points)**

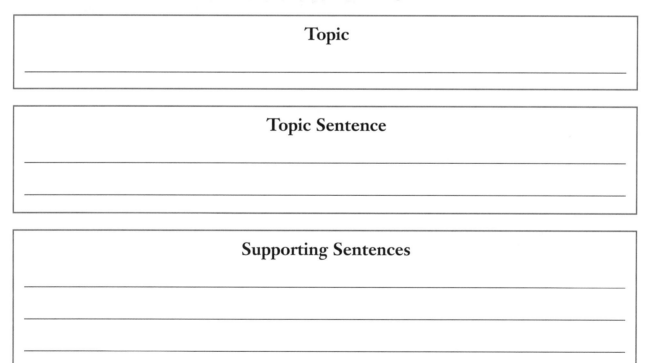

**Topic**

_____

**Topic Sentence**

_____

_____

**Supporting Sentences**

_____

_____

_____

_____

**Now, write your paragraph of information on a separate sheet of paper. Arrange your supporting sentences in a logical order, and make sure all of the sentences contain facts about the topic. (5 points)**

# Correcting Sentence Fragments

**A sentence fragment is a group of words that is missing either a subject or a predicate. The following groups of words are sentence fragments. Turn them into complete sentences by adding either a subject or a predicate. Write the complete sentence on the lines.** Responses will vary.

1. Many of the world's active volcanoes.

   Many of the world's active volcanoes are destructive. **(3 points)**

   _____

2. Clouds of hot ash.

   Clouds of hot ash fill the air. **(3)**

   _____

3. Buries plants and animals.

   Quick-moving lava buries plants and animals. **(3)**

   _____

4. The blast of an eruption.

   The blast of an eruption topples trees and buildings. **(3)**

   _____

5. Are seriously injured or killed.

   Hundreds of people are seriously injured or killed. **(3)**

   _____

Name _____

# Choosing the Best Answer

Use the test-taking strategies and tips you have learned to help you answer multiple-choice questions. This practice will help you when you take this kind of test.

**Read each question. Choose the best answer. Fill in the circle in the answer row.**

1   At the beginning of the story, why did Jonathan think that Moose was acting strangely?

   **A**   He thought Moose knew that Jonathan was worried about his mother.

   **B**   He thought Moose was looking for Mrs. Smith, who lived next door.

   **C**   He thought Moose knew there was going to be an earthquake.

   **D**   He thought Moose saw the children's father driving into the campground.

2   When did Jonathan plan to listen to the baseball game on the radio?

   **F**   After he hitched the car to the trailer

   **G**   After he found out how his mother was

   **H**   After he took Moose for a walk

   **J**   After Abby was in bed

3   When Jonathan and Abby first heard the rumbling noise, what did they think it was?

   **A**   An earthquake      **C**   A bomb

   **B**   Thunder          **D**   Rifles

4   Why couldn't Jonathan get to Abby during the earthquake?

   **F**   He couldn't see where she was.

   **G**   Birch trees fell on top of him.

   **H**   He couldn't keep his balance.

   **J**   He fell into the river.

ANSWER ROWS     A B C D **(5 points)**   3 A B C D **(5)**
2 F G H J **(5)**   4 F G H J **(5)**

Name _____

# Choosing the Best Answer

**continued**

5 What did Jonathan see right before the redwood almost fell on him?

   **A**  He saw the trunk tremble.

   **B**  He saw the roots rip loose from the ground.

   **C**  He saw the tree sway back and forth.

   **D**  He saw the trunk tilt toward him.

6 What did Jonathan do when he reached Abby?

   **F**  He helped her walk toward their trailer.

   **G**  He helped her look for their dog Moose.

   **H**  He helped her take shelter under a fallen tree.

   **J**  He helped her understand why earthquakes occur.

7 What did Jonathan think about as he hugged Moose after the earthquake?

   **A**  When he chose the dog

   **B**  The last earthquake his family had experienced

   **C**  His mother's broken ankle

   **D**  Bandaging his sister's cut knee

8 When did Abby realize that she and her brother could have been killed during the earthquake?

   **F**  When she saw the destruction around her

   **G**  When Jonathan told her

   **H**  When her parents got home

   **J**  When Grandma Whitney called from Iowa

ANSWER ROWS  5 Ⓐ **Ⓑ** Ⓒ Ⓓ **(5 points)**  7 **Ⓐ** Ⓑ Ⓒ Ⓓ **(5)**
               6 Ⓕ Ⓖ **Ⓗ** Ⓙ **(5)**  8 Ⓕ **Ⓖ** Ⓗ Ⓙ **(5)**

54   Theme 1: **Nature's Fury**
Assessment Tip: Total **40** Points

Name _____

# Spelling Review

**Write Spelling Words from the list on this page to answer the questions.**

Order of answers in each category may vary.

1–9. Which nine words have a short vowel sound?

1. fond **(1 point)**

2. swift **(1)**

3. slept **(1)**

4. staff **(1)**

5. grasp **(1)**

6. bunk **(1)**

7. dwell **(1)**

8. split **(1)**

9. crush **(1)**

10–19. Which ten words have the /ā/, /ē/, or /ī/ sound?

10. beast **(1)**

11. fleet **(1)**

12. thigh **(1)**

13. fade **(1)**

14. praise **(1)**

15. strike **(1)**

16. slight **(1)**

17. claim **(1)**

18. sway **(1)**

19. mild **(1)**

20–30. Which eleven words have the /ō/, /yo͞o/, or /o͞o/ sound?

20. flute **(1)**

21. dew **(1)**

22. clue **(1)**

23. slope **(1)**

24. boast **(1)**

25. stole **(1)**

26. stroll **(1)**

27. cruise **(1)**

28. mood **(1)**

29. youth **(1)**

30. thrown **(1)**

**Spelling Words**

1. fond
2. swift
3. beast
4. slept
5. fleet
6. staff
7. flute
8. grasp
9. thigh
10. dew
11. bunk
12. fade
13. dwell
14. strike
15. praise
16. slight
17. split
18. claim
19. sway
20. mild
21. clue
22. slope
23. boast
24. stole
25. stroll
26. cruise
27. mood
28. crush
29. youth
30. thrown

Theme 1: **Nature's Fury**   55
Assessment Tip: Total **30** Points

# Spelling Spree

**Puzzle Power** Use the Spelling Words to complete the sentences. Write the words in the puzzle. **(1 point each)**

**Across**

3. The animals _____ in the forest.
5. A lion is a large _____.

**Down**

1. I am in a good _____ today.
2. The _____ is very steep.
4. Don't _____ that flower with your foot!

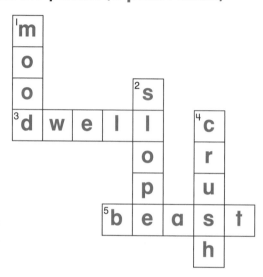

1. crush
2. mood
3. swift
4. dwell
5. fade
6. strike
7. cruise
8. sway
9. beast
10. thrown
11. slope
12. stole
13. flute
14. dew
15. youth

**Book Titles** Write the Spelling Word to complete each book title. Remember to use capital letters.

6. *My* Cruise **(1)** _____ *Down the River,* by C. Mann

7. *The Thief Who* Stole **(1)** _____ *the Diamonds,* by Tay Kitaway

8. *The* Swift **(1)** _____ *and Dangerous River,* by Can O. Tripp

9. *Earthquake:* Thrown **(1)** _____ *to the Ground!* by Shay Keeg Round

10. *Why Do Colors* Fade **(1)** _____ *in the Sun and Other Science Questions,* by Sy N. Tist

11. *Adventures of My Childhood and* Youth **(1)** _____, *by A. Jing X. Plorer*

12. *Flowers* Sway **(1)** _____ *in the Breeze* by Heather Rose Marigold

13. *Mist in the Air,* Dew **(1)** _____ *on the Grass* by I. M. Dampp

14. Flute **(1)** _____ *Music for Beginners,* by Mary Days

15. *The Clock Will* Strike **(1)** _____ *at Midnight,* by Miss Stear E. Yuss

Assessment Tip: Total **15** Points

# Proofreading and Writing

**Proofreading** **Circle the six misspelled Spelling Words in this newspaper article. Then write each word correctly.**

At 11:30 last night, a (milde) earthquake gently rocked the city. Little damage was reported, and some people (sleept) right through it. This morning Helen and Joe Dalton (boste) that they were not afraid. There was only (slite) damage downtown. With (prayse) for his workers, the mayor said, "My (staf) responded quickly to all questions."

1. mild **(1 point)**

2. slept **(1)**

3. boast **(1)**

4. slight **(1)**

5. praise **(1)**

6. staff **(1)**

**In the News** **A reporter takes notes after an earthquake. Complete his ideas by writing Spelling Words in the blanks.**

- No one is fond **(1)** of surprises like this.

- Scientists have no clue **(1)** about why this quake occurred at night.

- It is a strange time to stroll **(1)** through town!

- I'd rather be in my bunk **(1)** sleeping.

- A man has cuts on his thigh **(1)** and ankle.

- A large fleet **(1)** of fire trucks roars by.

- Large crevice in ground. Oak street is split **(1)** in two!

- It's hard to fully grasp **(1)** the power of a quake.

- Some people claim **(1)** that animals can predict earthquakes.

✎ **Write a Safety Plan** **On a separate sheet of paper, write about what you should do in an earthquake. Use the Spelling Review Words.**

Responses will vary.

**Spelling Words**

1. slept
2. praise
3. fond
4. clue
5. staff
6. thigh
7. stroll
8. slight
9. claim
10. fleet
11. mild
12. grasp
13. split
14. bunk
15. boast

Name _____

# You'll Never Believe Who I Just Met

**Think about characters you might find in a tall tale. Describe five tall tale characters by completing each sentence with an exaggeration.**

Sample answers shown.

1. This character is so tall that

   he has to duck whenever the space shuttle goes by. **(2 points)**

   _____

2. This character is so loud that

   when she clears her throat it causes an avalanche. **(2)**

   _____

3. This character is so old that

   he used to play hide-and-go-seek with the dinosaurs when he was

   a little boy. **(2)**

4. This character is so fast that

   she can run to the store, buy a quart of milk, and be back with the

   change before her father has finished writing *milk* on the

   shopping list. **(2)**

5. This character is so strong that

   when he loses something, he really *does* turn the house upside

   down to find it. **(2)**

Name _____

# That Could Never Happen!

**Each of the four selections in *Focus on Tall Tales* contains at least one exaggerated event. Write the event after each story title.**
Sample answers shown.

*Paul Bunyan, the Mightiest Logger of Them All*

Paul Bunyan chops down ten pine trees with one swing of his axe.

**(2 points)**

*John Henry Races the Steam Drill*

John Henry swings his hammer so hard and fast that it catches fire. **(2)**

*Sally Ann Thunder Ann Whirlwind*

Sally talks the grizzly bear into dancing with her, and at the same time

he churns her butter. **(2)**

*February*

McBroom saws chunks of the frozen wind during the winter and thaws

them out during the summer. **(2)**

Assessment Tip: Total **8** Points

Name _____

# Give It All You've Got

How do the characters in this theme "give their all"?  After reading each selection, answer the questions to complete the chart.

| | Michelle Kwan: Heart of a Champion | La Bamba |
|---|---|---|
| **What kind of writing is the selection an example of?** | autobiography **(2.5 points)** | fiction **(2.5)** |
| **What traits does the main character have? What actions or achievements help reveal those traits?** | Michelle is aggressive, determined to succeed, and physically strong and agile. Her desire to be a Senior skater and her Olympic victory reveal these traits. **(2.5)** | Manuel is a show-off, but he is also funny and creative. His desire to be up on stage and his creative solution to the sticking record needle reveal these traits. **(2.5)** |
| **Why does this selection belong in a theme called _Give It All You've Got_?** | Michelle tried her best to become a great skater, an achievement that required much hard work. **(2.5)** | Manuel keeps on dancing when the needle sticks, even though he is embarrassed and feels like hiding. **(2.5)** |
| **What advice might the main character give to others?** | Reach high for your goals. Work hard and you can accomplish anything. **(2.5)** | Check your equipment before every performance. Think twice before you volunteer for a talent show. **(2.5)** |

Assessment Tip: Total **10** Points per selection

Name _____

# Give It All You've Got

| | Mae Jemison: Space Scientist | The Fear Place |
|---|---|---|
| **What kind of writing is the selection an example of?** | biography **(2.5)** | fiction **(2.5)** |
| **What traits does the main character have? What actions or achievements help reveal those traits?** | Mae Jemison shows her intelligence through her educational achievements. She shows flexibility by changing careers. She shows artistic talent through dance, and leadership by forming a company. **(2.5)** | Doug is thoughtful and courageous. He forces himself to hike across a narrow ledge that terrifies him. He shows loyalty when he hikes alone to find his brother. **(2.5)** |
| **Why does this selection belong in a theme called *Give It All You've Got*?** | Mae Jemison succeeded at two very challenging careers, being a doctor and an astronaut. **(2.5)** | Doug hikes across the fear place even though it scares him. This takes great courage. **(2.5)** |
| **What advice might the main character give to others?** | Get a good education. Study what interests you and don't let others limit your goals or interests. **(2.5)** | Face your fear. **(2.5)** |

What have you learned in this theme about facing challenges?

People can meet and overcome very difficult challenges if they find the strength and

courage within them. **(2)**

Assessment Tip: Total **10** Points per selection and **2** points for the final question

Name _____

# Top Marks

**Read the word in each box from *Michelle Kwan: Heart of a Champion*.  Write a word from the list that is related in meaning.  Then use a dictionary to check if you were right.**

| **pressure** |
| --- |
| stress **(1 point)** |

| **required** |
| --- |
| specified **(1)** |

| **presentations** |
| --- |
| demonstrations **(1)** |

| **audience** |
| --- |
| spectators **(1)** |

| **elements** |
| --- |
| components **(1)** |

| **artistic** |
| --- |
| elegant **(1)** |

| **judges** |
| --- |
| officials **(1)** |

| **amateur** |
| --- |
| nonprofessional **(1)** |

| **technical** |
| --- |
| skilled **(1)** |

| **compete** |
| --- |
| perform **(1)** |

Name _____

# Is That a Fact?

| Passage | Fact or Opinion? | How I Can Tell |
|---|---|---|
| **Page 139, paragraph 1:** "I thought I was ready to become a Senior skater, at the age of twelve." | Opinion **(1)** | The words *I thought* are a clue that this is an opinion and cannot be proven. **(1)** |
| **Page 140, paragraph 5:** "Frank is one of the greatest coaches in the world." | Opinion **(1)** | The adjective *greatest* is a clue that this statement is an opinion. **(1)** |
| **Page 144, paragraph 6:** "The judges look for many required elements in a program." | Fact **(1)** | This fact could be proven by contacting the judging organization. **(1)** |
| **Page 146, paragraph 3:** "Elvis Stojko...does quadruple/triple combinations." | Fact **(1)** | This fact could be proven by watching a slow-motion videotape of Elvis. **(1)** |
| **Page 147, paragraph 1:** "Most elite skaters have three forty-five-minute-long practice sessions on the ice every day . . ." | Fact **(1)** | This fact could be proven by checking with all elite skaters. **(1)** |
| **Page 150, paragraph 4:** "And you can never forget how important school is." | Opinion **(1)** | This is Michelle's opinion—the words *how important* are clues that she is sharing a belief. **(1)** |

Assessment Tip: Total **12** Points

Name _____

# A Figure Skater's Trading Card

What if figure skaters were featured on trading cards as baseball players are? Complete the fact sheet so it gives vital information about Michelle Kwan. Then use the facts to write a paragraph that might appear on the back of a Michelle Kwan trading card.

**FACT SHEET**

Who Michelle Kwan is:

Ice skater **(1 point)**

Who her coach was:

Frank Carroll **(1)**

What she was especially good at when she was young:

She was a good jumper. **(1)**

Age at which she became a Senior skater:

12 years old **(1)**

How she had to improve in order to compete as a Senior skater:

Her skating had to become elegant and

she had to become a perfectionist in all

aspects. **(1)**

Her world records (see page 153):

Fifteen 6.0s for artistry **(1)**

Two pieces of advice she might give other young athletes:

1. Work hard. **(1)**

2. Be yourself. **(1)**

Michelle Kwan: Figure Skater

**(4)**

# Is That a Fact?

**Read the following passage. Then answer the questions on page 67.**

### A Track Legend

Wilma Rudolph was perhaps the greatest female track athlete of her time. She was the first American woman to win three gold medals in a single Olympics. She also received many honors, including the Sullivan Award as the country's top amateur athlete, and a place in the Women's Sports Hall of Fame, the Black Sports Hall of Fame, and the United States Olympic Hall of Fame.

Rudolph achieved success despite great personal obstacles. As a child, she was stricken with polio, pneumonia, and scarlet fever. Some doctors said she would never walk. Yet no one could have been more determined to beat the odds. After years of physical therapy, Rudolph put aside her leg brace at age eleven and went on to become a great athlete in high school and college.

At the 1960 Olympic Games, Rudolph was the star of the American team. She won gold medals and set world records in the 100-meter dash, the 200-meter dash, and the 400-meter relay.

Rudolph later became a coach and a teacher. She also wrote a book about her life that was made into a movie. There has never been an American athlete who overcame more obstacles in life than Wilma Rudolph. She should be an inspiration to all Americans, and to athletes everywhere.

Name _____

# Is That a Fact? continued

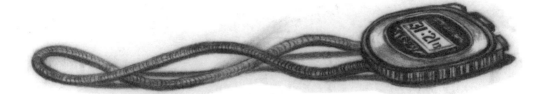

**Answer these questions about the passage on page 66.**

1. What opinion about Wilma Rudolph does the author give in the first paragraph? Write the sentence that states the opinion.

   Wilma Rudolph was perhaps the greatest female track athlete of her time.

   **(2 points)**

2. Which words in this sentence show that the statement is an opinion and not a fact?

   perhaps, greatest **(2)**

3. Which sentence from the second paragraph contains no opinions?

   As a child, she was stricken with polio, pneumonia, and scarlet fever. **(2)**

   _____

4. The third paragraph contains one opinion and several facts. Write them here.

   **Opinion:** Rudolph was the star of the American team at the 1960 Olympic

   Games. **(2)**

   **Facts:** She won gold medals and set world records in the 100-meter dash, the

   200-meter dash, and 400-meter relay. **(4)**

5. Reread the last paragraph to find two facts and two opinions. Write them here.

   **Opinion:** Rudolph overcame more obstacles than any other American athlete.

   She should be an inspiration. **(4)**

   **Facts:** She became a coach and a teacher. She wrote a book about her life that

   was made into a movie. **(4)**

Name _____

# Compound Creativity

**Read the pairs of sentences. Identify the compound word in the first sentence, and write the words it is made from.**

1. Even when my piano recital didn't go well, I believed in myself.
   <u>my</u> + <u>self **(1 point)**</u>

2. Jen will do whatever it takes to make the soccer team.
   <u>what</u> + <u>ever **(1)**</u>

3. Throughout the school year, I use the gym as often as I can.
   <u>through</u> + <u>out **(1)**</u>

4. I have to do my homework before I can go biking with my friends.
   <u>home</u> + <u>work **(1)**</u>

5. Philip spoke loudly from the stage so that everybody in the auditorium could hear him.
   <u>every</u> + <u>body **(1)**</u>

**Word Chain** **Play a compound word game. Start with a compound word. Use either of the words in it to form a new compound word. Then use part of the new word to form another compound. Keep your word chain going as long as you can.** Sample answers shown.

**Example:** anymore ⟶ anyway ⟶ freeway ⟶ wayside ⟶ ?
sideline ⟶ outline ⟶ outboard ⟶ boardwalk ⟶ sidewalk
walkup ⟶ upstage ⟶ stagecoach ⟶ coachman **(5)**

Assessment Tip: Total **10** Points

Name _____

# Compound Words

A **compound word** is made up of two or more smaller words. To spell a compound word correctly, you must remember if it is written as one word, as a hyphenated word, or as separate words.

**wheel + chair** = wheelchair     **up + to + date** = up-to-date

**first + aid** = first aid

**Write each Spelling Word under the heading that tells how the compound word is written.** Order of answers for each category may vary.

## One Word

basketball **(1 point)**

wheelchair **(1)**

cheerleader **(1)**

newscast **(1)**

weekend **(1)**

everybody **(1)**

grandparent **(1)**

wildlife **(1)**

highway **(1)**

daytime **(1)**

whoever **(1)**

turnpike **(1)**

shipyard **(1)**

homemade **(1)**

household **(1)**

salesperson **(1)**

## With a Hyphen

up-to-date **(1)**

brother-in-law **(1)**

## Separate Words

first aid **(1)**

test tube **(1)**

Assessment Tip: Total **20** Points

Name _____

# Spelling Spree

**Exchanging Word Parts** Write the Spelling Word that has one of the parts in each compound word below.

1. wildfire     wildlife **(1 point)**

2. dateline     up-to-date **(1)**

3. grandstand     grandparent **(1)**

4. sales tax     salesperson **(1)**

5. evergreen     whoever **(1)**

6. wayside     highway **(1)**

7. turnover     turnpike **(1)**

8. holdup     household **(1)**

**Clue Addition** Add the clues to create a Spelling Word.

9. large boat + play area =

10. comes before second + assist =

11. "Hooray!" + person in charge =

12. try out + hollow cylinder =

13. container made of twigs + sphere =

14. not night + what a watch measures =

15. circular frame with spokes + piece of furniture =

9. shipyard **(1)**

10. first aid **(1)**

11. cheerleader **(1)**

12. test tube **(1)**

13. basketball **(1)**

14. daytime **(1)**

15. wheelchair **(1)**

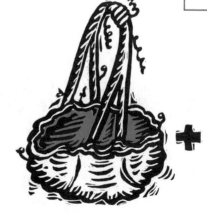

Assessment Tip: Total **15** Points

Name _____

# Proofreading and Writing

**Proofreading** Circle the five misspelled Spelling Words in this transcript of a television news report. Then write each word correctly.

To end tonight's (newskast,) we have a story about a local girl who made good. Debbie Martin, who started skating years ago on a pair of (homemad) skates, is going to the Junior Nationals. Debbie's parents, older sister, and (brother-in-lor) will accompany her to Seattle. For years, they have watched Debbie practice on the family's basketball court, which her father flooded in winter and allowed to freeze over. This (week-end) they will watch her in a world-class arena. We know that (everbody) in town will be rooting for Debbie!

1. newscast **(1 point)** _____
2. homemade **(1)** _____
3. brother-in-law **(1)** _____
4. weekend **(1)** _____
5. everybody **(1)** _____

## Spelling Words

1. basketball
2. wheelchair
3. cheerleader
4. newscast
5. weekend
6. everybody
7. up-to-date
8. grandparent
9. first aid
10. wildlife
11. highway
12. daytime
13. whoever
14. test tube
15. turnpike
16. shipyard
17. homemade
18. household
19. salesperson
20. brother-in-law

✏️ **Write a Comparison and Contrast** Think of a sport you enjoy playing or watching. Does it have anything in common with figure skating? How is it different from figure skating?

**On a separate piece of paper, write a paragraph in which you compare and contrast two sports. Use Spelling Words from the list.** Responses will vary. **(5)**

Name _____

# Word Family Matters

**Decide which word best completes each sentence. Write the word in the blank.**

1. When he realized that he had missed the team tryouts, Todd turned red with <u>fury **(1 point)**</u>.

   | furious | fury | infuriate |
   | --- | --- | --- |

2. Twenty school bands besides ours were entered in this year's state <u>competition **(1)**</u>.

   | compete | competition | competitive |
   | --- | --- | --- |

3. Vanilla ice cream with fudge sauce is a dessert I find <u>irresistible **(1)**</u>.

   | irresistible | resistance | resist |
   | --- | --- | --- |

4. Because the top math student receives a prize, my sister is <u>motivated **(1)**</u> to get a good grade on her next test.

   | move | motion | motivated |
   | --- | --- | --- |

5. Please wait <u>patiently **(1)**</u> until it is your turn to play the computer game.

   | impatient | patience | patiently |
   | --- | --- | --- |

**Now write two sentences, using two words you have not used yet.**
Sample answer shown.

6. <u>Waiting in line too long makes me impatient. **(2.5)**</u>

   _____

7. <u>I can't resist the sound of a parade. **(2.5)**</u>

   _____

Name _____

# Champion Michelle

**Common and Proper Nouns**  A **common noun** names any person, place, or thing.  A **proper noun** names a particular person, place, or thing.  Each important word in a proper noun begins with a capital letter.

> We met at the **statue**.  *statue:* common noun
>
> We met at the **Statue of Liberty.**  *Statue of Liberty:* proper noun
>
> **Coach Boe** taught me how to skate.  *Coach Boe:* proper noun
>
> A **coach** taught me how to skate.  *coach:* common noun
>
> She is from another **state**.  *state:* common noun
>
> She is from **California.**  *California:* proper noun

**Copy the nouns from the following sentences into the proper columns below.  When you rewrite a proper noun, be sure to capitalize correctly.**

1. debbie went to the skating rink on saturday.
2. In the winter, the pond is frozen.
3. miguel is fast when he puts on his skates.
4. I competed in the race at valley middle school.
5. Have you ever skated at rockefeller center?

| **Common Nouns** | **Proper Nouns** |
|---|---|
| rink **(1 point)** | Debbie **(1)** |
| winter **(1)** | Saturday **(1)** |
| pond **(1)** | Miguel **(1)** |
| skates **(1)** | Valley Middle School **(1)** |
| race **(1)** | Rockefeller Center **(1)** |

Name _____

# The People's Favorite

**Singular and Possessive Nouns** A **possessive noun** shows ownership or possession. To form a singular possessive noun, add an apostrophe and -*s* ('s). To form a plural possessive noun, add an apostrophe (') if the noun ends with *s*. Otherwise, add an apostrophe and -*s* ('s).

| Singular | Singular Possessive | Plural | Plural Possessive |
|---|---|---|---|
| cat | cat's | cats | cats' |
| country | country's | countries | countries' |
| Jones | Jones's | Joneses | Joneses' |
| woman | woman's | women | women's |
| mouse | mouse's | mice | mice's |

**Fill in the blank in each sentence below with the possessive form of the noun in parentheses. Write an S on the line at the end of the sentence if you wrote a singular possessive noun. Write a P on the line if you wrote a plural possessive noun.**

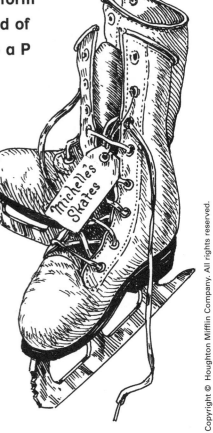

1. Our (school) ___school's **(1 point)**___ skating club
   sponsored a citywide competition. _S_ **(1)**

2. The fifth grade (classes) ___classes' **(1)**___
   skaters were great. _P_ **(1)**

3. The first event was the (seniors) ___seniors' **(1)**___
   short program. _P_ **(1)**

4. The (competition) ___competition's **(1)**___ rules were
   strict. _S_ **(1)**

5. The audience's favorite event was the (children)
   ___children's **(1)**___ competition. _P_ **(1)**

Assessment Tip: Total **10** Points

Name _____

# My Friend's Skating Pond

**Writing Possessive Phrases** It is easy to make a mistake when forming the possessive of a plural or a singular noun.  Therefore, when you proofread, pay special attention to possessive nouns.

**Chris in Maine wants to send this e-mail message to Joann in Florida. Proofread the message for errors in possessive nouns.  Write the correct possessive forms above the line, as shown.  (2 points for each word)**

               friends'

**Example:** My two friend's reports are about hockey.
             ^

To: joann@tropics.net
From: cwm@frozennorth.com
Re: Ice and Snow

Hi Joann!

                                 family's

    I have been ice-skating on my familys pond. The
                                 ^

pond froze solid last week. It is safe to skate on it
                  Tom's

now. Last evening, Toms family and my family skated
              ^
              families'

on the pond. Our families dogs played in the snow.
              ^
   dogs'

The dogs tails never stopped wagging. They enjoyed
        ^
   winter's

this winters snow as much as we did!
   ^

               Chris

Name _____

# Writing an Announcement

How can you find out when and where Michelle Kwan is going to skate in a competition or perform in an exhibition? You might read an announcement on a bulletin board or in a newsletter, or you might hear one on the radio or TV. An **announcement** is a short speech or notice that gives important information about an event.

**Fill in the chart below with details about an upcoming skating performance by Michelle Kwan or some other sporting event.**

| |
|---|
| **Date** (3 points) |
| **Time** (3) |
| **Place** (3) |
| **Cost** (3) |
| **Details about the program** (3) |

**Now write your announcement on a separate sheet of paper. State the purpose of the announcement at the very beginning. Then provide information that answers these questions: *who? what? where? when? why? how?* and *how much?* Be sure to include the exact date, time, location, and cost of the event as well as other details about the program. Use clear, interesting, and friendly language that the audience will understand. (5)**

Assessment Tip: Total **20** Points

Name _____

# Ordering Important Information

A careful writer makes sure that the information in an announcement is complete and presented in a clear order. Sequence words, such as *first*, *next*, and *last*, help clarify the order of events and call attention to what is most important.

**Somehow, this announcement has gotten scrambled. Reorder the sentences so that the announcement follows the sequence of events. Pay attention to sequence words that give clues to the order of the sentences. Then write the revised announcement on the lines below. (10 points)**

After the match, a victory party will be held in the cafeteria. Game time is 3 P.M. Following the pep rally, the Bloomington Wildcats will play against the Forest Lane Eagles for the regional championship at O'Neill Field. During the rally, Coach Strauss will introduce all of the players and hand out free T-shirts and banners. There will be a pre-game pep rally tomorrow at 2:20 in the gym before the most important soccer match of the season. Go Wildcats!

There will be a pre-game pep rally tomorrow at 2:20 in the gym before the most important soccer match of the season. During the rally, Coach Strauss will introduce all of the players and hand out free T-shirts and banners. Following the pep rally, the Bloomington Wildcats will play against the Forest Lane Eagles for the regional championship at O'Neill Field. Game time is 3 P.M. After the match, a victory party will be held in the cafeteria. Go Wildcats!

# Evaluating Your Personal Essay

**Reread your personal essay. What do you need to make it better? Use this page to help you decide. Put a checkmark in the box for each sentence that describes your personal essay.**

### Rings the Bell!

☐ My introduction catches the reader's attention.

☐ My main focus is clear throughout the essay.

☐ I wrote the essay in my own voice from my own point of view.

☐ The ending sums up the main focus of my essay.

☐ There are almost no mistakes.

### Getting Stronger

☐ My introduction could be more interesting.

☐ My main focus is not always clear.

☐ The point of view is sometimes unclear.

☐ The ending doesn't make the essay feel finished.

☐ There are a few mistakes.

### Try Harder

☐ My introduction is boring.

☐ The main focus is not clear.

☐ The point of view is unclear.

☐ There are a lot of mistakes.

Name _____

# Using Possessive Nouns

▶ Possessive nouns show ownership.

▶ To form the possessive of a singular noun add an apostrophe and *s*.

▶ To form the possessive case of a plural noun ending in *s*, add just an apostrophe.

**Rewrite each phrase, using a possessive noun. Then use the new phrase in a sentence of your own.**

1. the music of the composer _the composer's music **(1)**_

   Sentences will vary.

2. the skill of the musicians _the musicians' skill **(1)**_

   Sentences will vary.

3. the authority of the conductor _the conductor's authority **(1)**_

   Sentences will vary.

4. the hush of the spectators _the spectators' hush **(1)**_

   Sentences will vary.

5. the sore throat of the actress _the actress's sore throat **(1)**_

   Sentences will vary.

6. the big chance for the understudy _the understudy's big chance **(1)**_

   Sentences will vary.

7. the groan of the audience _the audience's groan **(1)**_

   Sentences will vary.

8. the surprise of the critics _the critics' surprise **(1)**_

   Sentences will vary.

Assessment Tip: Total **8** Points

Name _____

# Spelling Words

Look for familiar spelling patterns to help you remember how to spell the Spelling Words on this page. Think carefully about the parts that you find hard to spell in each word.

**Write the missing letters in the Spelling Words below.**

1. w o__ u__ l__ d (**1 point**)

2. w o__ u__ l__ dn't (**1**)

3. clo t__ h__ e__ s__ (**1**)

4. happ e__ n__ e__ d__ (**1**)

5. som e__ one (**1**)

6. sometim e__ s__ (**1**)

7. diff e__ r e__ nt (**1**)

8. an o__ ther (**1**)

9. w e__ i__ r__ d (**1**)

10. eig h__ t__ h__ (**1**)

11. c o__ m__ ing (**1**)

12. g e__ t__ t__ ing (**1**)

13. g o__ ing (**1**)

14. st o__ p__ p__ ed (**1**)

15. h e__ r__ e__ (**1**)

**Spelling Words**

1. would
2. wouldn't
3. clothes
4. happened
5. someone
6. sometimes
7. different
8. another
9. weird
10. eighth
11. coming
12. getting
13. going
14. stopped
15. here

**Study List On a separate piece of paper, write each Spelling Word. Check your spelling against the words on the list.** Order of words may vary.

Assessment Tip: Total **15** Points

Name _____

# Spelling Spree

**Find a Rhyme** **For each sentence write a Spelling Word that rhymes with the underlined word and makes sense in the sentence.**

1. The band _____ playing when the singer <u>dropped</u> his microphone.
2. When Alison <u>peered</u> out the window, she saw a _____ looking bird.
3. If my sweatshirt had a <u>hood</u>, I _____ definitely wear it on a day like this.
4. A <u>humming</u> sound was _____ from the car's engine.
5. We're _____ to the store after you finish <u>mowing</u> the lawn.
6. You <u>shouldn't</u> treat anyone in a way you _____ want to be treated yourself.
7. You have nothing to <u>fear</u> _____.

1. <u>stopped</u> **(1 point)**
2. <u>weird</u> **(1)**
3. <u>would</u> **(1)**
4. <u>coming</u> **(1)**

5. <u>going</u> **(1)**
6. <u>wouldn't</u> **(1)**
7. <u>here</u> **(1)**

**Spelling Words**

1. would
2. wouldn't
3. clothes
4. happened
5. someone
6. sometimes
7. different
8. another
9. weird
10. eighth
11. coming
12. getting
13. going
14. stopped
15. here

**Finding Words** **Each word below is hidden in a Spelling Word. Write the Spelling Word.**

8. pen
9. on
10. eight
11. tin
12. cloth
13. not
14. met
15. rent

8. <u>happened</u> **(1)**
9. <u>someone</u> **(1)**
10. <u>eighth</u> **(1)**
11. <u>getting</u> **(1)**
12. <u>clothes</u> **(1)**

13. <u>another</u> **(1)**
14. <u>sometimes</u> **(1)**
15. <u>different</u> **(1)**

*I'm letting her stay ahead of me until she starts getting tired.*

Theme 2: **Give It All You've Got** 81
Assessment Tip: Total **15** Points

Name _____

# Proofreading and Writing

**Proofreading** Circle the five misspelled Spelling Words in this certificate. Then write each word correctly.

1. would
2. wouldn't
3. clothes
4. happened
5. someone
6. sometimes
7. different
8. another
9. weird
10. eighth
11. coming
12. getting
13. going
14. stopped
15. here

### Certificate of Effort

This is to certify that Eduardo Díaz gave it all he had in the four hundred meter race held on the (eightth) day of May of this year. Just as the runners were (geting) to the first turn, Eduardo fell. (No one is sure just how it (happenned).) He could easily have (stoped) running there. Instead, he got back up, kept (goeing) and finished the race. We are proud to recognize him here for his extraordinary effort.

1. eighth **(1 point)**
2. getting **(1)**
3. happened **(1)**
4. stopped **(1)**
5. going **(1)**

**Writing Headlines** Write four headlines for newspaper stories about people who gave it all they had. The headlines can be about people in the theme's selections, can be about people you know of from somewhere else, or can be completely made up. Include a Spelling Word in each headline. Responses will vary. **(5)**

Assessment Tip: Total **10** Points

Name _____

# What a Performance!

**Words are missing in the sentences. Fill each blank with a word or words from the box.**

**Vocabulary**

talent

pantomime

forty-five record

limelight

applause

volunteered

rehearsal

embarrassed

duo

debut

1. If you are the only one on stage, you are in the
   limelight **(1 point)** .

2. If you are good at something, you have
   talent **(1)** .

3. If you buy an old record with one song on each side, you
   become the owner of a <u>forty-five record **(1)**</u> .

4. If you have agreed to help, you have
   volunteered **(1)** .

5. If you act without speaking, you
   pantomime **(1)** .

6. If you perform for the first time, you make your
   debut **(1)** .

7. If you go to practice a play, you attend a
   rehearsal **(1)** .

8. If you forget your lines during a play, you may feel
   embarrassed **(1)** .

9. If you please the audience, you may hear
   applause **(1)** .

10. If you perform with a partner, you are part of a
    duo **(1)** .

Name _____

# Talent Report

**Fill in the story map with information from the selection.**

| Characters | Setting |
|---|---|
| Manuel, Benny, Mr. Roybal, Manuel's family **(2 points)** | Manuel's school and his home **(2)** |

**Plot**

**Events**

1. Manuel volunteers to be in the school talent show. He plans to pantomime the words to "La Bamba." **(2)**

2. Manuel practices his act at rehearsal. His forty-five record slips out of his hand and rolls across the floor. **(2)**

3. On the night of the talent show, all the kids who go onstage before Manuel do fine. **(2)**

4. Finally, it's Manuel's turn to perform. He is nervous when he steps onstage, but he starts to relax and have fun as his performance goes on and he hears the audience clapping. **(2)**

**Problem**

5. When Manuel is in the middle of his routine, the record skips. Manuel is embarrassed and doesn't know what to do. **(2)**

**Solution**

6. Manuel keeps repeating the same steps and mouthing the same line over and over. The audience loves the act and thinks Manuel made the record skip on purpose. **(2)**

Assessment Tip: Total **16** Points

Name _____

# Manuel's Journal

**Manuel might have written about the talent show in his journal. Finish each sentence to show what he might have said about his performance.**

September _____, _____
        (today's date)            (year)

I can't believe I survived the talent show. Here's how it happened. I'd volunteered to pretend to sing Ritchie Valens's "La Bamba" before the entire school. **(1 point)** . Two things happened at rehearsal that should have made me nervous. First, Mr. Roybal's record player speed jammed **(1)** . Then, when Benny blew his trumpet, I dropped the record **(1)** .

On the night of the show, I had to wait for my turn onstage. A lot of other kids performed before me. As I watched them, I shivered with fear **(1)** . Finally it was my turn. At first, I took a dance step and the audience liked it and applauded. **(1)** .

Then, suddenly, something awful happened: the record got stuck, and repeated the same line over and over **(1)** .

I didn't know what to do, so I bowed to the audience, which applauded wildly **(1)** . As I left the stage, I tried hard to hold back the tears **(1)** .

Here's the funny thing. After the performance I received a burst of applause that was so loud it shook the walls of the cafeteria **(1)** .

I couldn't believe that people had actually liked my performance **(1)** .

Name _____

# A Class Act

**Read the story. Then complete the activity on page 87.**

## Horsing Around

Every year, the fifth grade classes held a big softball game and talent show. This year, Amy and Carmen decided to enter the talent show. Since their team was the Mustangs, the girls decided to dance in a horse costume. Amy would be the front half and Carmen the back half.

They spent an entire weekend making a papier-mâché horse's head. Carmen's dad sewed the body from fleecy brown cloth. The girls made the mane and tail out of thick black yarn. Amy's mom helped them learn a dance to a song called "Plains Pony."

At last it was the day of the show. But as the girls nervously galloped onto the softball diamond, they heard giggling from the audience. Someone called, "Hey, Horsey! You forgot something!" Carmen gasped, "Oh, no!" Peeking out from the horse's head, Amy saw something black near home plate. Their tail!

"What will we do?" Carmen whispered. Amy replied, "We'll pretend we planned it this way!" The next time they passed home plate, they danced around the tail and Amy snatched it up. Then she and Carmen danced backwards off the field, shaking their hooves to the music as Amy waved goodbye with the tail. The audience applauded noisily, screaming with laughter.

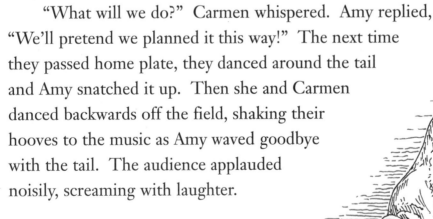

Name _____

# A Class Act continued

**Fill in the story map so it sums up the story on page 86. Write the characters' names, the setting, and the events that make up the plot.**

| **Main Characters** | **Setting** (time and place) |
|---|---|
| Amy and Carmen **(1 point)** | a school in modern times **(1)** |

**Plot**

The fifth graders hold an annual softball game and talent show. Amy and Carmen decide to dance in the show as a horse.  They work hard on a costume.  The girls face a problem during the show — their tail falls off. Through quick thinking, they solve their problem and are a success. **(4)**

**Problem**

As they go out onto the field to start their dance, their horse's tail falls off.  The girls are embarrassed. **(2)**

**Solution**

Amy tells Carmen to pretend that they planned to drop the tail.  They pick it up and use it to wave goodbye to the audience.  The audience loves it. **(2)**

Name _____

# Record Roots

Some words in the box contain the word root *spec*.
Others contain the root *opt*.  Write the words that match each
clue.  Then write each numbered letter in the space with the
matching number to find a message.

inspector

optician

optometry

respect

spectacle

suspect

1. a person who makes or sells eyeglasses

    <u>o</u>  <u>p</u>  <u>t</u>  <u>i</u>  <u>c</u>  <u>i</u>  <u>a</u>  <u>n</u>  **(1 point)**
     9            6

2. to look up to or regard highly

    <u>r</u>  <u>e</u>  <u>s</u>  <u>p</u>  <u>e</u>  <u>c</u>  <u>t</u>  **(1)**
     7

3. a remarkable or impressive sight

    <u>s</u>  <u>p</u>  <u>e</u>  <u>c</u>  <u>t</u>  <u>a</u>  <u>c</u>  <u>l</u>  <u>e</u>  **(1)**
       3           5

4. the profession of examining a person's vision

    <u>o</u>  <u>p</u>  <u>t</u>  <u>o</u>  <u>m</u>  <u>e</u>  <u>t</u>  <u>r</u>  <u>y</u>  **(1)**
                     10

5. to look upon someone as guilty without proof

    <u>s</u>  <u>u</u>  <u>s</u>  <u>p</u>  <u>e</u>  <u>c</u>  <u>t</u>  **(1)**
       4    1

6. a person who examines something closely and carefully

    <u>i</u>  <u>n</u>  <u>s</u>  <u>p</u>  <u>e</u>  <u>c</u>  <u>t</u>  <u>o</u>  <u>r</u>  **(1)**
     8           2

Manuel gained a lot of <u>p</u> <u>o</u> <u>p</u> <u>u</u> <u>l</u> <u>a</u> <u>r</u> <u>i</u> <u>t</u> <u>y</u> after
his performance.       1   2   3   4   5   6   7   8   9   10

**(4 points)**

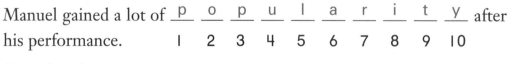

Assessment Tip: Total **10** Points

# The /ou/, /ô/, and /oi/ Sounds

When you hear the /ou/, the /ô/, and the /oi/ sounds, think of these patterns:

/ou/  *ou, ow*  **ou**nce, t**ow**er

/ô/  *aw, au, a* before *l*  cl**aw**, p**au**se, b**al**d

/oi/  *oi, oy*  m**oi**st, l**oy**al

Remember that the patterns *ou*, *au*, and *oi* are usually followed by a consonant sound.

**Write each Spelling Word under its vowel sound.**
Order of answers for each category may vary.

**Spelling Words**

1. hawk
2. claw
3. bald
4. tower
5. halt
6. prowl
7. loyal
8. pause
9. moist
10. ounce
11. launch
12. royal
13. scowl
14. haunt
15. noisy
16. coward
17. fawn
18. thousand
19. drown
20. fault

**/ou/ Sound**

tower **(1 point)**

prowl **(1)**

ounce **(1)**

scowl **(1)**

coward **(1)**

thousand **(1)**

drown **(1)**

**/ô/ Sound**

hawk **(1)**

claw **(1)**

bald **(1)**

halt **(1)**

pause **(1)**

launch **(1)**

haunt **(1)**

fawn **(1)**

fault **(1)**

**/oi/ Sound**

loyal **(1)**

moist **(1)**

royal **(1)**

noisy **(1)**

Theme 2: **Give It All You've Got**   89
Assessment Tip: Total **20** Points

Name _____

# Spelling Spree

**Contrast Clues** The second part of each clue contrasts with the first part. Write a Spelling Word after each clue.

1. not hairy, but <u>bald **(1 point)**</u>
2. not a traitor, but <u>loyal **(1)**</u>
3. not a smile, but a <u>scowl **(1)**</u>
4. not to dock, but to <u>launch **(1)**</u>
5. not an adult deer, but a <u>fawn **(1)**</u>
6. not a pound, but an <u>ounce **(1)**</u>
7. not a sparrow, but a <u>hawk **(1)**</u>
8. not lowly or common, but <u>royal **(1)**</u>
9. not quiet, but <u>noisy **(1)**</u>
10. not to move about openly, but to <u>prowl **(1)**</u>

**Finding Words** Each word below is hidden in a Spelling Word. Write the Spelling Words that contain these words.

11. aunt <u>haunt **(1)**</u>
12. tow <u>tower **(1)**</u>
13. sand <u>thousand **(1)**</u>
14. law <u>claw **(1)**</u>
15. use <u>pause **(1)**</u>

Assessment Tip: Total **15** Points

Name _____

# Proofreading and Writing

**Proofreading** Circle the five misspelled Spelling Words in this e-mail. Then write each word correctly.

| ☐ | **File** | **Edit** | **View** | **Toolbox** | **Help** | | ✉ |

To: Grandma

From: Manuel

Subject: Talent Show

    The show turned out okay, but I was pretty nervous beforehand. My hands were (moyst) with sweat. I'm no (cowerd,) though. I went out and started my act. Then the record stuck, and I had to sing the same words over and over. It was Benny's (falt) for making me scratch the record. When the music finally came to a (hault,) I ran offstage. I felt awful! At the end of the show, though, I got a round of applause noisy enough to (droun) out the names of the other acts. Nobody was more surprised than I was!

**Spelling Words**

1. hawk
2. claw
3. bald
4. tower
5. halt
6. prowl
7. loyal
8. pause
9. moist
10. ounce
11. launch
12. royal
13. scowl
14. haunt
15. noisy
16. coward
17. fawn
18. thousand
19. drown
20. fault

1. moist **(1 point)**

2. coward **(1)**

3. fault **(1)**

4. halt **(1)**

5. drown **(1)**

✏️➤ **Write an Announcement** Suppose that Manuel decided to give another performance of "La Bamba." How would you go about advertising it? What information would you need to include? How would you describe his act?

**On a separate piece of paper, write an announcement for this repeat performance. Use Spelling Words from the list.**
Responses will vary. **(5)**

Name _____

# Mixed Meanings

**Read the definitions of each word.  Then write one or two sentences that use different meanings of each word.**  Sample answers shown.

**fall** (fôl) *v.* **fell, fallen, falling, falls. 1.** To drop or come down. **2.** To suffer defeat or capture. **3.** *n.* The season of the year occurring between summer and winter.

1. During the fall, I love to watch leaves fall from the

   trees to the ground. **(2 points)**

**hand** (hănd) *n.* **1.** The part of the arm below the wrist. **2.** A round of applause. *v.* To give or pass with the hands; transmit.

2. The director handed Bonnie a bouquet of flowers as the audience

   gave her a hand. **(2)**

**stage** (stāj) *n.* **1.** A raised platform, especially one in a theater on which entertainers perform. **2.** A level or step in a process. *v.* To produce or direct a performance.

3. Sheila's school stages a musical every spring. My mother says my

   baby brother is at a difficult stage. **(2)**

**step** (stĕp) *n.* **1.** The movement of raising one foot and putting it down. **2.** An action taken to achieve a goal. *v.* To press the foot down or against.

4. If you follow the steps correctly, you'll make a perfect kite. Every

   step I take brings me a little closer to the campground. **(2)**

**stick** (stĭk) *n.* A long slender piece of wood. *v.* **1.** To fasten or attach, as with a pin or nail. **2.** To become fixed and unable to move.

5. Freddy's dog likes to chase sticks. Peanut butter sticks to the roof

   of my mouth. **(2)**

Assessment Tip: Total **10** Points

Name _____

# Mary Sings and Puppets Move

**Action Verbs** An **action verb** tells what the subject does or did. It is the main word in the complete predicate.

> The performers **bowed** to the audience.
>
> **action verb**

**Underline the action verb in each of the following sentences. (1 point each)**

1. Martin and Mary <u>built</u> a small theater for their puppet show.

2. Martin's father <u>cut</u> the wood for them.

3. Martin <u>painted</u> designs on the wooden theater.

4. Mary <u>picked</u> a song for their show.

5. On the night of the show, Martin <u>watches</u> the audience.

6. The audience <u>claps</u> for the tap dancer.

7. Martin and Mary <u>carry</u> their puppets on stage.

8. The puppets <u>dance</u> to the music.

9. The puppeteers <u>wait</u> for applause.

10. The crowd <u>cheers</u>!

Name _____

# He Gave a Speech

**Direct Objects** A **direct object** is a noun or pronoun in a predicate that receives the action of the verb. It answers the question *What?* or *Whom?*

The dancer tied his **shoes.**

The dancer tied *what?* His shoes. Therefore, *shoes* is the direct object.

**Underline the action verb and circle the direct object in each sentence below.**

1. Mr. Bruno <u>needed</u> a (volunteer) to give a speech. **(1 point)**

2. Sydney <u>raised</u> his (hand.) **(1)**

3. Mr. Bruno <u>thanked</u> (him) for volunteering. **(1)**

4. Sydney nervously <u>shuffled</u> his (notes.) **(1)**

5. Then he <u>cleared</u> his (throat.) **(1)**

6. He <u>projected</u> his (voice) throughout the room. **(1)**

7. Susan <u>heard</u> his (words) in the back of the classroom. **(1)**

8. After the speech, Mario <u>asked</u> a (question) of Sydney. **(1)**

9. Sydney <u>answered</u> the (query) politely. **(1)**

10. Then Sydney <u>set</u> his (notes) down. **(1)**

Assessment Tip: Total **10** Points

Name _____

# She Wrote and I Scribbled

**Using Exact Verbs** Your writing will be more vivid if you use action verbs that tell exactly what the subject of the sentence is doing. Look at the two sentences below. Which verb gives you a better idea of how Sandy made her way across the stage?

Sandy **moved** across the stage.

Sandy **twirled** across the stage.

**Pat is writing a review of the class play for the school newspaper. Replace each underlined verb with a more exact one. Choose from among the verbs in the box.** Answers may vary. **(1 point for each word)**

> stomped
> stumbled
> shouted
> fumbled
> scribbled

Last night I saw the class play *Ramshackle Inn*. There were five main

characters. The innkeeper was a loud man with a beard. When he <u>said</u> his
                              shouted

lines, others onstage covered their ears. The brother was clumsy. He
  stumbled                                      stomped

<u>walked</u> back and forth across the stage. His rude and angry sister <u>walked</u>
                                scribbled

up and down the stairs. The reporter <u>wrote</u> constantly in his pad. The
                                           fumbled

inept police officer was the funniest character of all. She <u>played</u> with her

radio, trying to get it to work. The plot of this play was silly, but the

actors were fun to watch.

Name _____

# Writing a Summary

If you were asked to summarize "La Bamba," you would probably tell who performed in the talent show and what happened during the performances. A **summary** is a brief account of a story or selection. Writing a summary is a good way to share what a story is about and to recall main events and characters.

**Choose a selection you have read, such as *Earthquake Terror* or *Michelle Kwan: Heart of a Champion*. Then fill in the graphic organizer below with the most important ideas or events in the selection.**

Selection: _____

| Idea/ Event | Idea/ Event | Idea/ Event | Idea/ Event |
|---|---|---|---|
| (3 points) | (3) | (3) | (3) |

**Now write your summary of the selection on a separate sheet of paper. Remember to leave out details and minor events. Briefly restate the most important ideas or events in your own words. (3)**

Assessment Tip: Total **15** Points

Name _____

# Paraphrasing

When you **paraphrase** a passage from a book, article, or story, you put it into your own words without changing the author's meaning. A careful writer makes sure to paraphrase without copying any passages word-for-word from the work of other writers.

**Read the following passage from "La Bamba."**

> But when Manuel did a fancy dance step, there was a burst of applause and some girls screamed. Manuel tried another dance step. He heard more applause and screams and started getting into the groove as he shivered and snaked around the stage. But the record got stuck, and he had to sing
>
> *Para bailar la bamba*
> *Para bailar la bamba*
> *Para bailar la bamba*
> *Para bailar la bamba*
> again and again.

**Now read one fifth grader's paraphrase of the passage.**

**Paraphrase**

*Manuel did one fancy dance step and then another. The audience applauded and screamed when he shivered and snaked across the stage. Then the record got stuck, and he sang one line of "La Bamba" again and again.*

**Improve the student's paraphrase by reducing it to a single sentence that tells what happened in the passage. You may want to reorder the information and reduce the number of details. Be sure to avoid repetition of whole phrases that appeared in the original passage. Write your improved version on the lines below.** Responses will vary. **(10 points)**

Even though Manuel was forced to lip-synch one line repeatedly when his record

got stuck, the audience responded enthusiastically to his pantomime of "La Bamba."

Name _____

# Have No Fear

Read the words in the chart. Then look in the word box to find a synonym and an antonym for each, and write these in the chart. Use a dictionary if you need help.

| | synonym | antonym |
|---|---|---|
| terrified | frightened **(1)** | unafraid **(1)** |
| dismayed | bewildered **(1)** | untroubled **(1)** |
| excitement | agitation **(1)** | monotony **(1)** |
| stamina | strength **(1)** | weakness **(1)** |
| concentrate | focus **(1)** | disregard **(1)** |
| discomfort | pain **(1)** | comfort **(1)** |
| unsure | uncertain **(1)** | sure **(1)** |
| cautious | careful **(1)** | reckless **(1)** |
| immobile | stationary **(1)** | mobile **(1)** |

Choose a word from the word box and write your own sentence.

**(2)** _____

_____

Assessment Tip: Total **20** Points

Name ______________________________

# I Predict . . .

**Fill in the chart with your predictions, based on details from the selection and on what you know from personal experience.**

| Predicting Outcomes | |
|---|---|
| selection details + personal knowledge + THINKING = prediction | |
| **Selection Details**<br>▶ Doug needs to get past a narrow ledge.<br>▶ The journey seems futile.<br>▶ Doug has made it to the narrow ledge before. | **Personal Knowledge**<br>▶ People who have done something before, even if it was difficult, know that they can do it again. |
| **Prediction:** Doug will make it back to the ledge. | |

| | |
|---|---|
| **Selection Details**<br>(2 points) ______________________<br>______________________ | **Personal Knowledge**<br>(2) ______________________<br>______________________ |
| **Prediction:** (1) ______________________<br>______________________ | |

| | |
|---|---|
| **Selection Details**<br>(2 points) ______________________<br>______________________ | **Personal Knowledge**<br>(2) ______________________<br>______________________ |
| **Prediction:** (1) ______________________<br>______________________ | |





Assessment Tip: Total **10** Points

Name _____

# Events Leading to the Climax

**The events in *The Fear Place* lead to a climax when Doug must face his fear. Fill in the event map with sentences that describe the events that lead up to and come after the climax. Start at the bottom of the page.**

7. Doug knows he is past the "fear place" when he comes to a part of the path that is wider and safer. **(2)**

⬆

6. When Doug reaches the narrowest part of the ledge, he edges his way across it carefully. **(2)**

⬆

5. Doug reaches the "fear place" and slowly begins to move across the ledge. **(2)**

⬆

4. Doug watches where Charlie goes and follows her up the path as it gets narrower and narrower. **(2)**

⬆

3. Charlie appears on the scene and startles Doug. **(2)**

⬆

2. Doug reaches the first ridge. He thinks about the weather to keep his mind off of his fear. **(2)**

⬆

1. Doug begins to climb, but every time he gains altitude he loses it again. **(2)**

Name _____

# Looking Forward

**Read the passage. Then complete the activity on page 102.**

## The Apology

Alexa hadn't meant to break the bowl. In fact, she'd always loved that china bowl and its pretty blue pattern. But she had broken it, and all week she'd listened with dread for the phone call she knew would come. It would be Mrs. Holabird, their neighbor, calling to tell her mother about the accident.

The Holabirds had no children of their own, so they were especially fond of Alexa. She had been helping Mrs. Holabird with chores for about two years. When they went out of town, the Holabirds always paid Alexa to cat-sit for Misty. Alexa would come twice a day and refill Misty's food and water bowls. She usually stayed for a while, holding the big, silky cat on her lap and scratching her behind the ears. Sometimes she helped Misty exercise. It was fun to toss a ball or a catnip mouse into the air and watch the fat, fluffy cat leap and grab for it with her paws. How was she to know that Misty would crash into the bowl and knock it off its stand?

Alexa had been so horrified that she had hidden the broken pieces under the sideboard. She went home and fearfully awaited the phone call. But three days later it still had not come, even though the Holabirds had returned two days ago.

On the fourth morning, Alexa awoke with her mind made up. She put on her coat and walked to the front door, calling, "Mom, I need to go see Mr. and Mrs. Holabird."

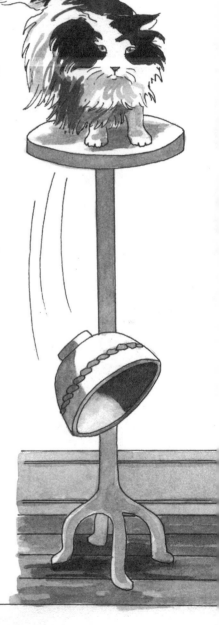

Name _____

# Looking Forward continued

**Answer these questions about the passage on page 101.**

1. What do you think Alexa will do next?

   She will go over to the Holabirds' house, tell them about the

   accident, and apologize. **(2 points)**

2. What clues in the passage helped you make this prediction?

   The first three paragraphs make clear that Alexa feels sorry about

   breaking the bowl and is afraid that Mrs. Holabird will call her

   mother. The fourth paragraph says that Alexa awoke with her mind

   made up and told her mother she needed to see the Holabirds. **(4)**

3. Do you think Alexa's mother will be glad that Alexa apologized to

   Mrs. Holabird? Why or why not?

   Yes, because that is what parents usually want their children to do

   if they have done something wrong. **(2)**

4. Do you think the Holabirds will ask Alexa to care for Misty again?
   Why or why not?

   Yes, because they are especially fond of Alexa and she has helped

   them with chores for two years. **(2)**

5. What might Alexa do to make up for breaking the bowl?

   She might offer to pay for it or to work off its value by doing

   chores. **(2)**

6. What is one thing Alexa might do differently the next time she plays
   with Misty?

   She might make sure to play with her outside or in a room that

   doesn't have breakable objects. **(2)**

Assessment Tip: Total **14** Points

Name _____

# Nervous? No, Onward!

**Read this diary page. Underline each word with the suffix *-ward***
**or *-ous*. (1 point** for each underlined word)

### The Hike

Climbing to the mountaintop was a frightening experience.
At first, it didn't seem so bad. The path <u>upward</u> was wide, even
<u>spacious</u>. After a while, though, I began to be <u>nervous</u>. The rise
was <u>continuous</u>, and the path began to narrow. When I looked
over the edge, I saw a <u>monstrous</u> gap between me and the canyon
bottom far below. Still, I made my way <u>toward</u> the top, pausing
only now and then. I knew that if I glanced <u>backward</u>, I would be
in trouble. Instead, I gazed <u>outward</u> to the golden plain in the
distance. It was a <u>marvelous</u> sight. I knew I would head <u>homeward</u>
in less than an hour.

**Now write each word you underlined next to its meaning.**

1. toward **(1 point)** _____ : in a direction nearer

2. nervous **(1)** _____ : uncomfortable

3. outward **(1)** _____ : in a direction away from

4. monstrous **(1)** _____ : huge

5. homeward **(1)** _____ : toward where one lives

6. upward **(1)** _____ : heading above

7. backward **(1)** _____ : to the rear

8. spacious **(1)** _____ : roomy

9. continuous **(1)** _____ : ongoing, with no break

10. marvelous **(1)** _____ : wonderful

Name _____

# The /ôr/, /âr/, and /är/ Sounds

When you hear the /ôr/ sound, think of the patterns *or, oar,* and *ore.* When you hear the /âr/ sound, think of the patterns *are* and *air.* When you hear the /är/ sound, think of the pattern *ar.*

/ôr/ **tor**ch, **s**oar, **s**ore     /âr/ **ha**re, fl**air**     /är/ sc**ar**

► The vowel sound + *r* spellings of the starred words differ from the usual spelling patterns. The /ôr/ sound is spelled *ar* in *warn* and *oor* in *floor.*

**Write each Spelling Word under its vowel + *r* sound.**
Order of answers for each category may vary.

| /ôr/ Sound | /âr/ Sound |
|---|---|
| torch **(1 point)** | hare **(1)** |
| soar **(1)** | flair **(1)** |
| sore **(1)** | lair **(1)** |
| lord **(1)** | snare **(1)** |
| warn **(1)** | fare **(1)** |
| floor **(1)** | flare **(1)** |
| tore **(1)** | rare **(1)** |
| bore **(1)** | **/är/ Sound** |
| gorge **(1)** | scar **(1)** |
| | harsh **(1)** |
| | carve **(1)** |
| | barge **(1)** |

| | Spelling Words |
|---|---|
| 1. | hare |
| 2. | scar |
| 3. | torch |
| 4. | soar |
| 5. | harsh |
| 6. | sore |
| 7. | lord |
| 8. | flair |
| 9. | warn* |
| 10. | floor* |
| 11. | tore |
| 12. | lair |
| 13. | snare |
| 14. | carve |
| 15. | bore |
| 16. | fare |
| 17. | gorge |
| 18. | barge |
| 19. | flare |
| 20. | rare |

Name _____

# Spelling Spree

**Word Hunt** Write the Spelling Word that you find in each of the longer words below.

**Example:** snowboarder *board*

1. torchlight — <u>torch **(1 point)**</u>
2. harebrained — <u>hare **(1)**</u>
3. warlord — <u>lord **(1)**</u>
4. scarcely — <u>scar **(1)**</u>
5. welfare — <u>fare **(1)**</u>
6. restored — <u>tore **(1)**</u>
7. floorshow — <u>floor **(1)**</u>

**Alphabet Puzzler** Write the Spelling Word that fits alphabetically between the two words in each group.

8. apple, <u>barge **(1)**</u>, bicycle
9. butter, <u>carve **(1)**</u>, dinner
10. ladder, <u>lair **(1)**</u>, loan
11. sock, <u>sore **(1)**</u>, stomach
12. father, <u>flair **(1)**</u>, flame
13. harmful, <u>harsh **(1)**</u>, kitchen
14. sneeze, <u>soar **(1)**</u>, solid
15. secret, <u>snare **(1)**</u>, snow

## Spelling Words

1. hare
2. scar
3. torch
4. soar
5. harsh
6. sore
7. lord
8. flair
9. warn*
10. floor*
11. tore
12. lair
13. snare
14. carve
15. bore
16. fare
17. gorge
18. barge
19. flare
20. rare

Assessment Tip: Total **15** Points

Name _____

# Proofreading and Writing

**Proofreading** Circle the five misspelled Spelling Words in this part of a note. Then write each word correctly.

To the Park Rangers:

I have to leave unexpectedly for a day. Will you keep an eye on my two boys, who are camping on the north ledge? They are experienced climbers, but their tempers sometimes (flar) when they're alone with each other. For that matter, it's (rair) for them to get along anytime! The younger one has a sore knee from sliding down a (gorg.) I won't (boar) you with the details, but I would appreciate it if you could check on them during the day. I'll (woarn) them to behave themselves.

1. flare **(1 point)** _____
2. rare **(1)** _____
3. gorge **(1)** _____
4. bore **(1)** _____
5. warn **(1)** _____

**Spelling Words**

1. hare
2. scar
3. torch
4. soar
5. harsh
6. sore
7. lord
8. flair
9. warn*
10. floor*
11. tore
12. lair
13. snare
14. carve
15. bore
16. fare
17. gorge
18. barge
19. flare
20. rare

✎ **Write a Prediction** Now that Doug has made it past the Fear Place, what do you think will happen next? Will he find his brother safe or in danger? Will Charlie continue to help him?

**On a separate piece of paper, write a paragraph giving your prediction of what will happen next in the story. Use Spelling Words from the list.** Responses will vary. **(5)**

Assessment Tip: Total **10** Points

Name _____

# Homophone Echoes

**Match the letter of the correct definition to the underlined word. Then write the homophone pairs at the bottom of the page.** (1 point each)

1. The hiker makes her way through a narrow canyon. __a__

2. As she climbs, objects below seem to get smaller __e__

3. She kneels beside the burrow of a ground squirrel. __f__

4. In the distance she can see a snow-capped peak. __h__

5. Will she freeze when she gets to the top? __i__

6. She takes a quick peek into the canyon. __c__

7. The seam in her boot rubs her heel. __d__

8. She's a long way from the borough of Brooklyn! __j__

9. If she threw a stone, it might cause a rockslide below. __b__

10. Watching an eagle fly frees her from her fear. __g__

a. in and out of
b. tossed
c. glance
d. stitch
e. appear
f. tunnel
g. liberates
h. summit
i. be cold
j. city section

11. through    threw _____

12. peek    peak _____

13. seam    seem _____

14. freeze    frees _____

15. burrow    burough _____

Name _____

# We Are Diving

**Main Verbs and Helping Verbs** A simple predicate can be more than one word. The **main verb** is the most important word in the predicate. The **helping verb** comes before the **main verb**.

I **have climbed** the rope.    main verb: *climbed*    helping verb: *have*

**Write the main verb and the helping verb in each of the following sentences.**

1. This summer camp program has challenged me.

**Main verb:** challenged **(1 point)**

**Helping verb:** has **(1)**

2. I am facing my fear of water in the swimming classes.

**Main verb:** facing **(1)**

**Helping verb:** am **(1)**

3. The swimming teacher has given me much encouragement.

**Main verb:** given **(1)**

**Helping verb:** has **(1)**

4. I have swum two laps so far this morning.

**Main verb:** swum **(1)**

**Helping verb:** have **(1)**

5. Next summer, I will learn to dive!

**Main verb:** learn **(1)**

**Helping verb:** will **(1)**

Assessment Tip: Total **10** Points

Name _____

# Jellyfish Are Nasty

**Linking Verbs** A **linking verb** links the subject to a word in the predicate that names or describes the subject. It does not show action. A **predicate noun** following a linking verb names the subject. A **predicate adjective** following a linking verb describes the subject.

---

**Common Linking Verbs**

| am | is | are | was | were | will be |
|-----|------|-------|-------|-------|---------|
| look | feel | taste | smell | seem | appear |

---

**Underline the linking verb in each sentence below. Circle each predicate noun or predicate adjective. Write *PN* on the line if the circled word is a predicate noun. Write *PA* if it is a predicate adjective.** (**1 point** for each)

**Example:** I <u>am</u> a (swimmer.) ___PN___

1. Susan <u>will be</u> a (lifeguard) someday. ___PN___

2. Lifeguards <u>are</u> (brave.) ___PA___

3. The ocean breeze <u>smells</u> (fresh.) ___PA___

4. I <u>am</u> (afraid) of jellyfish. ___PA___

5. A sea nettle <u>is</u> a (jellyfish.) ___PN___

6. Ocean water <u>tastes</u> (salty.) ___PA___

7. That boat <u>is</u> a (kayak.) ___PN___

8. My grandmother <u>was</u> a (diver.) ___PN___

9. That stroke <u>seems</u> (difficult) to me. ___PA___

10. Clayton and Rachel <u>are</u> (surfers.) ___PN___

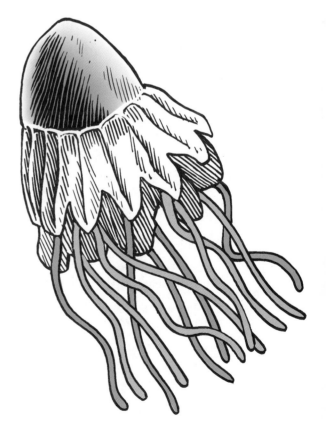

Name _____

# Are You Afraid?

**Using Forms of the Verb *be***  When using *be* as a linking verb, a writer
must use the correct form of the verb.  Like any other verb, a linking
verb must agree with its subject in number.

|  | The Verb *be* | |
| --- | --- | --- |
|  | **Present Tense** | **Past Tense** |
| I | am | was |
| You | are | were |
| She/he/it | is | was |
| We | are | were |
| You | are | were |
| They | are | were |

**Identify the five incorrect forms of the verb *be* in the draft.  Write the
correct form of the verb above the error. (2 points** for each correction)

                    was

A long time ago, I were afraid of dogs.  Every time I saw a dog I

would stand absolutely still.  Nobody could make me move until the dog

was                           were

were gone.  I don't know why, but dogs was just frightening to me.  My

                                      is

aunt said she would help me get to know her dog, Maggie.  Maggie are a

medium-sized dog.  Every day for a month my aunt came to our house

                    was

with Maggie.  She were right.  I began to trust Maggie and some other

dogs too.

Name _____

# Writing a Clarification Composition

Sometimes when you read, you will encounter a quote or statement that expresses a belief but whose meaning is not entirely clear. You can write a **clarification composition** to clarify the statement.

**Choose one of the following statements and write it on the clarification map:**

▶ *The only thing we have to fear is fear itself.*
   (Franklin D. Roosevelt)
▶ *Fools rush in where angels fear to tread.*
   (Alexander Pope)
▶ *Anything is possible, but not everything is probable.*
   (Doug Grillo)

**Then write what you think the statement means, and list reasons, details, and examples from *The Fear Place* that support your opinion.** Answers will vary.

| |
|---|
| **Statement (1 point)** |
| **Meaning (2)** |
| **Reasons, Details, and Examples (2)** |

**On a separate sheet of paper, write a three- to five-paragraph composition restating the statement in your own words and clarifying its meaning. Use examples from *The Fear Place* that support your opinion. (5)**

# Combining Sentences with Helping Verbs

Good writers avoid unnecessary repetition in their writing.
Sometimes you can improve your writing by combining
sentences that repeat the same helping verb into one sentence.

> Doug **had** reached the narrow ledge. He **had** glanced down
> at the rocky canyon.
>
> Doug **had** reached the narrow ledge and glanced down at the
> rocky canyon.

**Revise Doug Grillo's postcard by combining sentences that repeat
the same helping verb into a single sentence. Write the revised message
on the lines below. (2 points** for each combined sentence**)**

Dear Jim,

   We are finishing up our vacation in Colorado. We are coming home next week. I have
spotted a snowshoe rabbit. I have studied other wildlife for my merit badge. After a
fight, Gordie had hiked up a steep trail. My brother had pitched a tent on a high ridge.
I was very scared. I was determined to find my brother. I should have climbed with
someone else. I should have turned back before the narrow path curves sharply. Instead, I
faced my fear. With the help of Charlie the cougar, I reached my brother safely!

                    Your friend,

                    Doug

We are finishing up our vacation in Colorado and coming home next week. I have

spotted a snowshoe rabbit and studied other wildlife for my merit badge. After a

fight, Gordie had hiked up a steep trail and pitched a tent on a high ridge. I was very

scared but determined to find my brother. I should have climbed with someone else

or turned back before the narrow path curves sharply. Instead, I faced my fear. With

the help of Charlie the cougar, I reached my brother safely!

Name _____

# Space Is the Place

**Write each word from the box on the correct line.**

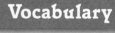

**Vocabulary**

artificial
satellite
launches *(verb)*
orbit
reusable
mission
specialist
space shuttle
astronaut
weightlessness

1. spacecraft

   satellite **(1 point)**

   space shuttle **(1)**

2. people

   specialist **(1)**

   astronaut **(1)**

3. descriptive words

   artificial **(1)**

   reusable **(1)**

4. words about movement

   launches **(1)**

   orbit **(1)**

5. a condition

   weightlessness **(1)**

**Now choose three words from the box. Use them to write a short paragraph about the launch of a spacecraft.**

(3) _____

_____

_____

_____

_____

_____

Name _____

# Main Idea Chart

| Topic: Mae Jemison | |
|---|---|
| **Page 211** | On September 12, 1992, Mae Jemison became the first African American woman to fly into space. |
| **Pages 212–213** | When Mae Jemison was growing up, she was interested in space travel, science, and math. **(2 points)** |
| **Pages 213–214** | Mae Jemison became a doctor and joined the Peace Corps. **(2)** |
| **Pages 215–216** | Mae Jemison returned to her medical practice, took engineering courses, and was accepted by NASA. **(2)** |
| **Page 217** | At the end of her training, Mae Jemison became a mission specialist astronaut. **(2)** |
| **Page 218** | Mae Jemison became an astronaut herself aboard the space shuttle *Endeavour*. **(2)** |
| **Pages 219–221** | Mae Jamison conducted important experiments on space sickness and the effects of zero gravity. **(2)** |
| **Pages 221–222** | Mae Jamison resigned from the astronaut corps and formed a company whose goal is to improve the quality of life through science and technology. **(2)** |

Assessment Tip: Total **14** Points

Name _____

# Is It True?

**The sentences below tell about Mae Jemison. Write T if the sentence is true, or F if the sentence is false. If a sentence is false, tell why it is false.**

1. Mae Jemison developed an interest in science at an early age.
   T **(2)**
   _____

2. Her parents and teachers all encouraged her to become a scientist.
   F One teacher told her she should try to become a nurse
   instead. **(2)**

3. When she graduated from Stanford University, she applied for admission to the astronaut corps.
   F She enrolled in medical school. **(2)**
   _____

4. Mae never gave up her childhood dream of traveling in space.
   T **(2)**
   _____

5. At the end of her year of intensive training, Mae Jemison rode a rocket into space.
   F After her year of training she had to wait four years to fly
   into space. **(2)**

6. On September 12, 1992, Mae Jemison became the first African American woman to journey into space.
   T **(2)**
   _____

Name _____

# Exploring the Topic

**Read the following passage. Then complete the activity on page 117.**

### Space Shuttle Science

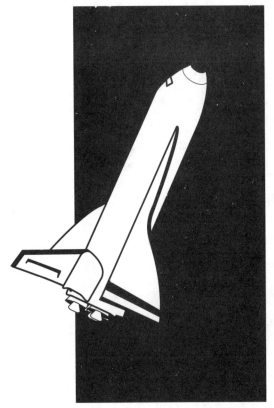

The space shuttle has many important uses. One use is for scientific research. In the weightless environment of space, scientists can carry out experiments they cannot do on Earth.

Inside the shuttle is a complete research laboratory called Spacelab. Spacelab is divided into two parts. One part is inside, where scientists can work. The other is outside and holds telescopes and other instruments that need to be exposed to space.

Most experiments take place in the inner section. Scientists on the space shuttle typically do experiments that make use of microgravity and weightlessness. They make new materials, such as crystals and silicon chips, and they also create medicines. Scientists even use themselves as test subjects, recording how weightlessness affects the human body.

Experiments in the outside section of Spacelab take advantage of being outside Earth's atmosphere. The atmosphere helps prevent radiation from reaching Earth, but it also makes radiation hard to study. Being outside the atmosphere also lets scientists use telescopes to get a clearer "view" of space.

Name _____

# Exploring the Topic continued

**Complete the chart below by filling in the topic and main ideas of the passage on page 116. Then write two details that support one of the main ideas.**

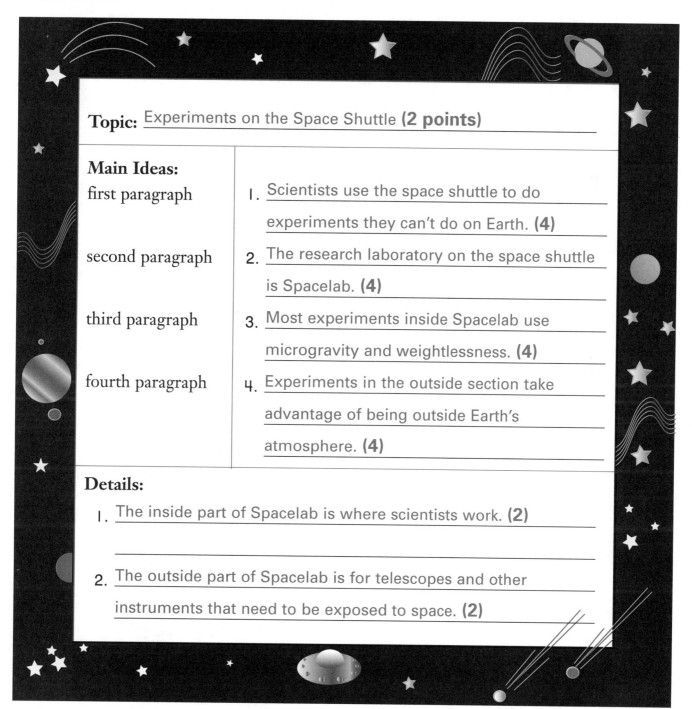

**Topic:** Experiments on the Space Shuttle **(2 points)**

| **Main Ideas:** | |
| --- | --- |
| first paragraph | 1. Scientists use the space shuttle to do experiments they can't do on Earth. **(4)** |
| second paragraph | 2. The research laboratory on the space shuttle is Spacelab. **(4)** |
| third paragraph | 3. Most experiments inside Spacelab use microgravity and weightlessness. **(4)** |
| fourth paragraph | 4. Experiments in the outside section take advantage of being outside Earth's atmosphere. **(4)** |

**Details:**

1. The inside part of Spacelab is where scientists work. **(2)**

2. The outside part of Spacelab is for telescopes and other instruments that need to be exposed to space. **(2)**

# Suffix Shuttle

**Choose words from the word boxes to write in the blanks in the paragraph below. Use the clue in parentheses to help you.**

| **-ic** |
|---|
| artistic |
| historic |
| periodic |
| realistic |

| **-ive** |
|---|
| inventive |
| massive |
| positive |
| supportive |

It was a truly (timely) <u>historic **(2 points)**</u> event

when the shuttle first went up.  The scientists who built it had

(clever) <u>inventive **(2)**</u> ideas.  They were

dreamers, but they were (aware of how things are)

<u>realistic **(2)**</u> about what was possible.

They knew the shuttle's flights would have to be

(now and then) <u>periodic **(2)**</u> during the

year.  But watching the (big) <u>massive **(2)**</u>

rocket rise into the air was breathtaking.  Its fiery trail in the

sky looked (made with style) <u>artistic **(2)**</u>.

The entire country was (in favor) <u>supportive **(2)**</u> of

their efforts.  They were (sure) <u>positive **(2)**</u>

they had a winner!

Assessment Tip: Total **16** Points

Name _____

# The /ûr/ and /îr/ Sounds

When you hear the /ûr/ sound, think of the patterns *er, ir, ur, ear,* and *or.* When you hear the /îr/ sounds, think of the patterns *eer* and *ear.*

/ûr/ g**er**m, st**ir**, ret**ur**n, **ear**ly, w**or**th

/îr/ st**eer**, sm**ear**

▶ The /îr/ sound in *pier* differs from the usual spelling patterns. In this word it is spelled *ier.*

**Write each Spelling Word under its vowel + *r* sound.**
Order of answers for each category may vary.

## /ûr/ Sound

germ **(1 point)**      burnt **(1)**

return **(1)**      term **(1)**

stir **(1)**      pearl **(1)**

squirm **(1)**      squirt **(1)**

nerve **(1)**      perch **(1)**

early **(1)**      hurl **(1)**

worth **(1)**      worse **(1)**

thirst **(1)**

## /îr/ Sound

smear **(1)**      rear **(1)**

peer **(1)**      steer **(1)**

pier **(1)**

**Spelling Words**

1. smear
2. germ
3. return
4. peer
5. stir
6. squirm
7. nerve
8. early
9. worth
10. pier*
11. thirst
12. burnt
13. rear
14. term
15. steer
16. pearl
17. squirt
18. perch
19. hurl
20. worse

Name _____

# Spelling Spree

**Hint and Hunt** **Write the Spelling Word that answers each question.**

1. What does a toy water pistol do?
2. What do you quench with a tall drink?
3. What is one thing you do with a spoon?
4. Where do you go to board a ship?
5. What might a diver find in an oyster?

1. squirt **(1 point)**
2. thirst **(1)**
3. stir **(1)**

4. pier **(1)**
5. pearl **(1)**

**Word Maze** **Begin at the arrow and follow the Word Maze to find ten Spelling Words. Write the words in order below.**

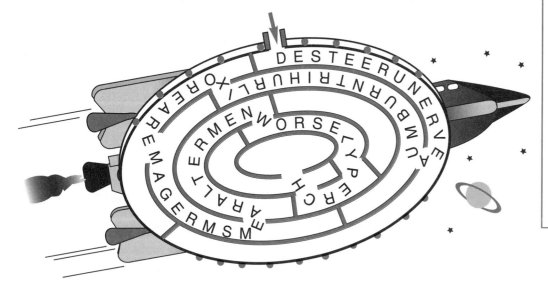

6. steer **(1)**
7. nerve **(1)**
8. burnt **(1)**

9. hurl **(1)**
10. rear **(1)**
11. germ **(1)**

12. smear **(1)**
13. term **(1)**
14. worse **(1)**
15. perch **(1)**

Assessment Tip: Total **15** Points

Name _____

# Proofreading and Writing

**Proofreading** Circle the five misspelled Spelling Words in this part of a script for a class skit. Then write each word correctly.

**Astronaut:**     Mission Control, when can we begin our (retern) to Earth?

**Mission Control:** Probably (erly) tomorrow morning. How's it going up there? How much fuel have you burnt?

**Astronaut:**     Not much—we've still got a few days' (werth.) We're all starting to (squerm) a bit up here, though. We're ready to go home. Actually, if I (per) closely through the glass here, I think I can see my house.

**Mission Control:** That's very funny.

1. return **(1 point)**
2. early **(1)**
3. worth **(1)**
4. squirm **(1)**
5. peer **(1)**

**Spelling Words**

1. smear
2. germ
3. return
4. peer
5. stir
6. squirm
7. nerve
8. early
9. worth
10. pier*
11. thirst
12. burnt
13. rear
14. term
15. steer
16. pearl
17. squirt
18. perch
19. hurl
20. worse

✏️ **Write a Newspaper Article** You have been asked to write a brief article about Mae Jemison's space shuttle mission for the school newspaper. Did any one of the experiments particularly interest you? Will you include any details about Jemison's personal life?

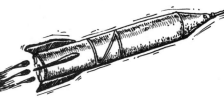

**On a separate piece of paper, write your article about Mae Jemison's mission. Use Spelling Words from the list.** Responses will vary. **(5)**

Name _____

# Stress on Syllables

**Read each dictionary entry. Sound out the entry word three ways, placing stress on a different syllable each time. Circle the choice with the correct stress. (1 point** each)

1. ad/ven/ture (ăd věn chər) *n.* A bold, dangerous, or risky undertaking.
   AD/ven/ture　　　(ad/VEN/ture)　　　ad/ven/TURE

2. en/gi/neer/ing (ĕn jə nîr ing) *n.* The practical use of scientific knowledge.
   EN/gi/neer/ing　　　en/GI/neer/ing　　　(en/gi/NEER/ing)

3. en/vi/ron/ment (ĕn vī rən mənt) *n.* Surroundings and conditions that affect the growth of living things.
   (en/VI/ron/ment)　　　en/vi/RON/ment　　　en/vi/ron/MENT

4. in/flu/ence (ĭn flo͞ons) *n.* The power to have an effect without using direct force.
   (IN/flu/ence)　　　in/FLU/ence　　　in/flu/ENCE

5. or/gan/i/za/tion (ôr gən ĭ zā shən) *n.* A group of people united for some purpose or work.
   OR/gan/i/za/tion　　　or/GAN/i/za/tion　　　(or/gan/i/ZA/tion)

6. par/tic/i/pate (pär tĭs ə pāt) *v.* To join with others in doing something; take part.
   (par/TIC/i/pate)　　　par/tic/I/pate　　　par/tic/i/PATE

7. tel/e/vi/sion (tĕl ə vĭ zhən) *n.* The transmission and reception of visual images and sounds as electrical waves through the air or through wires.
   (TEL/e/vi/sion)　　　tel/e/VI/sion　　　tel/e/vi/SION

8. vol/un/teer (vŏl ən tîr) *n.* A person who performs a service of his or her own free will.
   VOL/un/teer　　　vol/UN/teer　　　(vol/un/TEER)

Assessment Tip: Total **8** Points

Name _____

# Astronauts Travel into Space

**Verb Tenses** Verbs have forms, or tenses, that tell when the action occurs.

▶ A **present-tense** verb shows action that happens now, or that happens regularly over time.

▶ A **past-tense** verb shows that something already occurred.

▶ To form the **present tense,** add *-s* or *-es* to most verbs if the subject is singular. Do not add *-s* or *-es* if the subject is plural or *I* or *you.*

▶ To form the **past tense** of most verbs, add *-ed.*

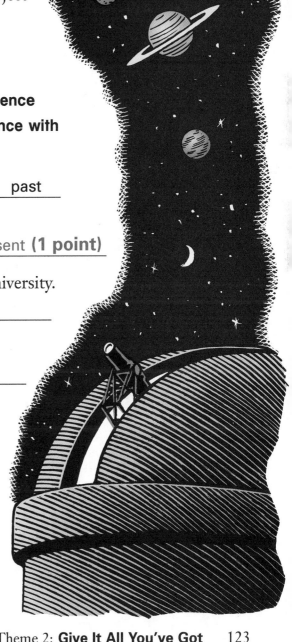

**On the line, write the tense of the verb in the first sentence of each pair. Then fill in the blank of the second sentence with the same verb, but change its tense.**

**Example:** Astronauts conducted experiments in space. __past__

Astronauts __conduct__ experiments in space.

1. My mother studies engineering at the university. __present **(1 point)**__

   My mother __studied **(1)**__ engineering at the university.

2. You learned about space travel in school. __past **(1)**__

   You __learn **(1)**__ about space travel in school.

3. I worked hard on my science project. __past **(1)**__

   I __work **(1)**__ hard on my science project.

4. Kate's father designs bridges. __present **(1)**__

   Kate's father __designed **(1)**__ bridges.

5. She followed her dreams. __past **(1)**__

   She __follows **(1)**__ her dreams.

Theme 2: **Give It All You've Got**    123

Assessment Tip: Total **10** Points

Name _____

# Astronauts Will Travel into Space

**More about Verbs** A **future-tense** verb shows that something is going to happen. Form the **future tense** by using the helping verb *will* or *shall* with the main verb.

**Present Tense:** I **see** many films about space.

**Future Tense:** I **will see** many films about space.

**Present Tense:** He **reads** about Jupiter.

**Future Tense:** He **shall read** about Jupiter.

**Rewrite each sentence. Change each verb from the present or past tense to the future tense.**

**Example:** You go to Cape Canaveral.

*You will go to Cape Canaveral.*

1. Astronauts fly the space shuttle.

   Astronauts will fly the space shuttle. **(2 points)**

2. The space probe landed on Mars.

   The space probe will land on Mars. **(2)**

3. You studied physics in college.

   You will study physics in college. **(2)**

4. Meteors shoot across the sky.

   Meteors will shoot across the sky. **(2)**

5. We think about the future.

   We will think about the future. **(2)**

**Assessment Tip: Total 10 Points**

Name _____

# I Joined

**Using the Right Tense** A good writer uses the correct tense to talk about a particular time. Look at the two examples below. The second sentence in each pair makes more sense than the first sentence.

**Incorrect:** I will clean my room yesterday.

**Correct:** I cleaned my room yesterday.

**Incorrect:** Next Thursday Jeremy listens to me on the radio.

**Correct:** Next Thursday Jeremy will listen to me on the radio.

**George has written a paragraph about his dream of joining the Peace Corps, like Mae Jemison and his teacher. Revise the paragraph to correct problems with verb tenses.**
**(2 points** each)

*will go*

**Example:** Next week, we went to South America.
                                                  ∧

              will join
   Someday, I joined the Peace Corps.  Last month, my teacher Mr.
  talked
        ∧
Stinson talks about his experience as a member of the Peace Corps in
     ∧ showed
Ghana.  He shows us photographs of the region too.  He made many
     ∧

new friends while he was there.  In the Peace Corps, my teacher
 worked                                       ask
will work to help build a school.  Every day now I asked him to tell us
  ∧                                                 ∧

more about it.

Name _____

# Writing a Business Letter

When Mae Jemison applied to the National Aeronautics and Space Administration to become an astronaut, she wrote a business letter. You write a **business letter** to apply for a job, to request or persuade someone to do something, to order a product from ads or catalogs, to ask for information, to complain about a product or service, or to express an opinion to a newspaper, or to a radio or TV station.

**On a separate sheet of paper, plan and organize a business letter. Either write a letter of recommendation to NASA telling why Mae Jemison would make an excellent astronaut, or write to a company asking for information. Follow these steps:**

1. Write a **heading** (your own address and the date) in the upper right corner.

2. Write the **inside address** (the address of the person or business you are writing to) at the left margin.

3. Write a **greeting** (*Dear Sir or Madam:* or *Dear [business name]:*) at the left margin below the inside address.

4. Write the **body** of your letter below the greeting. Be brief and direct, but present all of the necessary details clearly. If you state an opinion, support it with details. If you order a product, identify the item, size, color, price, and quantity you want. Make sure to use a formal and polite tone.

5. Write a formal **closing** such as *Sincerely, Cordially,* or *Yours truly* in the lower right corner.

6. Sign your full name under the closing. Then print or type your name below your **signature**.

**When you finish planning your business letter, copy it onto a clean sheet of paper. Then share it with a classmate or send it to the company you wrote to.** (**2 points** for each part of the letter)

Assessment Tip: Total **12** Points

Name _____

# Using the Right Tone

**Tone** is the attitude that a writer has toward a subject and is conveyed in the choice of words and details. Here are some tips to follow when you write a business letter:

► Use polite language and a formal tone.

► Use correct grammar and complete sentences.

► Avoid the use of slang.

► Do not include personal information.

**Fill in the chart with examples of language and details that do *not* strike the proper tone.**

144 Primrose Street

Evanston, IL 60201

October 23, 2001

Dr. Mae Jemison

P.O. Box 591455

Houston, TX 77259-1455

Dear Mae,

I am in the fifth grade at Primrose Elementary School. My class will be studying about space and space travel. I got a 91 on my last quiz. We hope you might be able to come talk to our class about your experiences as an astronaut.

It would be the bomb to meet an astronaut in person. My uncle is a pilot. We look forward to hearing from you. Do not give us some lame excuse about why you cannot speak here.

Love,

*Karen Aldrin*

**Slang:** the bomb **(2 points)**

**Impolite Language:** Do not give us some lame excuse about why you cannot speak here **(2)**

**Informal Tone:** Dear Mae, Love **(2)**

**Personal Information:** I got a 91 on my last quiz, My uncle is a pilot **(2)**

Name _____

# Filling in the Blank

Use the test-taking strategies and tips you have learned to help you complete these fill-in-the-blank sentences with the correct answer. You may go back to *The Fear Place* if you need to. This practice will help you when you take this kind of test.

**Read each item. In the answer row, fill in the circle that best completes each sentence.**

1 When Doug climbs higher than nine thousand feet, —

   **A**  he will be thirstier.

   **B**  it will be harder for him to breathe.

   **C**  he will not see any animals.

   **D**  it will be easier for him to climb the rocks.

2 Doug predicted that when he reached Gordon's camp, —

   **F**  Gordon would be okay.     **H**  Gordon's parents would be there.

   **G**  Gordon would be gone.     **J**  Gordon would be in serious trouble.

3 If Doug thought about all the people who had died climbing the mountain, he might —

   **A**  slip and fall.     **C**  find the climb more exciting.

   **B**  decide to turn back.     **D**  go in the wrong direction.

4 If Doug stopped a while before reaching the Fear Place, he might —

   **F**  have more time to conquer his fear.

   **G**  see Gordon coming down the mountain.

   **H**  find a safer way to climb the cliff.

   **J**  be too afraid to continue.

ANSWER ROWS    1 Ⓐ **Ⓑ** Ⓒ Ⓓ **(5 points)**    3 **Ⓐ** Ⓑ Ⓒ Ⓓ **(5)**

                2 **Ⓕ** Ⓖ Ⓗ Ⓙ **(5)**          4 Ⓕ Ⓖ Ⓗ **Ⓙ** **(5)**

Theme 2: **Give It All You've Got**     129

Name _____

# Filling in the Blank continued

**5** If Doug fell to the floor of the canyon —

    **A** the cougar would not be able to find him.

    **B** he would be killed.

    **C** his parents would be disappointed.

    **D** he would have to start the climb over.

**6** If he hadn't followed the cougar along the ledge, Doug might —

    **F** have gotten lost.

    **G** have found a safer way to go.

    **H** not have made it.

    **J** have gotten chased by the cougar.

**7** If Doug tied his shoelace while on the ledge, he might —

    **A** not have the energy to stand up again.

    **B** have lost his balance.

    **C** have caused the ledge to break.

    **D** not have been able to see the cougar.

**8** The next time Doug gets to the Fear Place, he will probably —

    **F** not be as frightened.

    **G** have to follow the cougar again.

    **H** be too afraid to make the journey.

    **J** need Gordon to help him make it past this point.

| ANSWER ROWS | 5 Ⓐ ● Ⓒ Ⓓ **(5 points)** | 7 Ⓐ ● Ⓒ Ⓓ **(5)** |
|---|---|---|
| | 6 Ⓕ Ⓖ ● Ⓙ **(5)** | 8 ● Ⓖ Ⓗ Ⓙ **(5)** |

Assessment Tip: Total **40** Points

Name _____

# Spelling Review

**Write Spelling Words from the list on this page to answer the questions.**

Order of answers in each category may vary.

1–8. Which eight words have the /ou/, /ô/, or /oi/ sounds?

1. halt **(1 point)**

2. thousand **(1)**

3. brother-in-law **(1)**

4. noisy **(1)**

5. launch **(1)**

6. hawk **(1)**

7. royal **(1)**

8. coward **(1)**

9–26. Which eighteen words have the /ôr/, /âr/, /är/, /ûr/, or /îr/ sounds?

9. gorge **(1)**

10. wheelchair **(1)**

11. soar **(1)**

12. tore **(1)**

13. snare **(1)**

14. flair **(1)**

15. carve **(1)**

16. barge **(1)**

17. steer **(1)**

18. first aid **(1)**

19. smear **(1)**

20. hurl **(1)**

21. perch **(1)**

22. early **(1)**

23. worth **(1)**

24. pearl **(1)**

25. stir **(1)**

26. return **(1)**

27–30. Which four compound words have one of these words in them?

end    wild    test    date

27. weekend **(1)**

28. wildlife **(1)**

29. test tube **(1)**

30. up-to-date **(1)**

## Spelling Words

1. halt
2. weekend
3. steer
4. gorge
5. first aid
6. smear
7. thousand
8. wildlife
9. hurl
10. brother-in-law
11. perch
12. test tube
13. wheelchair
14. early
15. noisy
16. launch
17. hawk
18. royal
19. worth
20. soar
21. pearl
22. up-to-date
23. tore
24. stir
25. snare
26. flair
27. carve
28. barge
29. coward
30. return

Assessment Tip: Total **30** Points

Name _____

# Spelling Spree

**Rhyme Time** **Write a Spelling Word that rhymes with the underlined word and makes sense in the sentence.**

1. Marge, do you see that <u>large</u> barge **(1 point)** ?

2. <u>Howard</u>, how did you spell the word
   coward **(1)** ?

3. If the plane will soar **(1)** , we will <u>roar</u>.

4. Let us <u>forge</u> ahead through the narrow
   gorge **(1)** .

5. I <u>wore</u> my new shirt until it tore **(1)** .

6. Please hurl **(1)** the ball to the girl with the <u>curl</u>.

7. Nate, please <u>rate</u> our new up-to-date **(1)** <u>gate</u>.

**The Third Word** **Write the Spelling Word that belongs in each group.**

8. to come back, to revisit, to return **(1)**

9. diamond, ruby, pearl **(1)**

10. sister-in-law, father-in-law, brother-in-law **(1)**

11. to balance, to wobble, to perch **(1)**

12. ten, hundred, thousand **(1)**

13. days off, holiday, weekend **(1)**

14. to start, to begin, to launch **(1)**

15. animals, nature, wildlife **(1)**

## Spelling Words

1. weekend
2. coward
3. soar
4. up-to-date
5. brother-in-law
6. gorge
7. tore
8. thousand
9. wildlife
10. barge
11. launch
12. return
13. perch
14. pearl
15. hurl

Assessment Tip: Total **15** Points

Name _____

# Proofreading and Writing

**Proofreading Circle the six misspelled Spelling Words in this diary entry. Then write each word correctly.**

*April 18—This weekend I woke up ⟨erly⟩ to go to the race. At the track, I passed the ⟨first ade⟩ station and steered my ⟨weelchair⟩ into place at the starting line. The crowd was ⟨noysy.⟩ I didn't win, but I felt like a ⟨royel⟩ princess when I came to a ⟨hault⟩ at the finish line.*

1. early **(1 point)**      4. noisy **(1)**

2. first aid **(1)**       5. royal **(1)**

3. wheelchair **(1)**      6. halt **(1)**

**Revise a Letter Write Spelling Words to complete the letter.**

**Spelling Words**

1. halt
2. noisy
3. early
4. hawk
5. test tube
6. snare
7. wheelchair
8. flair
9. steer
10. carve
11. stir
12. worth
13. smear
14. royal
15. first aid

You should have seen me steer **(1)** through the pack during the race! I flew like a hawk **(1)**. Then I felt like I was caught in a snare **(1)** when I hit some loose gravel. I recovered quickly. Racing is hard, but it is worth **(1)** the effort. I have a real flair **(1)** for it, I think.

School was fun today. For art class, I started to carve **(1)** a horse out of soap. Then in science I had to stir **(1)** a solution and put it in a test tube **(1)**. Last, we had to smear **(1)** pond water on a slide and look at it under a microscope.

✏️ **Write an Article On a separate sheet of paper, write a short newspaper article about a race or sport you enjoy. Use the Spelling Review Words.** Responses will vary. **(5)**

Name _____

# Two Poems

**Choose two poems: one that rhymes and follows a pattern, and one that is free verse. On the chart below, compare the two poems by answering the questions.** Sample answers shown.

| | **Rhyming Poem** <br> Travel _____ Title | **Free Verse Poem** <br> Lemon Tree _____ Title |
|---|---|---|
| What is the poem about? | It is about the poet's love of train travel. **(3 points)** | It is about climbing a tree, and using all your senses. **(3)** |
| What word or sound patterns are in the poem? | In each stanza, lines 1 and 3 rhyme and lines 2 and 4 rhyme. **(3)** | The poet repeats verbs and uses short phrases. **(3)** |
| What word pictures does the poem create? | It creates a word picture of a train at night, in the distance, puffing smoke and cinders. **(3)** | It creates a picture of a lemon tree with white blossoms and rough bark and branches. **(3)** |

Assessment Tip: Total **18** Points

Name _____

# Poetry Award

**You are the poetry editor for a magazine. Choose one poem from**
*Focus on Poetry* **as the Poem of the Year. Tell what makes it a**
**good poem and why people will want to read it.**

Answers will vary.

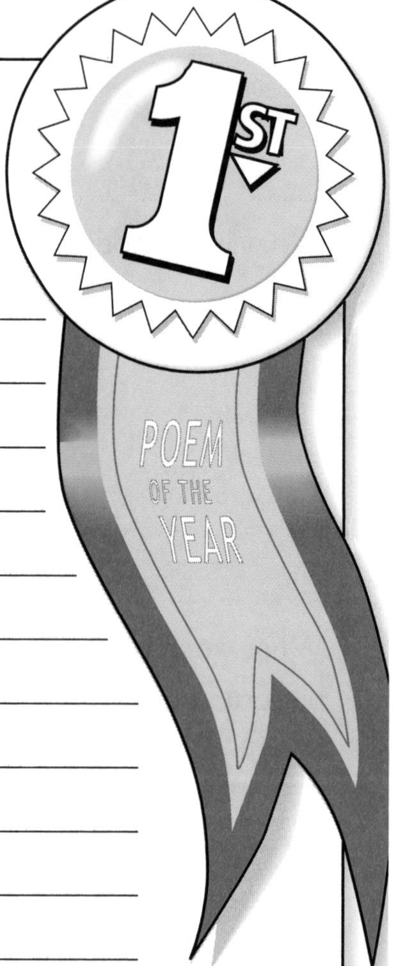

**Poem of the Year**

_____

I think this poem is the best because

_____

_____

_____

_____

_____

_____

_____

_____

_____

_____

_____

_____

_____

(Total **10 Points** for using details from the poem)

Name _____

# Voices of the Revolution

After reading each selection, complete the chart below and on the next page to show what you discovered.

| | And Then What Happened, Paul Revere? | Katie's Trunk | James Forten |
|---|---|---|---|
| **What kind of writing is this selection an example of?** | biography **(2 points)** | historical fiction **(2)** | biography **(2)** |
| **Why was this story important to tell?** | Paul Revere was a great American hero. It is important to tell his story so that people will remember him and his contributions. **(2)** | This story is important to tell because it helps readers understand that there were two sides to the American Revolutionary War, and that people on both sides suffered. **(2)** | James Forten's story is important to tell because it helps readers understand the contributions made by African-Americans before, during, and after the American Revolution. **(2)** |
| **What character traits are revealed by the character's actions?** | Paul Revere shows cleverness, courage, creativity, and intelligence. **(2)** | Katie shows fierce emotion, a strong sense of what is right and wrong, and a tendency to act without thinking. **(2)** | James Forten shows the ability to work hard, think for himself, and survive difficult challenges. **(2)** |

Assessment Tip: Total **10** Points per selection and **2** Points for the final question

Name _____

# Voices of the Revolution

| | **And Then What Happened, Paul Revere?** | **Katie's Trunk** | **James Forten** |
|---|---|---|---|
| **What details about colonial life did you learn from the selection?** | I learned more about the kinds of jobs people did. **(2)** | I learned more about daily life and about what colonial homes were like. **(2)** | I learned about jobs aboard ships, and about what cities such as Philadelphia were like. **(2)** |
| **What do you think the author's purpose for writing this selection was?** | The author wanted to teach readers about Paul Revere's life and work and help them understand his many talents and skills. **(2)** | The author wanted to entertain readers with an exciting story, and also help them see that there were real people on both sides of the conflict. **(2)** | The author wanted to help readers understand the contributions of African-Americans, and inform them about an African American not many people know about. **(2)** |

How did the selections in *Voices of the Revolution* increase your understanding of life in that period?

Possible response: I grew to understand how important the fight for independence

was in people's daily lives, and I learned that people had different points of view

about the war. **(2)**

Assessment Tip: Total **10** Points per selection and **2** Points for the final question

Name _____

# Resisting Oppression

**Use the words in the box to complete the paragraphs below.**

The residents of America's thirteen <u>colonies **(1 point)**</u> resented the new <u>taxes **(1)**</u> levied on them by the British government. A group of citizens in the Boston area formed a secret club to <u>oppose **(1)**</u> England's method of governing America. The organization was known as the Sons of Liberty, and every member was a <u>Patriot **(1)**</u>. The group won a place in history when its members dumped a <u>cargo **(1)**</u> of tea into Boston Harbor to protest the tax on that commodity.

As it became clear that England would never allow the colonists a voice in their own government, Americans began discussing the possibility of <u>revolution **(1)**</u>. That kind of talk was dangerous, though, so messages were carried secretly by <u>express **(1)**</u> riders from one city to another. The riders had to elude <u>sentries **(1)**</u> or they would be deprived of their <u>liberty **(1)**</u>. The communications network they established proved to be very valuable when war finally broke out.

**Choose one of the vocabulary words and write a sentence.**

**(1)** _____

_____

## Vocabulary

- revolution
- express
- cargo
- colonies
- oppose
- liberty
- Patriot
- sentries
- taxes

Assessment Tip: Total **10** Points

Name _____

# Fact or Opinion?

Fill in the chart with facts or opinions from the pages indicated in the first column. Where indicated, explain why the viewpoint is a fact or an opinion.

| Page | Statement | Fact or Opinion | Viewpoint Revealed |
|------|-----------|-----------------|--------------------|
| 263 | "Of all the busy people in Boston, Paul Revere would turn out to be one of the busiest." | Opinion | This statement shows that the author believes Paul Revere was busy all his life. She seems to be very impressed by him. |
| 264 | "In Boston there was always plenty to see." **(1 point)** | Opinion | The author seems to think Boston was a very interesting and engaging place to be. **(2)** |
| 266 | "You would think that with all Paul Revere did, he would make mistakes. But he always remembered to put spouts on his teapots... **(1)** | Fact | The author is amazed by Revere's abilities to do so much so well. She seems to think he is an exceptional individual. **(2)** |
| 269 | "He was back in Boston on the eleventh day, long before anyone expected him." **(1)** | Fact | Again, the author makes a statement that shows how impressive Revere's deeds were. **(2)** |
| 275 | "He did not stop to think that this might be the first battle of a war. His job was to move a trunk to safety, and that's what he did." **(1)** | Opinion and Fact | The author shows how dedicated Revere was to the cause of the Patriots. **(2)** |

Assessment Tip: Total **12** Points

Name _____

# When Did It Happen, Paul Revere?

The timeline below lists some important dates in Paul Revere's life. Answer the questions next to each date to help complete the timeline.

**1735**  What is Boston like when Paul Revere is born?

There are 42 streets, 4,000 houses, 12 churches, 4 schools, many

horses and dogs, and about 15,000 people. There is plenty to see;

many ships coming and going, and street vendors. **(1 point)**

**1756**  How does Revere respond when French soldiers and Indians attack the colonies?

He grabs his belongings, and goes to Fort Henry on Lake George. **(1)**

**1773**  On the night of December 16, Revere and the other Sons of Liberty are very busy in Boston Harbor. What are they doing?

They paint their faces, pretending to be Indians, and march on board

the British ships and dump the tea in the harbor. **(1)**

**1776**  On the night of April 18, Revere is sent to Lexington and Concord. What happens on his Big Ride?

He forgets the cloth to cover the oars, leaves his spurs at home, is

chased by two British officers, is detained and questioned by a British

patrol, is let go without his horse, and arrives in Lexington on foot. **(1)**

**1783**  By the end of the war, Revere is 48 years old. What does he do?

He goes back to silversmithing, he opens a hardware store, he sets up

a foundry, makes church bells, sets up a copper rolling mill. **(1)**

**1810**  What is Boston like now that Revere is 75 years old?

No one counts the streets, the horses, or the houses; everyone is busy

putting up new buildings, and making the city bigger. **(1)**

Theme 3: **Voices of the Revolution**     141

Assessment Tip: Total **6** Points

Name _____

# Viewing the Author

**Read the passage. Then answer the questions on page 143.**

### Traitor or Hero?

How should Benedict Arnold be remembered: as a traitor, or as a hero of the American Revolution? I'm not sure this question has a simple answer.

Arnold joined the Patriot militia in 1774. After the Revolutionary War began in 1775, he helped lead the capture of Fort Ticonderoga from the British. Later that year, he led over a thousand soldiers into Canada, was wounded in battle, and earned a promotion for bravery. In October of 1777, he was again seriously wounded as he led his soldiers against the forces of the British general Burgoyne. Arnold's courageous leadership helped the Americans win one of their most important victories in the war.

But in 1780, Arnold worked out a plan with the British to surrender an important American military base in exchange for money. After his plan was discovered, he escaped and joined the British army. Why did he do this? Many historians believe that Arnold felt his country had treated him unfairly. He was disappointed when he was passed over for a promotion. He was also accused of being too easy on Americans who were loyal to the British. This may have angered him.

The British never paid Arnold all the money he asked for. The land they gave him in Canada was not useful to him. When Arnold died in 1801, he had become poor, discouraged, and lonely, for he was a man few people trusted. Arnold was a traitor, it is true. But we should not forget that he performed several heroic acts that helped our nation win its independence.

Name _____

# Viewing the Author continued

1. What is the viewpoint of the author of this passage?   Sample answers shown.

   The author thinks Benedict Arnold was not just a traitor.  He should also be

   remembered as a hero. **(2 points)**

2. Which sentences reveal the author's viewpoint?

   the first two sentences and the last two sentences **(2)**

   _____

3. What do you think the author's purpose is for writing this passage?

   The author wants to inform us about different sides of Benedict Arnold. **(2)**

   _____

4. Write a sentence from the passage that shows the author's opinion.

   "I'm not sure this question has a simple answer." **(2)**

   _____

5. Write a fact from the passage that helps to support the author's viewpoint.

   Arnold helped lead the capture of Fort Ticonderoga. **(2)**

   _____

6. Write a fact from the passage that
   might support a different
   viewpoint about the subject.

   In 1780, Arnold worked out a plan

   with the British to surrender an

   important American military base.

   **(2)**

Name _____

# No Apostrophes!

**Your school is putting on a play of *And Then What Happened, Paul Revere?* You're sending an e-mail to the script writer, but the apostrophe (') on the computer doesn't work! Change each contraction or possessive to its longer form. Write P for possessive or C for contraction in each box.**

1. Paul makes a squirrel's silver collar.

   Paul makes a silver collar of a squirrel. **(1 point)** — [P] **(1)**

2. The writing's sloppy in the letters Paul writes.

   The writing is sloppy in the letters Paul writes. **(1)** — [C] **(1)**

3. Paul rings the church bells at a moment's notice.

   Paul rings the church bells at the notice of a moment. **(1)** — [P] **(1)**

4. The English are taxing tea, glass, and printers' inks.

   The English are taxing tea, glass, and the inks of printers. **(1)** — [P] **(1)**

5. Paul doesn't miss a chance to help the Sons of Liberty.

   Paul does not miss a chance to help the Sons of Liberty. **(1)** — [C] **(1)**

6. A messenger's job is to travel from place to place on horseback.

   The job of a messenger is to travel from place to place on horseback. **(1)** [P] **(1)**

7. Cloth to cover the oars isn't all Paul leaves behind.

   Cloth to cover the oars is not all Paul leaves behind. **(1)** — [C] **(1)**

8. He goes back to rescue the Patriots' papers.

   He goes back to rescue the papers of the Patriots. **(1)** — [P] **(1)**

Assessment Tip: Total **16** Points

Name _____

# Final /ər/

The **schwa sound** is a weak vowel sound that is often found in an unstressed syllable. It is shown as /ə/. When you hear the final /ər/ sound in words of more than one syllable, think of the patterns *er*, *or*, and *ar*.

/ər/   ang**er**, act**or**, pill**ar**

**Write each Spelling Word under the pattern that spells its final /ər/ sound.** Order of answers for each category may vary.

Copyright © Houghton Mifflin Company. All rights reserved.

**Spelling Words**

1. theater
2. actor
3. mirror
4. powder
5. humor
6. anger
7. banner
8. pillar
9. major
10. thunder
11. flavor
12. finger
13. mayor
14. polar
15. clover
16. burglar
17. tractor
18. matter
19. lunar
20. quarter

### er

theater **(1 point)**

powder **(1)**

anger **(1)**

banner **(1)**

thunder **(1)**

finger **(1)**

clover **(1)**

matter **(1)**

quarter **(1)**

### or

actor **(1)**

mirror **(1)**

humor **(1)**

major **(1)**

flavor **(1)**

mayor **(1)**

tractor **(1)**

### ar

pillar **(1)**

polar **(1)**

burglar **(1)**

lunar **(1)**

Assessment Tip: Total **20** Points

Name _____

# Spelling Spree

**Find a Rhyme** For each sentence write a Spelling Word that rhymes with the underlined word and makes sense.

1. Do me a <u>favor</u> and pick a different _____ of ice cream.
2. I <u>wonder</u> if we'll hear _____ during the rainstorm.
3. The town paved <u>over</u> a field of _____.
4. The butler hung a colorful _____ outside the <u>manor</u>.
5. Put the _____ in the coin <u>sorter</u>.
6. They hope to run the _____ station on <u>solar</u> power.
7. The _____ was a <u>factor</u> in the movie's success.

1. flavor **(1 point)**
2. thunder **(1)**
3. clover **(1)**
4. banner **(1)**
5. quarter **(1)**
6. polar **(1)**
7. actor **(1)**

**Puzzle Play** Write the Spelling Word that fits each clue. Then write the circled letters in order below. **(1 point each)**

8. a farm machine
9. a pointer or a pinky
10. fury
11. a column
12. a thief
13. a surface that reflects
14. place for movies
15. person in charge of a city

| t | r | a | c | (t) | o | r |
|---|---|---|---|---|---|---|
| f | i | n | g | (e) | r | |
| (a) | n | g | e | r | | |
| (p) | i | l | l | a | r | |
| b | u | r | g | l | (a) | r |
| m | i | r | r | o | (r) | |
| t | h | e | (a) | t | e | r |
| m | a | (y) | o | r | | |

**Mystery Words:** a  | t | e | a |  | p | a | r | t | y |

## Spelling Words

1. theater
2. actor
3. mirror
4. powder
5. humor
6. anger
7. banner
8. pillar
9. major
10. thunder
11. flavor
12. finger
13. mayor
14. polar
15. clover
16. burglar
17. tractor
18. matter
19. lunar
20. quarter

Assessment Tip: Total **15** Points

Name _____

# Proofreading and Writing

**Proofreading** Circle the five misspelled Spelling Words in this notice to British troops. Then write each word correctly.

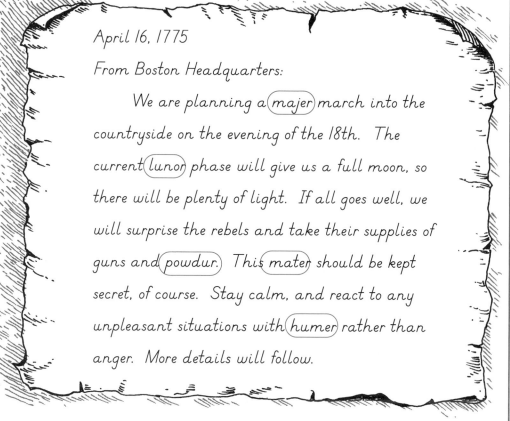

*April 16, 1775*

*From Boston Headquarters:*

*We are planning a (majer) march into the countryside on the evening of the 18th. The current (lunor) phase will give us a full moon, so there will be plenty of light. If all goes well, we will surprise the rebels and take their supplies of guns and (powdur.) This (mater) should be kept secret, of course. Stay calm, and react to any unpleasant situations with (humer) rather than anger. More details will follow.*

## Spelling Words

1. theater
2. actor
3. mirror
4. powder
5. humor
6. anger
7. banner
8. pillar
9. major
10. thunder
11. flavor
12. finger
13. mayor
14. polar
15. clover
16. burglar
17. tractor
18. matter
19. lunar
20. quarter

1. major **(1 point)**     4. matter **(1)**

2. lunar **(1)**     5. humor **(1)**

3. powder **(1)**

✏️ **Write Interview Questions** If you could interview Paul Revere, what questions would you ask him? Would you like to know more about his work as a silversmith or details of his famous ride?

**On a separate piece of paper, write some questions that you would like to ask this famous patriot about his life and the historical events in which he took part. Use Spelling Words from the list.**

Responses will vary. **(5)**

Name _____

# Synonym Switch

**Find a synonym in the box for each underlined word.**
**Rewrite the sentences using the synonyms.**

1. In Boston Harbor, ships constantly <u>came</u> and <u>left</u>.
   In Boston Harbor, ships constantly arrived and departed.
   **(2 points)**

2. Paul <u>found</u> that money could be <u>made</u> in many ways.
   Paul discovered that money could be earned in many
   ways. **(2)**

3. The men <u>hauled</u> the chests to the deck and <u>tossed</u> the tea
   overboard.
   The men dragged the chests to the deck and threw the tea
   overboard. **(2)**

4. Paul <u>slipped</u> past the sentries and <u>dashed</u> through the snow.
   Paul sneaked past the sentries and hurried through the
   snow. **(2)**

5. Paul <u>beat</u> on doors in Lexington and <u>aroused</u> the citizens.
   Paul pounded on doors in Lexington and woke the
   citizens. **(2)**

**Vocabulary**

arrived

departed

discovered

dragged

earned

hurried

pounded

sneaked

threw

woke

148    Theme 3: **Voices of the Revolution**
Assessment Tip: Total **10** Points

Name _____

# Where's Your House, Paul Revere?

**Subject-Verb Agreement** A verb must agree in number with its subject. In the present tense, add *-s* or *-es* to the verb if the subject is singular. Do not add *-s* or *-es* if the subject is plural or if the subject is *I* or *you*. If you are using *be* or *have* as helping verbs, use the form that agrees with the subject in number.

**Complete each sentence with the present-tense form of the verb in parentheses that agrees with the subject in number.**

1. We <u>are **(1 point)**</u> visiting Paul Revere's house in Boston. (be)

2. My cousin <u>likes **(1)**</u> the silver teapot on display. (like)

3. I <u>see **(1)**</u> tankards Paul Revere made. (see)

4. A 900-pound bell <u>stands **(1)**</u> in the courtyard of the Revere house. (stand)

5. The silver cup and tray <u>shine **(1)**</u> brightly. (shine)

6. You <u>walk **(1)**</u> to the Old North Church. (walk)

7. She <u>is **(1)**</u> gazing at the church steeple where the lanterns hung. (be)

8. I <u>imagine **(1)**</u> Revere's midnight ride to Lexington. (imagine)

9. Tourists <u>walk **(1)**</u> the Freedom Trail in Boston. (walk)

10. I <u>have **(1)**</u> learned about American patriots. (have)

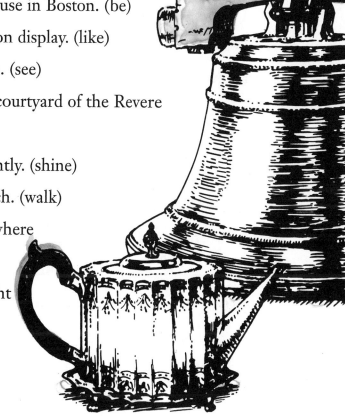

Theme 3: **Voices of the Revolution** 149
Assessment Tip: Total **10** Points

Name _____

# What Was Your Ride Like, Paul Revere?

**Regular and Irregular Verbs** To form the past tense of regular verbs, add -*ed* to the verb. Irregular verbs have special forms for the past tense. Do not add -*ed* to irregular verbs.

**Tracy and Kim have written an interview to perform in history class. To enjoy the interview, fill in the correct past-tense forms of the verbs in parentheses. You may have to check irregular verbs in your dictionary.**

**Reporter:** We are on the scene with the famous Patriot Paul Revere. Mr. Revere, you have returned from an important mission. What was it like on that ride, sir?

**Paul Revere:** My midnight ride __was **(1 point)**__ (be) exciting. I __rode **(1)**__ (ride) as fast as I __could **(1)**__ (can)! I don't think I have ever __ridden **(1)**__ (ride) so fast before!

**Reporter:** We have heard that you __forgot **(1)**__ (forget) your spurs. Is that true?

**Paul Revere:** Yes, I __did **(1)**__ (do), but my faithful dog __brought **(1)**__ (bring) them to me.

**Reporter:** You also __rowed **(1)**__ (row) across the river, right?

**Paul Revere:** I __ran **(1)**__ (run) as fast as I could, too, and I __warned **(1)**__ (warn) the people about the British.

**Reporter:** Paul Revere, American Patriot, your country is grateful.

Name _____

# What Did You See, Shirley Jensen?

**Choosing the Correct Verb Form** It is important for a writer to choose the correct form of a verb. For irregular verbs, you may have to check your dictionary.

**Shirley keeps a journal on her computer. She recently took a trip to Boston and wants to write an essay about her experience. To get started, she has printed out her journal entries. Proofread the journal entry below and circle the incorrect verb forms. Then write the correct form above the error.**

July 15

We arrived at Logan Airport this morning. We (taked)
took

a subway to Grandma's apartment in Boston. I had
taken
(took) a subway train before in New York City. I wish
had
we (haved) a subway in Allentown!
fixed
Grandma (fixes) us lunch, but I wasn't hungry
eaten
because I had (ate) too many peanuts on the plane. I
thought
(thinked) we might go to the beach in the afternoon, but
went                                            showed
we (goed) downtown instead. Grandma (shown) us the

State House with the golden dome. It was beautiful!
visited                              saw
Then we (visit) Paul Revere's house. We (seen) some of

the beautiful things he made.

Assessment Tip: Total **10** Points

Name _____

# Writing a Character Sketch

*And Then What Happened, Paul Revere?* gives many details about Paul
Revere, a hero of the American Revolution. These details help you
understand what he did and what kind of person he was. Using vivid
details in your writing can help bring a real person like Paul Revere or a
story character to life.

A **character sketch** is a written profile that describes how a real
person or a story character looks, acts, thinks, and feels.

**Choose a real person or a story character from another selection you
have read whom you think would make a good subject for a
character sketch. Then use the web to brainstorm details about the
character's physical appearance and personality traits. (2 points each)**

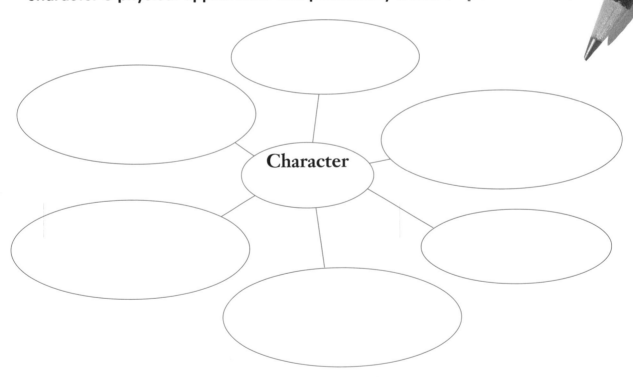

**On a separate sheet of paper, write your character sketch. Begin with
a quote or an anecdote about the character. Then write a sentence
that summarizes his or her most significant character traits. Next,
give two or three details from the web that support your summary.
Finally, conclude by restating the character's most significant traits. (2)**

Assessment Tip: Total **14** Points

Name _____

# Using Exact Nouns and Verbs

Which noun, *lights* or *chandeliers*, is more exact? Which verb, *galloped* or *rode*, is more exact? A good writer avoids using vague nouns and verbs. Exact nouns and verbs like *chandeliers* and *galloped* can make your writing clearer and help readers create a more vivid mental picture of the people, places, and events that you describe.

**One fifth-grader drafted these sentences for a character sketch about Paul Revere. Can you help her make her writing clearer and more vivid? Rewrite each sentence on the lines, replacing the underlined vague nouns and verbs with more exact ones from the list below.**

**More Exact Nouns and Verbs**

| | |
|---|---|
| crafted | careers |
| hardware store | colonists |
| opened | warned |
| tea | silver |
| pursued | dumped |

1. Throughout his life, Paul Revere <u>did</u> many different <u>things</u>.

   Throughout his life, Paul Revere pursued many different careers. **(2 points)**

   _____

2. He <u>made</u> pitchers, candlesticks, and buckles from <u>metal</u>.

   He crafted pitchers, candlesticks, and buckles from silver. **(2)**

   _____

3. With other patriots, he disguised himself as an Indian, boarded a British ship, and <u>put</u> <u>stuff</u> into Boston Harbor.

   With other patriots, he disguised himself as an Indian, boarded a British ship,

   and dumped tea into Boston Harbor.**(2)**

4. He became a hero when he <u>told</u> <u>people</u> that British troops were coming.

   He became a hero when he warned colonists that British troops were coming.**(2)**

   _____

Name _____

# Evaluating Your Story

Reread your story. What do you need to make it better? Use this page to help you decide. Put a checkmark in the box for each sentence that describes your story.

## Rings the Bell!

- [ ] The setting, characters, and plot are well defined.
- [ ] My story has a distinct beginning, middle, and end.
- [ ] The main character has an interesting conflict to resolve.
- [ ] I use dialogue and exact verbs to make the story's action clear.
- [ ] There are almost no mistakes.

## Getting Stronger

- [ ] The setting, characters, and plot could be more clear.
- [ ] My plot isn't always easy to follow.
- [ ] The main character's conflict could be more interesting.
- [ ] I could add more dialogue and exact verbs to make the action clear.
- [ ] There are a few mistakes.

## Try Harder

- [ ] The setting and plot are not easy to follow.
- [ ] There is no clear problem.
- [ ] I haven't included details or dialogue.
- [ ] There are a lot of mistakes.

Name _____

# Using Exact Verbs

**Replace each underlined verb. Circle the letter of the verb that best completes each sentence. (1 point each)**

1. Nina <u>rearranged</u> the cards in the deck.

   a. moved　　　b. mixed　　　**c.** shuffled　　　d. wrinkled

2. "<u>Have</u> one card," she said to Ted. "Then put it back into the deck."

   a. Replace　　　**b.** Remove　　　c. Repair　　　d. Deliver

3. "Is this your card?" she asked, <u>showing</u> the Queen of Hearts.

   **a.** flashing　　　b. flushing　　　c. hiding　　　d. presenting

4. Ted <u>moved</u> his head sadly. "No, it's not my card," he said.

   a. rotated　　　b. turned　　　c. stiffened　　　**d.** shook

5. "Oh goodness," Nina said. "I've <u>done</u> it again."

   a. smiled　　　**b.** misjudged　　　c. blundered　　　d. coughed

6. Then Nina's hand <u>went</u> behind her ear and pulled out a card.

   a. fell　　　**b.** darted　　　c. skipped　　　d. grasped

7. "That's my card," Ted <u>said</u>. "The deuce of clubs!"

   a. mentioned　　　b. noted　　　**c.** exclaimed　　　d. whispered

8. "Thank you very much," Nina said. She bowed to her audience and <u>ran</u> off the stage.

   **a.** scampered　　　b. slinked　　　c. wriggled　　　d. skipped

Name _____

# Spelling Words

**Words Often Misspelled** Look for familiar spelling patterns to help you remember how to spell the Spelling Words on this page. Think carefully about the parts that you find hard to spell in each word.

**Write the missing letters in the Spelling Words below.**

1. happ <u>i</u> ly **(1 point)**

2. min <u>u</u> t <u>e</u> **(1)**

3. b <u>e</u> a <u>u</u> t <u>i</u> ful **(1)**

4. usua <u>l</u> <u>l</u> y **(1)**

5. inst <u>e</u> a <u>d</u> **(1)**

6. stre <u>t</u> c <u>h</u> **(1)**

7. l <u>y</u> ing **(1)**

8. e <u>x</u> c <u>ite</u> **(1)**

9. mil <u>l</u> i <u>meter</u> **(1)**

10. d <u>i</u> v <u>i</u> d <u>e</u> **(1)**

11. unt <u>i</u> l **(1)**

12. wri <u>t</u> i <u>ng</u> **(1)**

13. tr <u>i</u> e <u>d</u> **(1)**

14. b <u>e</u> f <u>o</u> r <u>e</u> **(1)**

15. <u>S</u> at <u>u</u> r <u>day</u> **(1)**

**Study List** **On a separate piece of paper, write each Spelling Word. Check your spelling against the words on the list.**

Order of words may vary.

Assessment Tip: Total **15** Points

Name _____

# Spelling Spree

**Phrase Fillers** **Write the Spelling Word that best completes each phrase.**

1. a _____ and true method
2. to yawn and _____
3. wait a _____
4. _____ down for a nap
5. to _____ into two pieces
6. dinner comes _____ dessert
7. _____ a letter

1. happily
2. minute
3. beautiful
4. usually
5. instead
6. stretch
7. lying
8. excite
9. millimeter
10. divide
11. until
12. writing
13. tried
14. before
15. Saturday

1. tried **(1 point)**     5. divide **(1)**
2. stretch **(1)**     6. before **(1)**
3. minute **(1)**     7. writing **(1)**
4. lying **(1)**

**Syllable Scramble** **Rearrange the syllables to write a Spelling Word. One syllable in each item is extra.**

8. til un till
9. ur date day Sat
10. cite ite ex
11. ly u al fer su
12. pi hap an ly
13. in ted stead
14. ti ness ful beau
15. mil time ter li me

8. until **(1)**
9. Saturday **(1)**
10. excite **(1)**
11. usually **(1)**
12. happily **(1)**
13. instead **(1)**
14. beautiful **(1)**
15. millimeter **(1)**

Assessment Tip: Total **15** Points

# Proofreading and Writing

**Proofreading** Circle the five misspelled Spelling Words in this open letter. Then write each word correctly.

**Spelling Words**

> Fellow Countrymen:
>
> I am (riting) these words to urge you all to action. This land cannot spend another (minut) under the tyrannical rule of the British King! We have (tride) to plead and reason with him, but he will not listen. Now, (insted) of talking, we must fight! If we do, it will not be long before we are living (hapilly) in our own nation. Join the struggle for liberty now!

**Spelling Words**

1. happily
2. minute
3. beautiful
4. usually
5. instead
6. stretch
7. lying
8. excite
9. millimeter
10. divide
11. until
12. writing
13. tried
14. before
15. Saturday

1. writing **(1 point)**
2. minute **(1)**
3. tried **(1)**
4. instead **(1)**
5. happily **(1)**

✏️➤ **Slogan Writing** Pick three Spelling Words. Then, with each one, write a slogan (such as "Don't Tread on Me" or "Liberty or Death") that could have been used during the Revolutionary War.
Responses will vary. **(5)**

Name _____

# Some Talk of Revolution

**Answer each of the following questions by writing a vocabulary word.**

1. Which word means "right" or "fair"?
   just **(1 point)**

2. Which word names individuals fighting against their government? rebels **(1)**

3. Which word means "giving weapons to"?
   arming **(1)**

4. Which word means "practicing for battle"?
   drilling **(1)**

5. Which word is a synonym for *nervous*?
   skittish **(1)**

6. Which word means "looked"?
   peered **(1)**

7. Which word is an antonym for *meek*?
   fierce **(1)**

8. Which word means "a brief battle"?
   skirmish **(1)**

9. Which word is a synonym for *relatives*?
   kin **(1)**

## Vocabulary

arming

skittish

just

fierce

skirmish

peered

rebels

kin

drilling

**Write a different question using one of the vocabulary words.**

**(1)** _____

_____

Name _____

# Why Did It Happen?

**Fill in the columns where indicated with the cause or the effect of the events included in the chart.**

| Causes | Effects |
|---|---|
| Fights have broken out in the colonies, and rebels have called for independence from British rule. **(2)** | The uneasiness and fighting make Katie's family feel skittish, nervous, and worried. |
| Friends and neighbors disagree about whether to fight or be loyal to British rule. **(2)** | The family has lost friends and neighbors. |
| Armed rebels come to Katie's home. | The family goes to the woods to hide. **(2)** |
| Katie feels that it is not just for their neighbors to break into their house and ruin their things. | Katie rushes back to the house to protect it. **(2)** |
| Katie becomes afraid when she hears the rebels tearing off the knocker on the door. **(2)** | Katie hides inside her mother's wedding trunk. |
| When John Warren searches the trunk and discovers Katie, he calls the rebels away and leaves the lid open so she can breathe. | Katie realizes that goodness still exists in people, despite the conflicts they might have with each other. **(2)** |

Assessment Tip: Total **12** Points

Name _____

# In the Characters' Words

**Read the characters' words in the left column. In the right column, write why each character said what he or she did.**

| What the Character Said | Why the Character Said It |
|---|---|
| **Mama:** "It makes me as skittish as a newborn calf." | There was talk of war with England. Neighbors were no longer speaking. **(2 points)** |
| **Papa:** "Get your mother! Hide in the woods." | The rebels were coming to Katie's house and the family had to hide. **(2)** |
| **Katie:** "It was not right. It was not just. It was not fair." | Katie became angry when she thought about her family's rebel neighbors ruining their things. **(2)** |
| **The rebels:** "This'll be fine pickings!" | The house was full of English goods, and the rebels were trying to steal the valuables to sell for arms. **(2)** |
| **John Warren:** "Out! The Tories are coming. Back to the road! Hurry!" | John Warren found Katie in the trunk and he didn't want her to get hurt by the rebels, so he made up a lie. **(2)** |
| **Katie:** "He'd left one seam of goodness there, and we were all tied to it." | John Warren proved there was goodness left in him, and Katie felt there was some good in everyone. **(2)** |

Assessment Tip: Total **12** Points

Name _____

# Making Connections

**Read the story. Then complete the activity on page 163.**

## A Dangerous Day

My name is Margaret Tompkins. I work as a nurse in a field hospital here in Virginia. When my brother enlisted as a soldier in the Union army, I, too, wanted to join and help the cause. I decided to become a nurse. I came to this area three months ago when my brother's company was sent here.

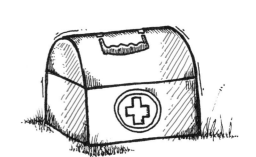

For the past few hours, our soldiers have been involved in a fierce battle. After almost ten hours of fighting, they are exhausted and very hungry. Some of the wounded have been brought to the hospital, where the other nurses and I have been treating them. It is hard, heartbreaking work.

It is now just past three in the afternoon. Over the noise, I suddenly hear my brother's voice calling "Margaret!" I grab a medical bag and run out onto the field. When I reach James, he is sitting next to a cannon, holding his left shoulder.

"What has happened?" I ask him.

"The cannon recoiled and twisted my shoulder out of its socket," he tells me. I tell James I will lead him to the hospital so he can be treated. He shakes his head. "I can't leave here," he says. "Someone has to fire the cannon."

I look around and realize that, for the moment, no one else is nearby. Finally I say, "James, you cannot fire a cannon with a dislocated shoulder. You go. I have watched cannons being fired. I'll take a turn here." He goes.

I feel afraid. But I prepare the cannon. Here is a chance to do more to win the war than just unroll bandages.

# Making Connections continued

**Complete the cause-effect chain to show what caused the events described on page 162, and what happened as a result.** Sample answers shown.

| Causes | Effects |
|---|---|
| Margaret wants to help the Union effort. | Margaret becomes a nurse. **(2 points)** |
| Margaret's brother's company is sent to Virginia. **(2)** | Margaret travels to Virginia to work in a field hospital and be near him. |
| The cannon James is firing recoils into him. **(2)** | James's shoulder is dislocated. |
| James refuses to get his shoulder treated because he is the only soldier at the post. | Margaret tells him she will fire the cannon and sends him to the hospital. **(2)** |
| Margaret wants to help the Union win the war. **(2)** | Margaret prepares the cannon even though she feels afraid. |

Name _____

# Signalling Syllables

**Rewrite each underlined word, adding slashes between its syllables.
Then write a definition of the word.** Sample answers shown.

1. The family usually sat and talked with visitors in the <u>parlor</u>.
   par/lor **(1 point)**; a room for entertaining visitors **(1)**

2. Katie's mother is <u>skittish</u> because of the fighting in the area.
   skit/tish **(1)**; nervous, uneasy **(1)**

3. <u>Dragonflies</u> would land briefly on the rocks before flying away again.
   drag/on/flies **(1)**; large flying insects **(1)**

4. As she hid in the trunk, Katie heard <u>faraway</u> voices and footsteps.
   far/a/way **(1)**; distant **(1)**

5. The incident was just a <u>skirmish</u>, not a major battle.
   skir/mish **(1)**; a minor conflict **(1)**

6. A large horse went <u>thudding</u> by on the road.
   thud/ding **(1)**; making a heavy, dull sound **(1)**

Assessment Tip: Total **12** Points

Name _____

# VCCV and VCV Patterns

A **syllable** is a word part with one vowel sound. To spell a two-syllable word, divide the word into syllables. Divide a VCCV word between the consonants. Divide a VCV word before or after the consonant. Look for spelling patterns you have learned, and spell the word by syllables.

| VC \| CV | VC \| CV |
|----------|----------|
| **ar \| rive** | **par \| lor** |

| VC \| V | V \| CV |
|---------|---------|
| **val \| ue** | **a \| ware** |
| **clos \| et** | **be \| have** |

**Write each Spelling Word under the heading that tells how it is divided.** Order of answers for each category may vary.

### Spelling Words

1. equal
2. parlor
3. collect
4. closet
5. perhaps
6. wedding
7. rapid
8. value
9. arrive
10. behave
11. shoulder
12. novel
13. tulip
14. sorrow
15. vanish
16. essay
17. publish
18. aware
19. subject
20. prefer

**VC | CV**

parlor **(1 point)**

collect **(1)**

perhaps **(1)**

wedding **(1)**

arrive **(1)**

shoulder **(1)**

sorrow **(1)**

essay **(1)**

publish **(1)**

subject **(1)**

**VC | V**

closet **(1)**

rapid **(1)**

value **(1)**

novel **(1)**

vanish **(1)**

**V | CV**

equal **(1)**

behave **(1)**

tulip **(1)**

aware **(1)**

prefer **(1)**

Theme 3: **Voices of the Revolution**   165
Assessment Tip: Total **20** Points

Name _____

# Spelling Spree

**Syllable Match** Match each of the following syllables with one of the numbered syllables to create Spelling Words. Then write the words on the blanks provided.

| ar | qual | have | par | a |
|---|---|---|---|---|
| et | wed | pre | lish | el |

1. **nov** — novel **(1 point)**

2. **lor** — parlor **(1)**

3. **fer** — prefer **(1)**

4. **clos** — closet **(1)**

5. **e** — equal **(1)**

6. **ding** — wedding **(1)**

7. **be** — behave **(1)**

8. **ware** — aware **(1)**

9. **rive** — arrive **(1)**

10. **pub** — publish **(1)**

**The Third Word** Write the Spelling Word that belongs with each group.

11. sadness, grief, sorrow **(1)**

12. possibly, maybe, perhaps **(1)**

13. worth, price, value **(1)**

14. gather, accumulate, collect **(1)**

15. fast, speedy, rapid **(1)**

16. rose, daffodil, tulip **(1)**

17. topic, field, subject **(1)**

18. paper, report, essay **(1)**

19. wrist, elbow, shoulder **(1)**

20. fade, disappear, vanish **(1)**

Assessment Tip: Total **20** Points

Name _____

# Proofreading and Writing

**Proofreading** Circle the five misspelled Spelling Words in this speech. Then write each word correctly.

Fellow Townspeople!

Recent events have made it clear. The flag of England will soon (vannish) from our land. We are aware, however, that certain people (prefur) to remain loyal to King George. This has made some of us angry. Indeed, some people (behav) as if they don't know their own neighbors. The (rappid) changes of the past months have stirred up strong feelings, but everyone must remain calm! If you (vallue) the freedoms of our new land, you will respect your neighbors' homes and property whether or not you share their beliefs.

**Spelling Words**

1. equal
2. parlor
3. collect
4. closet
5. perhaps
6. wedding
7. rapid
8. value
9. arrive
10. behave
11. shoulder
12. novel
13. tulip
14. sorrow
15. vanish
16. essay
17. publish
18. aware
19. subject
20. prefer

1. vanish **(1 point)**
2. prefer **(1)**
3. behave **(1)**
4. rapid **(1)**
5. value **(1)**

✏️ **Write a Bulletin-Board Notice** You want your classmates to join you in some activity, perhaps organizing a pep rally or raising money for disaster relief or some other worthy cause. How will you get their attention?

**On a separate piece of paper, write a notice to tack up on a school bulletin board giving reasons why students should join you in the activity.** Responses will vary. **(5)**

Name _____

# Turning the Key

**Use the spelling table/pronunciation key to figure out how to pronounce the underlined words. Then find a word in the box with the same vowel sound as the underlined word, and write it after the sentence.**

| Sounds | Spellings | Sample Words |
|--------|-----------|--------------|
| /ĕ/ | e, ea | shed, breath |
| /î/ | ea, ee, ie, e | dear, deer, pier, mere |
| /ŭ/ | o, u, ou, oo | cut, rough, flood |
| /o͝o/ | u, oo, o | full, book, wolf |
| /ou/ | ou, ow | about, crown |

**Vocabulary**

meant

steer

blood

took

town

flour

1. Crouched in the underbrush, I felt like an animal in a trap.
   flour or town **(2 points)**
   _____

2. In a fierce whisper, Mama was trying to call me back.
   steer **(2)**
   _____

3. The men ripped the knocker off the wood.
   took **(2)**
   _____

4. The rustle of the clothing in the trunk drowned their words.
   town or flour **(2)**
   _____

5. I could hear the drums of the rebels who were marching in

   town.
   blood **(2)**
   _____

6. A sudden thread of a song ran through my head.
   meant **(2)**
   _____

Assessment Tip: Total **12** Points

Name _____

# Katie's Adventure

**Verb Phrases with *have*** Many verb phrases begin with a form of *have*, *has*, or *had*. Use *has* with singular subjects. Use *have* with plural subjects or with *I* or *you*. Use *had* with either singular subjects or plural subjects.

**Underline the verb phrase in the following sentences.**

1. Katie and her family <u>had been friends</u> with their neighbors before the revolution. **(1 point)**

2. Political differences now <u>have come</u> between them. **(1)**

3. It <u>has been</u> difficult for everyone. **(1)**

4. The rebels <u>have entered</u> the house. **(1)**

5. Katie <u>has hidden</u> in a trunk. **(1)**

**Fill in the correct form of the verbs in parentheses to complete the following sentences.**

6. They have <u>broken **(1)**</u> (break) a precious teapot.

7. It has <u>been **(1)**</u> (be) a trying time for the family.

8. I have <u>enjoyed **(1)**</u> (enjoy) reading the story about British loyalists.

9. You have <u>made **(1)**</u> (make) me think.

10. Mr. Roby had <u>hoped **(1)**</u> (hope) the class would like the story.

Name _____

# Let Us Learn About Lexington

*teach, learn; let, leave; sit, set; can, may*   Some pairs of verbs can be confusing.  The meanings of these verbs are related but different.  Study the definitions carefully.

teach—to instruct            let—to allow

learn—to be instructed        leave—to go away

sit—to rest or stay in one place     can—to have the ability to

set—to put              may—to have permission

**Choose between the two verbs in parentheses to correctly complete each sentence.**

1. We will <u>learn **(1 point)**</u> (teach, learn) about the American Revolution.

2. Ms. Amata will <u>teach **(1)**</u> (teach, learn) us about the Tories.

3. In Lexington, our class <u>can **(1)**</u> (can, may) see a statue of a Minuteman.

4. You <u>may **(1)**</u> (can, may) take my picture beside the statue.

5. In Boston, we <u>can **(1)**</u> (can, may) see the harbor where the rebels dumped the tea.

6. We will <u>sit **(1)**</u> (sit, set) on a bench at the harbor.

7. I'll <u>set **(1)**</u> (sit, set) my camera on the bench.

8. <u>May **(1)**</u> (Can, May) I borrow your history book?

9. My teacher <u>lets **(1)**</u> (lets, leaves) me ask many questions.

10. They will <u>leave **(1)**</u> (let, leave) before lunch.

**Assessment Tip: Total 10 Points**

Name _____

# Uncle Warren's Trunk

**Choosing the Correct Verb** **Michael is writing a letter to his cousin, but he is uncertain about the correct verb to use. Choose the correct verbs from the list to fill in the blanks.**

| |
|---|
| teach |
| learn |
| let |
| leave |
| sit |
| set |
| can |
| may |

Dear Kenya,

I read a story about a girl who had to hide in a trunk. It reminded me of the trunk we saw in Uncle Warren's attic. Do you remember? I talked to Uncle Warren on Sunday, and he said that we __may **(1 point)**__ open it next time we visit. I hope we find a Revolutionary War sword inside! If we do, we __can **(1)**__ try to find out who owned it. We would __learn **(1)**__ a lot about history that way. Uncle Warren doesn't think we will find anything that old, but he said he will __teach **(1)**__ us about the history of our family.

__Can **(1)**__ you come next Saturday? If not, will your parents __let **(1)**__ you come the following Saturday? If you __leave **(1)**__ your house before noon, we __can **(1)**__ have lunch. I will __sit **(1)**__ on the porch and wait for you. I better __set **(1)**__ down my pen now and turn out the light.

     Your cousin,

     Michael

Name _____

# Writing a Friendly Letter

Katie Gray in *Katie's Trunk* lived in the 1700s during the Revolutionary War — long before the invention of either the telephone or the computer. If she wanted to share her experience of hiding in the trunk, Katie could not have called a friend or sent an e-mail message. However, she might have written a friendly letter.

A **friendly letter** is a letter that you write to a friend to share news about your life.

**Use this page to help you plan and organize a friendly letter. Either write to a friend of yours, or write a letter that Katie might have written to a friend. Use a separate sheet of paper, and follow these steps: (2 points each)**

1. Write a **heading** (your address and the date) in the upper right corner.

2. Write a **greeting** (*Dear* and the person's name followed by a comma) at the left margin.

3. Write the **body** of your letter below the greeting. Begin by writing something that demonstrates you care about your friend. Include your personal thoughts, feelings, or news. Make sure to use a friendly tone and informal language. At the end of the letter, ask your friend to write back soon.

4. Write an informal **closing** such as *Love* or *Your friend* followed by a comma in the lower right corner.

5. Sign your name under the closing.

**When your friendly letter is finished, address an envelope and mail it or share it with a classmate.**

*Heading*

*Greeting*
*Body*

*Closing*
*Signature*

Assessment Tip: Total **10** Points

Name _____

# Voice

Every writer has a **voice,** or a unique way of expressing himself or herself. A writer's voice helps reveal what he or she is like as a person. You can sometimes also "hear" a narrator's or a character's voice when you read a work of literature. For example, listen for Mama's voice as you read this sentence from *Katie's Trunk:* "Tea! In the harbor! Wasting God's good food."

You can strengthen your own writing voice when you write by showing more of what you think and feel, and by including expressions you commonly use when speaking, such as *No way!* or *I'm psyched* or *You've got to be kidding.*

**On the lines below, write ten expressions that you commonly use when speaking.**

## My Common Expressions

| **(1 point)** | **(1)** |
|---|---|
| (expression of fear) | (expression of disgust) |
| **(1)** | **(1)** |
| (expression of surprise) | (expression of embarrassment) |
| **(1)** | **(1)** |
| (expression of encouragement) | (expression of affection) |
| **(1)** | **(1)** |
| (expression of confusion) | (expression of pleasure) |
| **(1)** | **(1)** |
| (expression of doubt) | (expression of concern) |

**When you revise your friendly letter, use these expressions to strengthen your writing voice. By adding a few of these expressions, you can make your writing sound more natural — as if you are talking directly to your friend.**

Name _____

# Drama on the High Seas

**Complete each sentence below by writing a vocabulary word from the box.**

1. Those opposing slavery were called <u>abolitionists</u> **(1 point)**.

2. A group whose views are respected by leaders is considered
   to be <u>influential</u> **(1)**.

3. If you have helped a person, you have
   <u>assisted</u> **(1)** him or her.

4. An argument is one type of <u>conflict</u> **(1)**.

5. Changing direction while sailing is <u>tacking</u> **(1)**.

6. If you have told a group that their plan seems solid, you have
   <u>encouraged</u> **(1)** them to carry it out.

7. Another word for *prisoners* is <u>captives</u> **(1)**.

8. If you feel strong fear, you feel <u>dread</u> **(1)**.

9. <u>Enslavement</u> **(1)** is preventing people from living
   in freedom.

10. A <u>privateer</u> **(1)** was a private ship given papers
    by a government allowing it to attack ships of another country.

11. A person learning a trade is an <u>apprentice</u> **(1)**.

**Choose one of the vocabulary words and write a sentence.**

**(1)** _____

_____

Name _____

# James Forten and the Revolutionary War

**Complete the chart as you read the selection.**

| What I <u>K</u>now | What I <u>W</u>ant to Know | What I <u>L</u>earned |
|---|---|---|
| Answers will vary. | Answers will vary. | **(2 points each)** |
| Samples provided. | Samples provided. | |
| | | |
| James Forten was an | What was James | |
| African American boy. | Forten's job on the ship? | |
| He served on a ship | Did he fight in any | |
| during the American | battles? | |
| Revolution. | What did he do after the | |
| | war? | |

Name _____

# Did It Really Happen?

**The sentences below tell about James Forten. Write T if the sentence is true, or F if the sentence is false. If a sentence is false, correct it to make it true.**

1. __F **(1)**__ New York, where James Forten was born, was home
to many significant abolitionists.

   Philadelphia, where James Forten was born, was home to many significant

   abolitionists.

2. __F **(1)**__ James became a foot soldier when he was 14 years old.

   His mother finally let him become a sailor when he was 14 years old.

   _____

3. __T **(1)**__ On his second voyage, James Forten and the crew of the *Royal Louis* were

   captured and held captive on board the British prison ship *Jersey*.

   _____

   _____

4. __F **(1)**__ James feared he would be killed by the British.

   James feared he would be sold into slavery by the British.

   _____

5. __T **(1)**__ It was probably George Washington's victory over the British
that saved Forten.

   _____

   _____

6. __F **(1)**__ After the war, James Forten became a wealthy politician and
an influential abolitionist.

   After the war, James Forten became a wealthy sailmaker and an influential

   abolitionist.

Assessment Tip: Total **6** Points

Name _____

# Step by Step

**Read the directions.  Then answer the questions on page 178.**

## "Wild Snake" Marble Game

This marble game provides good marble-shooting practice.

**Players:** Two or more

**Materials:** One marble per player; a stick or a piece of chalk

**Object:** The winner is the last player left in the game.

**How to Play:**

1. If the game is played on sand, scratch seven circles to form a course. If it is played on cement, draw seven circles with chalk.  The course may go in any direction.

2. Make a starting line and place all players' marbles behind it.

3. Taking turns, players try to land their marble in the first circle by flicking it with their thumb or finger.

4. A player who lands a marble in the first circle proceeds to the second one, and so on.

5. A player who gets to the seventh circle must complete the course in reverse.

6. Players who complete the course forward and backward are "wild snakes."  This means that they may shoot at the other players' marbles.

7. If a player's marble is hit by the marble of a wild snake, that player is out of the game (even if that player is also a wild snake).

8. If a wild snake's marble lands in a circle while trying to shoot another player's marble, the wild snake is out of the game.

Name _____

# Step by Step continued

**Answer these questions about the directions on page 177.**

1. What do the directions teach readers?

   how to play a marble game called "Wild Snake" **(2 points)**

   _____

2. In order to follow these directions, what should you do first?

   Read the directions all the way through. **(2)**

   _____

3. What does each player need before play can begin?

   a marble **(2)**

   _____

4. Why do you need chalk if you are playing the game on cement?

   You need to draw seven circles on the cement. **(2)**

   _____

5. How does a player become a "wild snake"?

   The player moves through the course, first forward, then in

   reverse, by flicking a marble into each circle. **(2)**

6. What can cause a wild snake to be out of the game?

   being hit by another wild snake's marble; landing in a circle **(2)**

   _____

7. What would happen if you did step number two before doing step
   number one?

   The marbles would be lined up, but there would be no course to

   follow. **(2)**

Assessment Tip: Total **14** Points

Name _____

# Prefix Plus

**Use the charts to figure out the meaning of each underlined word.**
**Then rewrite the word in the blank space, using the clues.  The first**
**one has been done for you.**  Sample answers shown.

| Prefix | Meaning |
|--------|---------|
| sub- | under, below |
| sur- | over, above |

| Word Root | Meaning |
|-----------|---------|
| mit | to cause to go |
| ject | to throw |
| vey | to look |
| merge | to plunge |

| Base Words |
|------------|
| mount (climb) |
| standard (usual quality) |
| face (part) |
| pass |

1. The rebels would not <u>submit</u> to unfair British laws.

   The rebels would not _____go under_____ unfair British laws.

2. The naval officer <u>surveyed</u> the harbor.

   The naval officer __looked over **(2)**__ the harbor.

3. A harbor seal <u>submerged</u> near the ship.

   A harbor seal __plunged under **(2)**__ near the ship.

4. Soon, the seal came to the <u>surface</u> of the ocean.

   Soon, the seal came to the __above part **(2)**__ of the ocean.

5. The prisoners were <u>subjected</u> to punishment.

   The prisoners were __thrown under **(2)**__ punishment.

6. James thought the tattered sailcloth was <u>substandard</u>.

   James thought the tattered sailcloth was __below the usual quality **(2)**__.

7. With his positive attitude, James could <u>surmount</u> any problem.

   James could __climb over **(2)**__ any problem.

8. James's sails <u>surpassed</u> any others.

   James's sails __passed above **(2)**__ any others.

Name _____

# Final /l/ or /əl/

The final /l/ or /əl/ sounds are usually spelled with two letters. When you hear these sounds, think of the patterns *le*, *el*, and *al*.

/l/ or /əl/    spark**le**, jew**el**, leg**al**

► The spellings of *fossil* and *devil* differ from the usual spelling patterns. The /əl/ sounds in these words are spelled *il*.

**Write each Spelling Word under its spelling of the final /l/ or /əl/ sound.** Order of answers for each category may vary.

1. jewel
2. sparkle
3. angle
4. shovel
5. single
6. normal
7. angel
8. legal
9. whistle
10. fossil*
11. puzzle
12. bushel
13. mortal
14. gentle
15. level
16. label
17. pedal
18. ankle
19. needle
20. devil*

*le*

sparkle **(1 point)**

angle **(1)**

single **(1)**

whistle **(1)**

puzzle **(1)**

gentle **(1)**

ankle **(1)**

needle **(1)**

*el*

jewel **(1)**

shovel **(1)**

angel **(1)**

bushel **(1)**

level **(1)**

label **(1)**

*al*

normal **(1)**

legal **(1)**

mortal **(1)**

pedal **(1)**

**Another Spelling**

fossil **(1)**

devil **(1)**

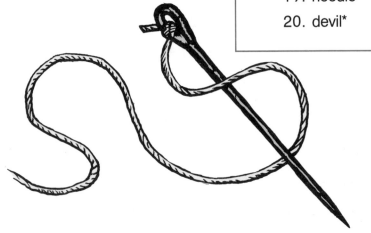

Assessment Tip: Total **20** Points

Name _____

# Spelling Spree

**Ending Match** For each beginning syllable, choose the correct spelling of the /l/ or /əl/ sound to form a Spelling Word. Then write each word correctly.

1. spar-   -kel   (-kle)   -kal          1. sparkle **(1)**
2. gen-    (-tle)   -tal   -til          2. gentle **(1)**
3. fos-    -sle   -sal   (-sil)          3. fossil **(1)**
4. puz-    -zel   (-zle)   -el           4. puzzle **(1)**
5. la-     (-bel)   -bal   -ble          5. label **(1)**
6. whis-   -tel   (-tle)   -tal          6. whistle **(1)**
7. mor-    -tle   -tel   (-tal)          7. mortal **(1)**

**Crack the Code** Some Spelling Words have been written in the following code. Use the code to figure out each word. Then write each word correctly.

| CODE:   | R | E | N | O | T | V | A | G | B | F | Y | M |
|---------|---|---|---|---|---|---|---|---|---|---|---|---|
| LETTER: | A | D | E | G | I | J | K | L | N | P | V | W |

8.  RBAGN    ankle **(1)**
9.  GNYNG    level **(1)**
10. RBONG    angel **(1)**
11. BNNEGN   needle **(1)**
12. RBOGN    angle **(1)**
13. VNMNG    jewel **(1)**
14. ENYTG    devil **(1)**
15. FNERG    pedal **(1)**

1. jewel
2. sparkle
3. angle
4. shovel
5. single
6. normal
7. angel
8. legal
9. whistle
10. fossil*
11. puzzle
12. bushel
13. mortal
14. gentle
15. level
16. label
17. pedal
18. ankle
19. needle
20. devil*

Name _____

# Proofreading and Writing

**Proofreading** Circle the five misspelled Spelling Words in the following Help Wanted advertisement. Then write each word correctly.

   **Are you tired** of doing dirty work with a (shovle?) Maybe you're sick of hauling (bushal) baskets of vegetables to market. We're looking for a hard-working, (singel) young man or woman to be an apprentice in the sailmaking business. You must be of (legil) working age, and you should be willing to work with a large needle.

**Please apply in person during (normel) business hours at the office of James Forten, Sailmaker.**

1. shovel **(1 point)**
2. bushel **(1)**
3. single **(1)**
4. legal **(1)**
5. normal **(1)**

**Write a Character Sketch** James Forten had an unusual life. At various times he was a sailor in the Revolutionary War, a sailmaker, a successful businessman, and an abolitionist. Is there anything about his personality that you think would have helped him in the different parts of his life?

**On a separate sheet of paper, write a brief character sketch of James Forten. Use Spelling Words from the list.**

Responses will vary. **(5)**

Name _____

# Journal of Opposites

**Read the journal. In each blank, write an antonym of the clue word.**
Sample answers shown.

December 31, 1781

This summer I set sail aboard the *Royal Louis*. We were ready to

fight the ___powerful **(1 point)**___ British navy. Soon we were caught up
(powerless)

in battle with the ___heavily **(1)**___ armed ship *Active*. I carried
(lightly)

gunpowder from ___below **(1)**___ the decks to the guns. In time,
(above)

the *Active* surrendered by ___lowering **(1)**___ its flag. I'll never
(raising)

forget the crowd's excited ___cheering **(1)**___ as we took the ship
(booing)

back to Philadelphia. But our next trip out was ___unlucky **(1)**___.
(lucky)

Our ship surrendered to three British ships, and we crew members were

___captured **(1)**___ as prisoners. At least the boys were
(set free)

___allowed **(1)**___ to play marbles. The captain's son joined us,
(forbidden)

and we became ___friends **(1)**___. I wonder if this friendship
(enemies)

saved me from being ___sold **(1)**___ into slavery.
(bought)

Name _____

# What Kind? How Many? Which One?

**Adjectives**  A word that describes a noun or a pronoun is called an **adjective**. It tells what kind or how many. *A*, *an*, and *the* are special adjectives called **articles**. *A* and *an* refer to any item. *The* refers to a particular item. *This*, *that*, *these*, and *those* are **demonstrative adjectives**. They tell which one. *This* and *these* refer to nearby items; *that* and *those* refer to farther away items.

**Circle all of the adjectives in the following sentences, including articles and demonstrative adjectives.**

1. James sewed (straight) seams on (large), (square) sails. **(3 points)**
2. (Those) ships needed (many) sails. **(2)**
3. (Six) sailors are pulling on (the) (thick) ropes. **(3)**
4. (This) (huge) vessel is (impressive.) **(3)**
5. (Tired) merchants closed (the) shops. **(2)**
6. (Grateful) citizens will raise (a) cheer for (these) sailors. **(3)**
7. (An) anchor is thrown overboard. **(1)**
8. (A) (white) seagull dives for (the) (slippery) fish. **(4)**
9. (That) shop sells sails and (other) equipment for ships. **(2)**
10. Philadelphia has (a) (proud) heritage. **(2)**

Assessment Tip: Total **25** Points

Name _____

# Who Settled Where?

**Proper Adjectives** A **proper adjective** is formed from a proper noun and always begins with a capital letter.

**Fill in the blank with the proper adjective formed from the proper noun in parentheses. Check a dictionary if you need to. (Number four is tricky!)**

1. The state of Louisiana was once a <u>French **(1)**</u> colony. (France)

2. The <u>American **(1)**</u> Revolution was a fight for independence from England. (America)

3. King George III sat on the <u>English **(1)**</u> throne. (England)

4. There were <u>Dutch **(1)**</u> settlers in New York. (Holland)

5. <u>Spanish **(1)**</u> explorers settled parts of Florida. (Spain)

6. Margaret's <u>German **(1)**</u> ancestors settled in Pennsylvania. (Germany)

7. Many <u>Irish **(1)**</u> immigrants came to America in the nineteenth century. (Ireland)

8. James Forten's ancestors were <u>African **(1)**</u>. (Africa)

9. Alaska was once a <u>Russian **(1)**</u> territory. (Russia)

10. General Washington fought <u>British **(1)**</u> soldiers. (Britain)

Name _____

# Marvelous Marbles

**Expanding Sentences with Adjectives** Good writers add interest to their writing by adding adjectives that help readers visualize a scene.

**Add adjectives to the following sentences to make them more lively and interesting. Use your imagination!** Answers will vary.

1. These __(1 point)_____ children are playing with marbles.

2. That __(1)_____ bag holds __(1)_____ marbles.

3. Alfred sits on the __(1)_____ ground to play.

4. Carla shows Tony a __(1)_____ marble.

5. The players enjoy the __(1)_____ sunshine.

6. Kinley doesn't play marbles, but he collects __(1)_____ cards.

7. That __(1)_____ girl usually wins.

8. The __(1)_____ boy in the __(1)_____ jacket won today!

Assessment Tip: Total **10** Points

Name _____

# Writing a Biography

In *James Forten*, you read about an African American sailor who served during the Revolutionary War. A **biography** is a written account of important events and significant experiences in a person's life. Before you write a biography of your own, follow these steps:

► Choose a real person whom you admire or a person who lived during the American Revolution.

► Research important facts, dates, places, events, and accomplishments in this person's life. Use the Internet, reference books, or history books in your library to gather information.

**Record and organize important dates, locations, and events in this person's life on the timeline below. (2 points each)**

The Life of _____

| DATE | EVENT |
|------|-------|
| _____ | |
| _____ | |
| _____ | |
| _____ | |

**Now write your biography on a separate sheet of paper. Start with an anecdote or a famous quotation from this person's life. Then work from your timeline. Write about important events and experiences, using chronological order, time-order words, and key dates. Highlight the events that you think best reveal this person's character or major accomplishments. Finally, conclude by summarizing why this person is remembered. (5)**

Name _____

# Capitalizing Names of People and Places

Good biographers proofread their writing to check for correct
capitalization of proper names. Imagine you have written a biography
of James Forten. The book jacket will include information to interest
readers in the book.

**Proofread the following book-jacket sentences. Underline the
names of people and places that should be capitalized and write
them correctly on the lines. (1 point each)**

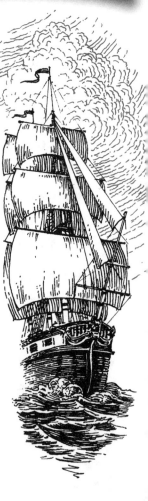

African American sailor james forten was born in philadelphia in 1766.

James Forten, Philadelphia
_____

Living on the shores of the atlantic ocean, he dreamed of glory on the
high seas.

Atlantic Ocean
_____

When he was only fourteen years old, he joined the crew of a vessel that
was commanded by captain stephen decatur.

Captain Stephen Decatur
_____

The *royal louis* was a privateer, or a privately owned ship that the united
states used in the war against england.

*Royal Louis*, United States, England
_____

After the British captured his ship in 1781, the teenaged sailor was
imprisoned in the filthy hold of a prison ship, the *jersey*, which was
anchored off new york.

*Jersey*, New York
_____

This young patriot feared little — except the bitter chance that he would
be sent to the west indies and enslaved.

West Indies
_____

Assessment Tip: Total **10** Points

Name _____

# Writing a Personal Response

Use the test-taking strategies and tips you have learned to help you answer personal response questions. Take the time you need to decide which topic you will write about and to write an answer. Then read your answer and see how you may make it better. This practice will help you when you take this kind of test.

**Write one or two paragraphs about one of the following topics.**

**a.** Many Patriots in the time of the American Revolution took strong actions, such as dumping tea, to protest the taxes imposed by the British. If you had lived in the time of Paul Revere, would you have protested against British laws? If so, what would you have done? If not, why not?

**b.** Paul Revere interrupted his regular job as a silversmith to do dangerous work as an express rider for the Sons of Liberty. Do you think interrupting your routine to help others is a good definition for heroism? Explain why or why not.

Answers will vary. **(15 points)**

_____

_____

_____

_____

_____

_____

_____

_____

_____

_____

Name _____

# Writing a Personal Response continued

**Read your response. Check to be sure that it**

- focuses on the topic
- is well organized
- has details that support your response
- includes vivid and exact words
- has few mistakes in capitalization, punctuation, grammar, or spelling

**Now pick one way you can improve your response. Make your changes below.**

Answers will vary. **(5)**

_____

_____

_____

_____

_____

_____

_____

_____

_____

_____

_____

_____

_____

Assessment Tip: Total **20** Points

Name _____

# Spelling Review

**Write Spelling Words from the list on this page to answer the
questions.** Order of answers in each category may vary.

1–12. Which twelve words have the final /ər/ sounds?

1. polar **(1 point)**

2. humor **(1)**

3. mayor **(1)**

4. lunar **(1)**

5. tractor **(1)**

6. quarter **(1)**

7. parlor **(1)**

8. powder **(1)**

9. actor **(1)**

10. matter **(1)**

11. shoulder **(1)**

12. burglar **(1)**

13–23. Which eleven words have the final /l/ or /əl/ sounds?

13. jewel **(1)**

14. needle **(1)**

15. legal **(1)**

16. gentle **(1)**

17. equal **(1)**

18. mortal **(1)**

19. sparkle **(1)**

20. bushel **(1)**

21. single **(1)**

22. whistle **(1)**

23. pedal **(1)**

24–30. What syllable is missing from each word? Write
each word.

24. sor— sorrow **(1)**

25. —have behave **(1)**

26. wed— wedding **(1)**

27. rap— rapid **(1)**

28. —ware aware **(1)**

29. —ue value **(1)**

30. pub— publish **(1)**

## Spelling Words

1. jewel
2. polar
3. needle
4. humor
5. legal
6. mayor
7. gentle
8. lunar
9. sorrow
10. tractor
11. quarter
12. behave
13. parlor
14. wedding
15. powder
16. actor
17. rapid
18. equal
19. mortal
20. aware
21. matter
22. sparkle
23. shoulder
24. bushel
25. value
26. publish
27. single
28. whistle
29. burglar
30. pedal

Name _____

# Spelling Spree

**Syllable Rhymes** **Write the Spelling Word that has a first syllable that rhymes with each word below.**

1. win    <u>single **(1 point)**</u>

2. car    <u>sparkle **(1)**</u>

3. rub    <u>publish **(1)**</u>

4. push    <u>bushel **(1)**</u>

5. fur    <u>burglar **(1)**</u>

6. den    <u>gentle **(1)**</u>

7. map    <u>rapid **(1)**</u>

Spelling Words

1. humor
2. gentle
3. lunar
4. tractor
5. quarter
6. rapid
7. mortal
8. sparkle
9. bushel
10. publish
11. single
12. burglar
13. pedal
14. jewel
15. mayor

**Word Fun** **Write a Spelling Word to fit each clue.**

8. Change the last three letters in *jelly* to make a word meaning "gem." <u>jewel **(1)**</u>

9. Change the first three letters of *final* to make a word describing what you do to make a bicycle move. <u>pedal **(1)**</u>

10. Add a consonant to *moral* to make a word meaning "human being." <u>mortal **(1)**</u>

11. Change the word *quartz* to make it mean "twenty-five cents." <u>quarter **(1)**</u>

12. Remove two letters from *detractor* to form a word for a farm machine. <u>tractor **(1)**</u>

13. Replace two consonants in *lunch* to form a word having to do with the moon. <u>lunar **(1)**</u>

14. Replace two letters in *humid* to make a word that tells what makes people laugh. <u>humor **(1)**</u>

15. Change one letter in *major* to make the head of a city. <u>mayor **(1)**</u>

Assessment Tip: Total **15** Points

Name _____

# Proofreading and Writing

**Proofreading** Circle the five misspelled Spelling Words in this report. Then write each word correctly.

Betsy Ross sat in her (parler) with a few scraps of cloth, a (needel), and some thread. She usually made jackets, (weding) dresses, and lacy shirts. That day, she made a flag with great (valyew) for the new nation. It made the colonial army (equel) to the British.

1. parlor **(1 point)**

2. needle **(1)**

3. wedding **(1)**

4. value **(1)**

5. equal **(1)**

1. powder
2. polar
3. matter
4. parlor
5. equal
6. aware
7. behave
8. sorrow
9. shoulder
10. value
11. whistle
12. needle
13. legal
14. actor
15. wedding

**Title Trouble** Correct the following book titles. Replace each underlined word with a rhyming Spelling Word.

6. *Soldiers, Keep Your Chowder Close By* Powder **(1)**

7. *Just Thistle, I'll Come Running!* Whistle **(1)**

8. *The Factor Who Makes History Come Alive* Actor **(1)**

9. *One Soldier's Borrow; Another's Joy* Sorrow **(1)**

10. *Be Compare of Danger Signs* Aware **(1)**

11. *Manners: How a Soldier Should Shave* Behave **(1)**

12. *Valley Forge—Cold as Solar Ice* Polar **(1)**

13. *He Carried His Musket on His Boulder* Shoulder **(1)**

14. *The New Flag Really Does Flatter!* Matter **(1)**

15. *The Regal Papers* Legal **(1)**

✎ **Write a Diary Entry** On a separate sheet of paper, write a diary entry telling about a colonial American's day. Use the Spelling Review Words. Responses will vary.

Name _____

# Person to Person

**The characters in this theme learn about themselves and others. After reading each story, complete the chart below to show what you have learned about the characters. (10 points per selection)**

|  | **Mariah Keeps Cool** | **Mom's Best Friend** |
|---|---|---|
| **Who is the main character or characters?** | Mariah | Mom and her daughter, the narrator. |
| **How do the story characters try to help each other?** | Mariah throws a surprise party for her sister Lynn. The guests help by bringing gifts for the homeless shelter where Lynn volunteers. | The family helps Mom by taking care of the house while Mom is away learning how to work with her new dog guide. |
| **How do the story characters communicate with each other?** | The characters spend a lot of time talking together and planning for the party. | The narrator and Mom write letters back and forth. Also, Mom communicates with her dog guide through words and gestures. |

Name _____

# Person to Person  continued

| | **Yang the Second and Her Secret Admirers** | **Dear Mr. Henshaw** |
|---|---|---|
| **Who is the main character or characters?** | Yingtao and Yinglan, or Second Sister | Leigh Botts |
| **How do the story characters try to help each other?** | Yingtao and his sister try to help Second Sister feel more at home in America by matching her up with Paul Eng, a boy from school. | Angela Badger tries to encourage students to be better writers. |
| **How do the story characters communicate with each other?** | The characters talk to each other. Yingtao and his sister stage conversations for Second Sister and Paul. | Leigh writes letters to Mr. Henshaw. The characters also talk to each other. |

What have you learned about working together in this theme?

Sample answer: There are many ways people can work together.

Communication exists in many forms. **(2)**

_____

Assessment Tip: Total **22** Points

Name _____

# Guests of Honor

**Answer each of the following questions by writing a vocabulary word.**

1. Which word means "make something look nice"?
   decorate **(1 point)**

2. Which word tells what people do when they stop someone and delay him or her for a while? detain **(1)**

3. Which word means "people who make up an audience"?
   spectators **(1)**

4. Which word means "express a willingness to help"?
   volunteer **(1)**

5. Which word describes an event with lively music and colorful decorations? festive **(1)**

6. Which word is another word for *party*? celebration **(1)**

7. Which word means "unwilling"? reluctant **(1)**

8. Which word has the same meaning as *astonishingly*?
   amazingly **(1)**

9. Which word means "believes something is wrong"?
   suspects **(1)**

10. Which word means "to show respect for someone publicly"?
    honor **(1)**

**Now write the first letter of each of the last five words you wrote above to answer this question.**

What noise might tip off a person that he or she is about to be surprised? crash **(2)**

Name _____

# This Was Their Solution!

**Read the problem stated in the left-hand column. Fill in the Solution
column with information from the selection.**

| Problem | | Solution |
|---------|---|----------|
| Lynn overhears Mariah say "See you later" to Denise and is curious about why they were going to be together. | → | Mariah tells Lynn that she is going to see Denise when she gets back home. **(2 points)** |
| Lynn shows up unexpectedly at Brandon's house while they're making decorations. | → | Mariah, Brandon, and the girls convince Lynn that she cannot stay to watch. **(2)** |
| Lynn doesn't want a birthday celebration; she just wants to stay in bed all day. | → | Mariah asks her mother to take Lynn to the bookstore to get her out of the house. **(2)** |
| Mariah forgets to get music for the party. | → | Mariah's father calls Brandon's father because he has music equipment he can bring over. **(2)** |
| Mariah and the rest of the Friendly Five don't have anyone to dance with. | → | Mariah suggests that they dance together, or by themselves. **(2)** |

198    Theme 4: **Person to Person**

Assessment Tip: Total **10** Points

Name _____

# Surprise Party Advice

**Based on what you've learned from the selection, complete the sentences below giving advice about how to throw a successful surprise party. (Answers will vary.)**

▶ On the party invitations, make sure everyone knows that the party is a surprise, when and where it is taking place, and any other special instructions about what to bring or do. **(1 point)**

▶ Speak carefully when you're around the guest of honor, so you don't accidentally give away the surprise. **(1)**

▶ If you say something that makes the guest of honor suspicious, be ready to tell a story that gives another explanation for what you've said. **(1)**

▶ A few days before the party, get others to help you make party decorations. **(1)**

▶ If the guest of honor unexpectedly appears while party preparations are taking place, figure out another way to explain what is going on. **(1)**

▶ On the day of the party, ask others to help you set up for the party. **(1)**

▶ If the party is taking place at the guest of honor's house, ask someone to get that person out of the house while you set up the party. **(1)**

▶ Be sure to have plenty of food and drinks **(1)** available for your guests.

▶ If you want to have music at the party, be sure that you have all the musical equipment you will need. **(1)**

▶ And remember to have fun **(1)** yourself!

Name _____

# Think It Through

**Read the passage.   Then complete the activity on page 201.**

## Munching on Leaves

Julie's little brother Pablo was obsessed with the movie *Bugs*.  This wouldn't have been a problem, except that Aunt Elena bought him the soundtrack, and Pablo listened to it nonstop, especially one song called "The Caterpillar Crawl."  The chorus went: "Merrily we crawl along, crawl along, munchin' leaves all day!"  It had one of those catchy tunes that sticks in your mind even though it is the last song in the world that you want to sing.  Last week Julie's friend Diana had looked at her strangely and asked, "What are you singing?  Something about munching *leaves*?"  Julie knew she had to do something.

"I can't listen to that CD anymore," she told her father.  "Not one more time.  If I hear it one more time, I will scream."

Dad sighed. "Yes, I know," he said.  "Yesterday at the office I started singing 'Don't Bug Me' during a meeting."

"Can't you tell him not to play it anymore?"

"Well, would it be fair if I told you not to play one of your CDs?"

"It would be if I played one CD over and over and over again."

"What about the time I asked you to stop playing that Screaming Purple Rhinos CD?" Julie could see that her dad had a point.

She went to the library and searched until she found an audiotape of folk songs that she had loved when she was six.  She checked it out, brought it home, and started playing it on her own tape player.  When Pablo asked what it was, she said, "Never mind," and shut her door.

Soon she heard him tapping. "Can't I listen to that?"

"No, it's mine. Go listen to your *Bugs* CD."  She heard him complaining to Dad.  Julie came out of her room and said, "Oh, all right. You can listen to it, but you have to give it back right afterwards."  Of course, he didn't, which had been her plan all along.

By the time Julie was sick of the folk song tape, it was due back at the library.

Name _____

# Think It Through  continued

**Answer these questions about the passage on page 200.**

Answers may vary. Sample answers shown.

1. What problem does Julie have in the story? She is sick of the CD
   her little brother keeps playing again and again. **(3 points)**

2. What solution does Julie think of first? She asks her dad to tell
   Pablo not to play the CD anymore. **(3)**

3. After thinking about that solution, what does Julie decide? She
   decides that it's not really fair to ask Pablo to stop listening to
   the CD. **(3)**

4. What solution does she think of next? She draws Pablo's attention
   to a recording of folk songs she used to like, so that he forgets
   about the *Bugs* CD. **(3)**

5. Do you think her solution is a good one? Why or why not?
   Yes. It solves the problem without being unfair or making Pablo
   feel bad. **(3)**

6. Think about the steps to solving a problem. Which steps did Julie
   follow, and how well did she follow them? First, she identified the
   problem. Then, she thought about different solutions. Finally, she
   picked the best solution and followed through on it. Julie did a
   good job of following the steps. **(3)**

Name _____

# Divide and Define

**Read each sentence. Rewrite the underlined word with a slash (/) to divide the syllables. Then, after it, write a definition or synonym for the word.** Sample answers shown. Accept all reasonable definitions.

1. As you <u>approach</u> the yard, you will smell the hot dogs.

   ap/proach; to come near **(2 points)**

2. I'll be ready for the party in an <u>instant</u>.

   in/stant; moment **(2)**

3. Lynn is always <u>hungry</u> when she wakes up in the morning.

   hun/gry; starved **(2)**

4. I'll call you when the decorations are <u>complete</u>.

   com/plete; finished **(2)**

5. On his vacation in Maine, Brendan went out on a <u>lobster</u> boat.

   lob/ster; a sea animal **(2)**

6. Will you please <u>increase</u> the volume on the CD player?

   in/crease; make greater **(2)**

7. Mariah decided to <u>confront</u> Denise about the rumor she had heard.

   con/front; meet face to face **(2)**

8. The balloons and colored paper make a beautiful <u>display</u>.

   dis/play; exhibit **(2)**

Assessment Tip: Total **16** Points

# VCCCV Pattern

Spelling Words

Two-syllable words with the VCCCV pattern have two consonants that spell one sound, as in *laughter*, or that form a cluster, as in *complain*. Divide a VCCCV word into syllables before or after those consonants. Then look for familiar patterns that you have learned, and spell the word by syllables.

VCC | CV    **laugh | ter**        VC | CCV     **com | plain**

**Write each Spelling Word under the heading that shows where it is divided.** Order of answers for each category may vary.

## VC|CCV

district **(1 point)**          mischief **(1)**

address **(1)**                complex **(1)**

complain **(1)**               orphan **(1)**

explain **(1)**                constant **(1)**

improve **(1)**                dolphin **(1)**

farther **(1)**                employ **(1)**

simply **(1)**                 monster **(1)**

hundred **(1)**               orchard **(1)**

although **(1)**

## VCC|CV

laughter **(1)**               sandwich **(1)**

partner **(1)**

**Spelling Words**

1. district
2. address
3. complain
4. explain
5. improve
6. farther
7. simply
8. hundred
9. although
10. laughter
11. mischief
12. complex
13. partner
14. orphan
15. constant
16. dolphin
17. employ
18. sandwich
19. monster
20. orchard

Theme 4: **Person to Person**    203
Assessment Tip: Total **20** Points

Name _____

# Spelling Spree

**Syllable Addition** **Combine the first syllable of the first word with the final syllable of the second word to write a Spelling Word.**

1. addition + headdress = _____
2. parting + runner = _____
3. monsoon + youngster = _____
4. farsighted + father = _____
5. command + floodplain = _____
6. concern + instant = _____
7. empire + deploy = _____

1. address **(1 point)**
2. partner **(1)**
3. monster **(1)**
4. farther **(1)**
5. complain **(1)**
6. constant **(1)**
7. employ **(1)**

**Word Clues** **Write a Spelling Word to fit each clue.**

8. a child whose parents have died
9. two pieces of bread and a slice of cheese
10. an area set aside for a specific purpose
11. where you can find apple trees
12. a reaction to a joke
13. an aquatic mammal
14. a word meaning "even though"

8. orphan **(1)**
9. sandwich **(1)**
10. district **(1)**
11. orchard **(1)**
12. laughter **(1)**
13. dolphin **(1)**
14. although **(1)**

Assessment Tip: Total **14** Points

Name _____

# Proofreading and Writing

**Proofreading** Circle the six misspelled Spelling Words in this birthday card. Then write each word correctly.

Dear Lynn,

Let me (explane) why we threw you a surprise party. It wasn't to create (mischeif) Although you said you (simplie) wanted to stay in bed on your birthday, we had to show how much we care about you. That's why we decided on something more (complecks) than a simple party. By having the guests bring things for your friends at the shelter, we might be able to (improove) the lives of the people there. I hope it's the best party you'll ever have, even if you live to be a (hunderd!)

Your loving sister,
Mariah

1. explain **(1 point)**
2. mischief **(1)**
3. simply **(1)**
4. complex **(1)**
5. improve **(1)**
6. hundred **(1)**

## Spelling Words

1. district
2. address
3. complain
4. explain
5. improve
6. farther
7. simply
8. hundred
9. although
10. laughter
11. mischief
12. complex
13. partner
14. orphan
15. constant
16. dolphin
17. employ
18. sandwich
19. monster
20. orchard

✎ **Write About an Experience** Have you ever worked together with your family or friends to surprise someone? What was the surprise? How did you organize it? Were you able to keep it a secret until the end? How did the person being surprised react?

**On a separate piece of paper, write a paragraph describing the experience. Use Spelling Words from the list.** Responses will vary. **(4)**

Name _____

# Inflection Connection

**Read each word and its definition. Pay attention to inflected endings
such as *-s, -es, -ed, -ing, -er, -est*. Then use inflected forms of each
word to complete the sentences below.**

> *dance* (dăns) *v.* danced, dancing, dances. To move in time to music.
>
> *happy* (hăp´ ē) *adj.* happier, happiest. Showing or feeling joy or pleasure.
>
> *noisy* (noi´ zē) *adj.* noisier, noisiest. Full of or accompanied by noise.
>
> *party* (pär´ tē) *n.*, pl. parties. A social gathering for pleasure or entertainment.
>
> *supply* (sə plī´) *v.* supplied, supplying, supplies. To make available for
>    use; provide.

1. Everyone agreed that Rosa's birthday celebration was one of the

   best __parties **(2 points)**__ they had been to.

2. Gabe shouted to Danny that he had never been to a

   __noisier **(2)**__ party.

3. Conchita __supplied **(2)**__ the music from her large CD

   collection.

4. Singing and __dancing **(2)**__ went on late into the night.

5. Rosa's big smile showed that she was the __happiest **(2)**__

   person there.

Assessment Tip: Total **10** Points

Name _____

# Strong, Stronger, Strongest

**Comparing with Adjectives** Add -*er* to most adjectives to compare two
people, places, or things. Use *more* with long adjectives to compare two
items. Add -*est* to most adjectives to compare three or more. Use *most*
with long adjectives to compare three or more.

1. **Most Adjectives**          Tanya is strong.

   Add -*er* or -*est* to the adjective.    Chris is **stronger** than Tanya.

   Pat is the **strongest** of all.

2. **Adjectives with Two or More**    It is a beautiful view.

   **Syllables**          It is a **more beautiful** view from here.

   Use *more* or *most*.        It is the **most beautiful** view of all.

**Complete each sentence with the correct form of the adjective in
parentheses.**

1. She is the <u>most generous **(1 point)**</u> person I know. (generous)

2. Denise is a <u>more skillful **(1)**</u> artist than I am. (skillful)

3. Her mother was the <u>calmest **(1)**</u> one there. (calm)

4. It was the <u>greatest **(1)**</u> night of the year. (great)

5. I'd like a <u>smaller **(1)**</u> slice of cake than that,
   please. (small)

6. LaToya is the <u>kindest **(1)**</u> person I know. (kind)

7. Of all our houses, Marco's house is the <u>nearest **(1)**</u>
   one to the school. (near)

8. Marsha is a <u>more talented **(1)**</u> singer than Carlos. (talented)

9. However, Carlos is the <u>most gifted **(1)**</u> bass player
   in the school. (gifted)

10. I am a <u>faster **(1)**</u> reader than a writer. (fast)

Name _____

# 'Tis Better to Give Than to Receive

**Comparing with *good* and *bad*** The adjectives *good* and *bad* have irregular comparative forms. Use *better* to compare two things, and *best* to compare three or more. Use *worse* to compare two things, and *worst* to compare three or more.

| | **Good** | **Bad** |
|---|---|---|
| **Comparing two** | This lunch is **better** than yesterday's. | I did **worse** on this test than the last one. |
| **Comparing three or more** | It is the **best** lunch I've ever had. | In fact, this is the **worst** I've ever done. |

**Fill in each blank with the correct form of *good* or *bad*.** Answers may vary.

1. Donating used clothing is a ___better **(1 point)**___ act than throwing it away.

2. In fact, it is probably the ___best **(1)**___ thing you can do with old clothing.

3. Icy sidewalks are a ___worse **(1)**___ hazard for frail people than for others.

4. Last winter was the ___worst **(1)**___ winter on record.

5. Hooray! This month's food drive was a ___better **(1)**___ one than last month's.

6. In fact, it was the ___best **(1)**___ food drive we've ever had.

7. What is the ___worst/best **(1)**___ thing that has ever happened to you?

8. Uncle Sal has a ___better **(1)**___ garden than my mother.

9. In fact, he won an award for the ___best **(1)**___ garden in the neighborhood.

10. She has a ___worse **(1)**___ cold than I had.

Assessment Tip: Total **10** Points

Name _____

# Lighter and Warmer

**Combining Sentences with Adjectives**  To avoid having too many short, comparing sentences, you can combine sentences to make one sentence with two or more comparative adjectives.  Here is an example:

> **Two sentences**: This year's swim team is **more enthusiastic** than last year's team.  It is a **stronger** team too.

> **One sentence**: This year's swim team is **more enthusiastic and stronger** than last year's team.

**Mark wrote a draft of an article for the school paper.  Revise the five underlined pairs of sentences by combining them to form sentences with more than one comparative adjective.**

I am a member of the swim team.  Being on the team has given me a busier life. It has given me a better life too.  I get up at 6 A.M. for practice.  In the winter, it was darker outside than it had been in the fall. It was colder too.  That was hard, but when I got to school I saw my teammates.  Pat would tell funny jokes.  Dale would tell even funnier jokes.  Dale told sillier jokes too.

Now that spring is here, warmer days have arrived.  Lighter days have arrived too.  It is easy to practice a lot when it is light. We will have a stronger team for our next meet.  We will have a faster team too. I love to swim, but the best part of being on the team is working with great friends.

1. Being on the team has given me a busier and better life. **(2 points)**

2. In the winter, it was darker and colder outside than it had been in the fall. **(2)**

3. Dale would tell even funnier and sillier jokes. **(2)**

4. Now that spring is here, warmer and lighter days have arrived. **(2)**

5. We will have a stronger and faster team for our next meet. **(2)**

Name _____

# Writing a Memo

A **memo** is a brief, informal message sent from one person to others in the same company, group, or organization.  Sometimes people write memos to each other when they work together as a team.

**Use this page to plan a memo to your classmates or other students at school about an important event.  Follow these steps:**

▶ **Name the person or the persons to whom you are writing**

▶ **Tell who is writing the memo.**

▶ **Write the date.**

▶ **Identify the subject of the memo.**

▶ **Write the body of the memo.  Begin by stating why you are writing. Use clear, direct language and a businesslike tone.  Be brief but include all the important information.  If you want a response, end by asking a question or by requesting an action.**

---

### MEMORANDUM

To: (2 points) _____

From: (2) _____

Date: (2) _____

Subject: (2) _____

(4) _____

_____

_____

_____

_____

**When you finish your memo, check it for correct grammar and punctuation and for complete sentences. Then copy your memo on a clean sheet of paper and post it or send it.**

Assessment Tip: Total **12** Points

Name _____

# Changing Positions of Adjectives

An **adjective** describes a noun or pronoun. Adjectives may come before or after the nouns or pronouns they describe. Good writers place adjectives in different positions in a sentence to add variety to their writing.

**First, circle the adjectives in the following memo from Denise to the other party organizers. Then rewrite the body of the memo on the lines, changing the positions of some adjectives to add variety. Either place the adjectives before or after the nouns they describe. (1 point** for each adjective)

To: All Party Organizers

From: Denise

Date: July 15

Subject: Surprise Party Decorations

We will meet at Brandon's house on Wednesday, July 18, at 1 P.M. We will create decorations that are (pretty) yet (inexpensive). Bring scissors to make flowers that are (paper), signs that are (handmade), and banners that are (long) and (colorful). Sometimes decorations that are (simple) and (easy) to make are the most effective. I know the backyard will look like a garden that is (beautiful). Lynn and the other guests will be (happy)!

Responses will vary. **(10)**

We will meet at Brandon's house on Wednesday, July 18, at 1 P.M. We will create

decorations that are pretty yet inexpensive. Bring scissors to make paper flowers,

handmade signs, and long, colorful banners. Sometimes decorations that are

simple and easy to make are the most effective. I know the backyard will look like a

beautiful garden. Lynn and the other guests will be happy!

Theme 4: **Person to Person**   211
Assessment Tip: Total **20** Points

Name _____

# Evaluating Your Personal Narrative

**Reread your personal narrative. What do you need to do to make it better? Use this page to help you decide. Put a checkmark in the box for each sentence that describes your personal narrative.**

### Rings the Bell!

☐ My story starts with an attention-grabbing beginning.

☐ My voice comes through in my telling of the story.

☐ I included details that help the reader picture what happened.

☐ My use of dialogue makes the story more interesting.

☐ I vary the types of sentences in my writing.

☐ There are very few mistakes.

### Getting Stronger

☐ I could have a stronger beginning.

☐ Most of it sounds like me, but some of it doesn't.

☐ I use details, but I could include more.

☐ Maybe I should add more dialogue.

☐ I could vary my sentences a bit more.

☐ There are quite a few errors that need to be fixed.

### Try Harder

☐ My beginning needs work.

☐ This doesn't sound like the way I would tell a story.

☐ I need to add details so it isn't so hard to picture what's happening.

☐ I haven't varied the sentence types in my writing.

☐ Too many mistakes make the story hard to read.

Name _____

# Varying Sentence Types

**Read the paragraph.  All the sentences are declarative sentences.**

Yesterday I had a bad day. I overslept.  I didn't have time for breakfast.
I missed the bus.  I yelled at it to stop.  It was too late.  No one heard
me.  I walked all the way to school.  I wondered what I had done to
deserve this.  I was late, and I didn't have a note from my mom.
The day went downhill from there.

**Now rewrite the paragraph, varying the sentence types.  Include
at least one question, one exclamation, and one command.
You will need to add or delete words to revise the sentences.**

Answers will vary. **(10 points)**

_____

_____

_____

_____

_____

_____

_____

_____

_____

_____

_____

_____

Theme 4: **Person to Person**    213
Assessment Tip: Total **10** Points

Name _____

# Spelling Words

**Words Often Misspelled** Look for familiar spelling patterns to help you remember how to spell the Spelling Words on this page. Think carefully about the parts that you find hard to spell in each word.

**Write the missing letters in the Spelling Words below.**
Order of answers for 12–13 may vary.

1. <u> a </u> lot **(1 point)**

2. bec <u> a </u> <u> u </u> se **(1)**

3. s <u> c </u> <u> h </u> ool **(1)**

4. it <u> s </u> **(1)**

5. it ' <u> </u> <u> s </u> **(1)**

6. ton <u> i </u> <u> g </u> <u> h </u> t **(1)**

7. m <u> i </u> <u> g </u> <u> h </u> t **(1)**

8. r <u> i </u> <u> g </u> <u> h </u> t **(1)**

9. <u> w </u> <u> r </u> ite **(1)**

10. ag <u> a </u> <u> i </u> n **(1)**

11. t <u> o </u> **(1)**

12. t <u> o </u> <u> o </u> **(1)**

13. t <u> w </u> <u> o </u> **(1)**

14. th <u> e </u> <u> y </u> **(1)**

15. tha <u> t </u> ' <u> s </u> **(1)**

**Study List On a separate piece of paper, write each Spelling Word. Check your spelling against the words on the list.**

Order of words may vary. **(5)**

Assessment Tip: Total **20** Points

# Spelling Spree

**Homophone Blanks** The blanks in each of the following sentences can be filled with homophones from the Spelling Word list. Write the words in the correct order.

1–2. I think _____ too bad that the park lost the funding for _____ swimming pool.

3–5. The _____ football players decided that they would try _____ play on the basketball team, _____.

6–7. After she broke her arm, Leslie couldn't _____ with her _____ hand.

1–2. it's **(1 point)** _____ its **(1)** _____

3–5. two **(1)** _____ to **(1)** _____ too **(1)** _____

6–7. write **(1)** _____ right **(1)** _____

**Crack the Code** Some Spelling Words have been written in the code below. Use the code to figure out each word. Then write the words correctly.

| **CODE:** | B | P | Y | L | A | T | R | F | D | W | Z | X | V | I | O |
|-----------|---|---|---|---|---|---|---|---|---|---|---|---|---|---|---|
| **LETTER:** | a | b | c | e | g | h | i | l | m | n | o | s | t | u | y |

8. DRATV
9. B FZV
10. XYTZZF
11. VTBV'X
12. BABRW
13. VTLO
14. PLYBIXL
15. VZWRATV

8. might **(1)**
9. a lot **(1)**
10. school **(1)**
11. that's **(1)**
12. again **(1)**
13. they **(1)**
14. because **(1)**
15. tonight **(1)**

**Spelling Words**

1. a lot
2. because
3. school
4. its
5. it's
6. tonight
7. might
8. right
9. write
10. again
11. to
12. too
13. two
14. they
15. that's

Assessment Tip: Total **15** Points

Name _____

# Proofreading and Writing

**Proofreading** Circle the five misspelled Spelling Words in this advertisement. Then write each word correctly.

Has it been (two) long since you talked to your best friend? Do you feel like you don't have the time to (wright) to the people you care about? Then (its) time to call them, person to person! There's nothing like a conversation to get you back in touch. And it doesn't cost (alot,) either! Call (tonite) — you'll be glad you did.

Spelling Words:
1. a lot
2. because
3. school
4. its
5. it's
6. tonight
7. might
8. right
9. write
10. again
11. to
12. too
13. two
14. they
15. that's

1. too **(1 point)**
2. write **(1)**
3. it's **(1)**
4. a lot **(1)**
5. tonight **(1)**

✏ **Write a Conversation** Work with one or more classmates to create a conversation. One person writes a sentence, using a Spelling Word, to open the conversation. The next person writes the second sentence, using a Spelling Word. From here, take turns writing sentences, using Spelling Words from the list. Responses will vary. **(5)**

Name _____

# A Friend and a Helper

**Use words from the box to complete the paragraphs below.**

**Vocabulary**

attachment

dog guide

mastered

obedience

memorizing

obstacles

instinct

mature

braille

layout

A person who cannot see may use a <u>dog guide</u> **(1 point)** as a helper when going from place to place. In order to do this important work, a dog must go through <u>obedience</u> **(1)** training. It must learn to ignore its <u>instinct</u> **(1)** to chase other dogs. It must also learn to help its master avoid <u>obstacles</u> **(1)** and cross streets safely. Only a <u>mature</u> **(1)** dog can be trained effectively. Once a dog has <u>mastered</u> **(1)** the basic skills, it can go to live with its master and begin developing an <u>attachment</u> **(1)** to that person.

Dogs are helpful in a number of ways, but people who cannot see still must spend time <u>memorizing</u> **(1)** the <u>layout</u> **(1)** of a building in which they will be spending time. They also must depend on their listening skills and their ability to read <u>braille</u> **(1)** in order to acquire new knowledge and be more independent.

Assessment Tip: Total **10** Points

Name _____

# Tell Me All the Details!

**Look for details in the selection, and fill in each Details column. Read
the prompts in the far left-hand column to determine if the details belong
*before*, *while*, or *after* Mom went to The Seeing Eye.** Sample details shown.

| | Details about Mom | Details about Narrator | Details about Ursula |
|---|---|---|---|
| **Before Mom returns to The Seeing Eye** | she's blind; misses Marit has sensitive hearing **(1 point)** | **(1)** | **(1)** |
| **While Mom is at The Seeing Eye** | **(1)** | misses Mom; divided house chores; wonders if she'll love Ursula **(1)** | sprang up on the narrator; every day learned one route in the neighborhood **(1)** |
| **After Mom returns from The Seeing Eye** | **(1)** | **(1)** | started "loneliness training" **(1)** |

**Write one sentence with details about The Seeing Eye.**

**(1)** _____

_____

Assessment Tip: Total **10** Points

Name _____

# Trace the "Route" of the Selection

**Complete the sentences in the boxes below to show the steps in Ursula's training process.** Sample answers are shown.

1. Mom returns to
   The Seeing Eye training
   school in Morristown,
   New Jersey **(2 points)**
   where she gets her new guide
   dog, Ursula.

2. After making mistakes in her early lessons, Ursula
   starts to get better at
   guiding Mom. **(2)**

3. In addition to training with Ursula, Mom spends her time at The Seeing Eye
   talking with her new
   blind friends. **(2)**

4. When Mom brings Ursula home, she continues
   her training by teaching
   Ursula new routes and
   giving her obedience
   lessons. **(2)**

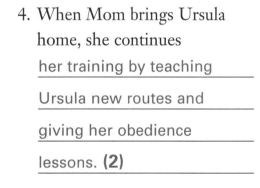

5. When Ursula finally feels comfortable in her new home,
   Mom starts loneliness
   training **(2)**

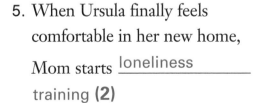

6. Ursula soon becomes
   a beloved and important
   part of Mom's family. **(2)**

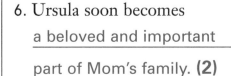

Name _____

# Reading Carefully

**Read the passage. Then complete the activity on page 221.**

## Louis Braille

Louis Braille was born in France in 1809. At the age of three, he had an accident in his father's workshop and became blind. His father wanted young Louis to become educated and successful, so he enrolled Louis in the Royal Institute for Blind Youth in Paris when Louis was ten years old. The Institute was a school that specialized in teaching blind students.

Louis proved himself to be an outstanding student. He learned to read, though books for people who were blind were rare and hard to use at that time. The Institute had only three books in its library. Each book was divided into twenty parts, and each part weighed more than twenty pounds. A person read the text by touching the huge raised letters on each page.

Shortly after Louis came to the Institute, a military officer named Charles Barbier brought his own system of writing to the attention of the school. He had invented a system he called "night writing." It consisted of raised dots and dashes on thin cardboard and was used by night watchmen to send and receive messages. Louis was fascinated with the system, and he decided to try to improve it.

Louis worked day and night. He used only the dots and found that a "cell" made up of up to six dots could be changed to form sixty-three different patterns. Using his six-dot cell, Louis made a separate pattern for each letter of the alphabet, for numbers, punctuation marks, and even musical notes. This system, which became known as *braille*, is used in countries throughout the world.

Name _____

# Reading Carefully continued

**Read each statement below.  Write a detail from the passage on page 220 to support the statement.** Sample answers shown.

| Conclusions | Supporting Details |
|---|---|
| 1. Louis was intelligent and hard-working. | 1. He proved himself to be an outstanding student. **(3 points)** |
| 2. Louis had sensitive fingers and could learn new things. | 2. He learned to read through touch. **(3)** |
| 3. Before the invention of braille, books for people who were blind were hard to read. | 3. These books were rare, hard to use, and heavy. **(3)** |
| 4. Louis was creative and liked to try new things. | 4. He helped invent a new way of writing. **(3)** |
| 5. Louis was patient and determined. | 5. He worked day and night to find the six-dot system. **(3)** |
| 6. The invention of braille affects the lives of many people. | 6. Braille is used in countries throughout the world. **(3)** |

Name _____

# Viva Vowels!

**Read the letter. Notice that each underlined word has two vowels with the VV pattern. If the vowels should be kept together in a syllable, circle the vowels. If the vowels should be divided between syllables, draw a line between the vowels. Two examples have been done for you. (1 point each)**

actual
believer
pause
create
complains
librarian
laziest

Dear kids,

   Today could not have been much crazier! I spent so much time with Prince, my dog guide, that both of us were exhausted. And Prince still had to see the veterinarian.

   I can't wait for you to meet Prince. He is a golden retriever. I wish I could explain to him what our routine at home will usually involve. I do not think he realizes that he is soon going to end his training.

                              Love, Mom

**Now use the VV words in the word box to complete these sentences.**

1. After a short __pause **(1)**___ for a sip of water, the speaker continued.

2. The __librarian **(1)**___ told me that the latest *Billy Burton* mystery just came in!

3. "You are the __laziest **(1)**___ animal I've ever known," I said to my sleeping cat.

4. I didn't think you could win the race, but you've made me a __believer **(1)**___.

5. Our neighbor __complains **(1)**___ that the garbage collector comes too early in the morning.

6. This is not a copy of the Gilroy diamond; it is the __actual **(1)**___ jewel!

7. I asked the puppeteer how she was able to __create **(1)**___ such lifelike puppets.

Assessment Tip: Total **12** Points

Name _____

# VV Pattern

When the two vowels in a VV pattern spell two vowel sounds, divide the word into syllables between the vowels. Look for familiar patterns that you have learned, and spell the word by syllables.

V | V          V | V
**po | em     cre | ate**

▶ The word *quiet* has three vowels that appear together. In this word, the *u* goes with *q* to make the consonant sound /kw/.

**Write each Spelling Word. Draw a line between the two vowels in each VV syllable pattern.** Order of answers may vary.

**V | V**

| | |
|---|---|
| po \| em **(1 point)** | di \| et **(1)** |
| ide \| a **(1)** | li \| ar **(1)** |
| cre \| ate **(1)** | fu \| el **(1)** |
| di \| ary **(1)** | ri \| ot **(1)** |
| are \| a **(1)** | actu \| al **(1)** |
| gi \| ant **(1)** | li \| on **(1)** |
| usu \| al **(1)** | ru \| in **(1)** |
| radi \| o **(1)** | tri \| al **(1)** |
| cru \| el **(1)** | rode \| o **(1)** |
| qui \| et **(1)** | sci \| ence **(1)** |

### Spelling Words

1. poem
2. idea
3. create
4. diary
5. area
6. giant
7. usual
8. radio
9. cruel
10. quiet*
11. diet
12. liar
13. fuel
14. riot
15. actual
16. lion
17. ruin
18. trial
19. rodeo
20. science

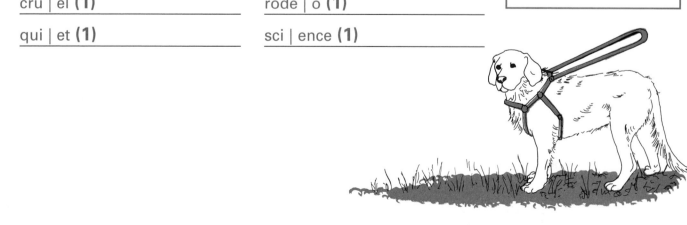

Name _____

# Spelling Spree

**Phrase Fillers** **Write the Spelling Word that best completes each phrase.**

1. a nutritious, low-fat _____

2. to call an untruthful person a _____

3. a _____ by jury

4. the _____ of biology

5. a _____ with four verses

6. an ancient, crumbling _____

7. a fairy tale with a towering _____

8. the mane of a _____

9. an _____ for a new product

1. diet **(1 point)**

2. liar **(1)**

3. trial **(1)**

4. science **(1)**

5. poem **(1)**

6. ruin **(1)**

7. giant **(1)**

8. lion **(1)**

9. idea **(1)**

**Syllable Scramble** **Rearrange the syllables to write a Spelling Word.  One syllable in each item is extra.**

**Example:** ish ble fin    *finish*

10. ra dis o di      radio **(1)**

11. al u ent su      usual **(1)**

12. ru ot ri         riot **(1)**

13. a di sci ry      diary **(1)**

14. tu re ac al      actual **(1)**

15. de o ro ant      rodeo **(1)**

Spelling Words

1. poem
2. idea
3. create
4. diary
5. area
6. giant
7. usual
8. radio
9. cruel
10. quiet*
11. diet
12. liar
13. fuel
14. riot
15. actual
16. lion
17. ruin
18. trial
19. rodeo
20. science

Assessment Tip: Total **15** Points

Name _____

# Proofreading and Writing

**Proofreading Circle the five misspelled Spelling Words in this set of guidelines. Then write each word correctly.**

1. poem
2. idea
3. create
4. diary
5. area
6. giant
7. usual
8. radio
9. cruel
10. quiet*
11. diet
12. liar
13. fuel
14. riot
15. actual
16. lion
17. ruin
18. trial
19. rodeo
20. science

## Tips on Caring for Your New Dog Guide

1. Be sure to (creat) a comfortable home environment for your dog. A calm and (quiete) atmosphere is best.

2. Feed your dog a healthy diet. Just as food gives you energy, a dog's food is its (fule) too.

3. Discipline your dog firmly but kindly.

4. Never be (crual) to your dog—or to any animal!

5. Focus on walks in the (areea) around your neighborhood until your dog becomes familiar with the territory. Then try some longer trips.

1. create **(1 point)**

2. quiet **(1)**

3. fuel **(1)**

4. cruel **(1)**

5. area **(1)**

✏ **Write a Want Ad** What qualities make a good dog guide? What natural instincts does a dog guide have to learn to overcome?

**On a separate sheet of paper, write a want ad for *Working Dog Weekly* describing the job of dog guide. Use Spelling Words from the list.** Responses will vary. **(5)**

Name _____

# The Meaningful Word

**Read the advertisement.  Then use each underlined word to complete the numbered sentences.  Be careful!  The underlined words have more than one meaning.**

**Dog Walkers Wanted**

Helping Hound, the biggest guide dog school in the state, is looking for young people like you.  We need your help to train our future guide dogs.  You can take a dog on a trip to the park or around the block.  You can play with your dog, teach it not to bark at other dogs, and help break it of other bad habits.  You'll be training your dog to suit a new owner.  You'll have fun as you help your helping hound pass its final exams!  Apply today.

1. I covered my ears to <u>block **(1 point)**</u> out the sound of the jackhammer.

2. Be careful not to <u>trip **(1)**</u> on that curb.

3. If you <u>hound **(1)**</u> your teacher for less homework, you might get more instead!

4. My father bought us tickets for a <u>train **(1)**</u> ride this weekend.

5. If you get tired, take a <u>break **(1)**</u> before you go back to work.

6. Could you please <u>pass **(1)**</u> me the potatoes?

7. Every day, my mother wears a <u>suit **(1)**</u> to work.

8. We drove around looking for a place to <u>park **(1)**</u> the car.

9. Speak into the microphone and <u>state **(1)**</u> your name clearly.

10. The thin white <u>bark **(1)**</u> of the birch tree feels soft, like tissue paper.

Assessment Tip: Total **10** Points

Name _____

# Commas, Commas, and More Commas!

**Commas in a Series** A **series** is a list of three or more items. Use commas to separate the items in a series. Put a comma after each item in a series except the last one. Use *and* or *or* before the last item in a series.

I like cats, dogs, rabbits, **and** all kinds of animals.

**Add commas to the sentences below that have items in a series. If the sentence does not contain a series, write *none* after the sentence. (1 point** for each correct sentence)

1. German shepherds, golden retrievers, and other breeds can be trained as dog guides.

2. Dogs and monkeys are trained to help people with disabilities. none

3. Our dogs are named Riley, Maggie, and Midnight.

4. My cousin takes her dog to visit nursing homes, retirement centers, and hospitals.

5. Parakeets, parrots, cockatoos, and mynah birds can learn to talk.

6. In our classroom are fish, turtles, and a snake.

7. Other classrooms have guinea pigs, hamsters, and gerbils.

8. Our calico cat is black, brown, white, and orange.

9. Marla's cat is orange and white. none

10. Tim's cat is black, gray, and white.

Name _____

# Yes, I Can

**More Uses for Commas**  Use commas to set off the words *yes*, *no*, and
*well* when they appear as introductory words at the beginning of a
sentence.  Also use a comma or commas to set off the names of people
who are addressed directly.

| | |
|---|---|
| **Introductory word:** | **Yes,** Mr. Baxter's dog is devoted to him. |
| **Direct address:** | **Kristin,** please help Mr. Baxter with the door. |
| | Would you walk the dog, **Jamie**? |
| **Introductory word** | |
| **and direct address:** | **Well, Kristin,** that is a good idea. |

**Add commas where needed in the sentences below.**
**(1 point** for each correct sentence)

1. I'm afraid I'm not feeling well today, Jamie.

2. Well, Mr. Baxter, I'll walk Buster for you.

3. Thank you, Jamie.

4. Why isn't Mr. Baxter walking Buster, Kristin?

5. Well, I guess Jamie wants to help him.

6. It's nice of you, Jamie, to help Mr. Baxter.

7. Well, Kristin, Mr. Baxter is a helpful neighbor.

8. Yes, he is, Jamie.

9. Kristin, have you ever walked Buster?

10. No, Myron, I haven't.

Assessment Tip: Total **10** Points

Name _____

# I Feed, Groom, and Pet My Cat

**Combining Sentences by Creating a Series** A good writer puts items in a series in one sentence, instead of mentioning them in separate sentences.

**Awkward:** Dogs make good pets. Cats make good pets. Birds do too.

**Revised:** Dogs, cats, and birds make good pets.

**Sophie is drafting an essay. Revise the essay by putting items into a series where needed. Write your revision below. (10 points)**

> My cat, Buzz, greets me at the door when I come home from school. He greets me when I come home from a friend's house. He greets me when I come home from an appointment. Buzz meows. He purrs. He rubs against my legs. Then I pick him up. Buzz purrs while I tell him about the spelling test. He purrs while I tell him about my friend's cat or events of the day.
>
> I like to take care of Buzz. I feed him. I groom him. I play with him. He can make me feel calm. He can make me feel loved. He can make me feel special. Buzz is like a patient person with fur. He is like a person with long whiskers. He is like a person with a tail.

My cat, Buzz, greets me at the door when I come home from school, a friend's house, or an appointment. Buzz meows, purrs, and rubs against my legs. Then I pick him up. Buzz purrs while I tell him about the spelling test, my friend's cat, or events of the day.

I like to take care of Buzz. I feed him, groom him, and play with him. He can make me feel calm, loved, and special. Buzz is like a patient person with fur, long whiskers, and a tail.

Name _____

# Writing Instructions

In *Mom's Best Friend*, Pete Jackson at The Seeing Eye gives Leslie's mother verbal instructions for training her new dog guide, Ursula. **Instructions** tell you how to do or make something. When you are trying to learn a new skill, written instructions are helpful. Good written instructions clearly explain all of the steps to be followed and the order in which the steps are to be done.

**Complete the graphic organizer below to help you plan and organize written instructions for doing something you know how to do, such as a dance, a particular sports move, or a game. If possible, do the activity yourself and use the graphic organizer to outline each step.**

Instructions for **(1 point)** _____

Materials **(1)** _____

Step 1 **(1)** _____

    Step 2 **(1)** _____

       Step 3 **(1)** _____

    Step 4 **(1)** _____

       Step 5 **(1)** _____

**Using the information you recorded, write your instructions on a separate sheet of paper. First, write a title that describes what the instructions are for. Then list any materials that are needed. Explain each step in order, using sequence words such as *first, next,* or *last.* Include diagrams or pictures if they help clarify the process. When you finish your instructions, share them with your classmates. (5)**

Assessment Tip: Total **12** Points

Name _____

# Combining Sentences by Using Introductory Phrases

Good writers avoid using a string of short, choppy sentences to express their ideas. One way to streamline your writing is to combine two choppy sentences into one sentence with an introductory phrase.

> Mom will walk solo with Ursula. She will do this after ten practice runs with Pete.
>
> **After ten practice runs with Pete,** Mom will walk solo with Ursula.

**Read the instructions for acting as a sighted guide. Then revise them by combining two short sentences into a single sentence with an introductory phrase. Punctuate introductory phrases correctly.**
Responses may vary slightly. **(12 points)**

### Techniques for Being a Sighted Guide

Touch the person's elbow, forearm, or hand lightly. Do this at the start. Stand still a moment. Let the person grasp your arm just above the elbow. Walk where the person wants to go. Use a comfortable pace. Stay slightly ahead. Guide with your words and body movement. Tell the person what is ahead, such as stairs or a curb. Do this when approaching an obstacle. State whether you will turn right or left. This should be done just before turning. When you reach your destination, the person will release his or her grasp.

### Techniques for Being a Sighted Guide

At the start, touch the person's elbow, forearm, or hand lightly. Standing still a moment, let the person grasp your arm just above the elbow. Using a comfortable pace, walk where the person wants to go. Staying slightly ahead, guide with your words and body movement. When approaching an obstacle, tell the person what is ahead, such as stairs or a curb. Just before turning, state whether you will turn right or left. When you reach your destination, the person will release his or her grasp.

Name _____

# It's a Secret

**Write each word from the box in the correct category.**

**things done in front of an audience**

opera **(1 point)**

demonstration **(1)**

**parts of a culture**

heritage **(1)**

traditions **(1)**

**describing words**

noble **(1)**

rhythmic **(1)**

**action word**

impressed **(1)**

**word for musical support**

accompaniment **(1)**

**Choose two words from the box and write a sentence using both words.**

**(2)** _____

_____

### Vocabulary

heritage

impressed

traditions

opera

accompaniment

demonstration

noble

rhythmic

Assessment Tip: Total **10** Points

Name _____

# Different and Alike

**Fill in the diagram to compare and contrast Second Sister and Yingtao.** Sample answers shown.

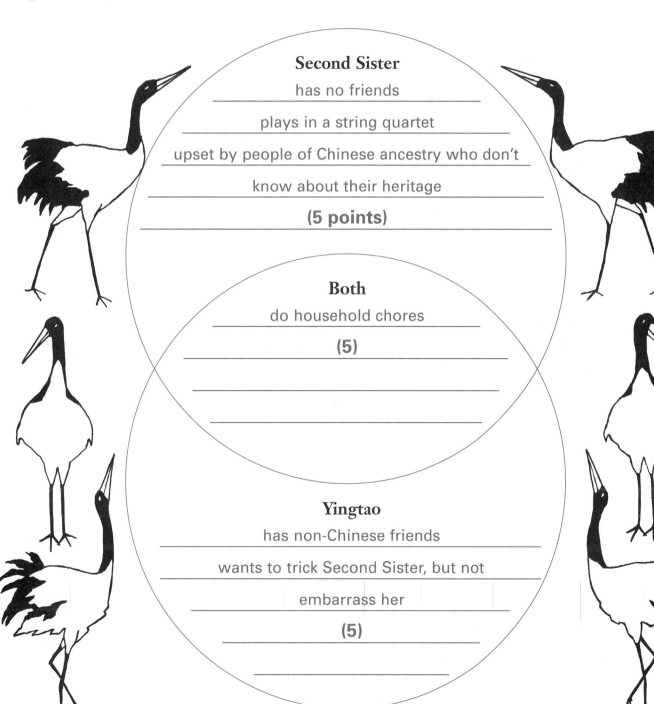

**Second Sister**

has no friends

plays in a string quartet

upset by people of Chinese ancestry who don't

know about their heritage

**(5 points)**

**Both**

do household chores

**(5)**

**Yingtao**

has non-Chinese friends

wants to trick Second Sister, but not

embarrass her

**(5)**

Name _____

# Plot the Trick

**Complete the story map below to show the main elements of the story.**

| Characters | Setting |
|---|---|
| **Main Characters:** Second Sister, Third Sister, Yingtao, Paul Eng **(1)** | **First Setting:**<br> **Time:** during and after dinner<br> **Place:** the family's home **(1)** |
| **Minor Characters:** Father, Mother, Eldest Brother, Kim O'Meara, Mrs. O'Meara, Melanie Eng **(1)** | **Second Setting:**<br> **Time:** during spring vacation<br> **Place:** the Science Center **(1)** |

**Plot**

**Problem:** Second Sister has made no friends. She is angry at Paul Eng for not knowing as much about Chinese customs and traditions as she thinks he should.

**Events:**

1. During a family dinner, Second Sister tells about her erhu demonstration and her scorn for Paul Eng's lack of cultural knowledge. **(1)**

2. After dinner, Third Sister and Yingtao let Second Sister overhear them saying that Paul asked if she goes on dates. **(1)**

3. At the Science Center, Third Sister, Yingtao, and Kim let Paul overhear them talking about how Second Sister is impressed by Paul's baseball and math skills. **(1)**

4. Later in the cafeteria, Paul asks if Second Sister goes out on dates. **(1)**

**Resolution:** Paul and Second Sister think that the other would like to go out on a date. **(2)**

Assessment Tip: Total **10** Points

Name _____

# Similarity Search

**Read the passage.   Then complete the activity on page 236.**

## Trevisa's Favorite Teachers

Trevisa had two favorite teachers: Mr. Yetto, her third-grade teacher, and the fifth-grade teacher, Mrs. McIlvaine, who was Trevisa's teacher now.

Mr. Yetto was young and athletic.  He had played football in college and still liked sports, just like Trevisa.  He was kind and often called on Trevisa to answer questions during class discussions to help her get over her shyness.  But Mr. Yetto could also be strict, and he did not accept excuses.  If a student didn't turn in his or her homework on time, he marked that student's grade down.  On Fridays Mr. Yetto did yo-yo tricks for the class after lunch.  He saved new tricks to show them for the weeks when they had worked especially hard.

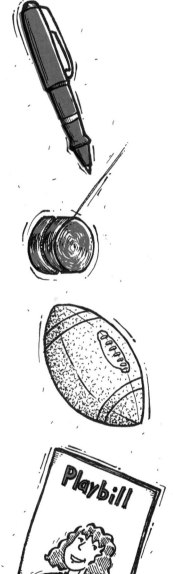

Unlike Mr. Yetto, Mrs. McIlvaine was older.  She did not like sports, but she loved stories and plays.  On Fridays she allowed her students to perform skits during class.  Once Danny Pine and David Ginsburg performed a skit in which Danny wore a white wig and played the role of Mrs. McIlvaine herself.  He imitated her voice and even remembered certain phrases she used.  Mrs. McIlvaine laughed and laughed.  But like Mr. Yetto, Mrs. McIlvaine could also be strict.  Once, when Trevisa tried writing a book report in very tiny handwriting, just to see if she could do it, Mrs. McIlvaine made her rewrite it.  "I can't even read this!" she wrote across the page in red ink.  But after Trevisa rewrote her report and turned it in again, Mrs. McIlvaine wrote, "I'm glad I can read this now, because it is just marvelous!"

Name _____

# Similarity Search continued

**Fill in the Venn diagram below to show some ways Mr. Yetto and Mrs. McIlvaine are alike and different.**

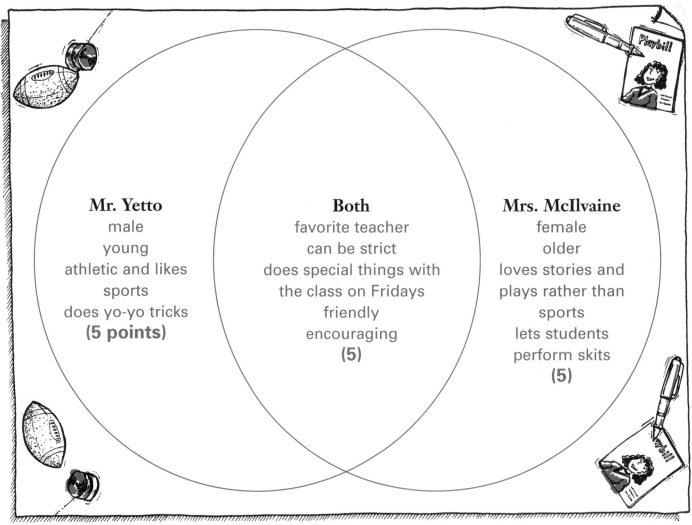

**Mr. Yetto**
male
young
athletic and likes
sports
does yo-yo tricks
**(5 points)**

**Both**
favorite teacher
can be strict
does special things with
the class on Fridays
friendly
encouraging
**(5)**

**Mrs. McIlvaine**
female
older
loves stories and
plays rather than
sports
lets students
perform skits
**(5)**

**Now write a paragraph in which you describe how the two teachers are alike.**
Sample answer shown. **(5)**

Mr. Yetto and Mrs. McIlvaine are both teachers Trevisa likes a lot. Both are friendly,

kind, and encouraging, but can also be strict. Both plan special events to do with

their class on Fridays.

Assessment Tip: Total **20** Points

Name _____

# Tricky Endings

**Read the speech below.  Circle the *-ed* and *-ing* endings of the underlined words.  Then write those words on the lines with each *-ing* ending changed to an *-ed*, and each *-ed* to an *-ing*.  Use the new words to complete the sentences at the bottom of the page.**

It's too bad that Tanya keeps <u>ignoring</u> Raul!  He was <u>admiring</u> how hard she <u>studied</u> for the math test.  He's always <u>dropping</u> by to say, "Do you think she <u>noticed</u> me at the <u>wrestling</u> match?" **(6 points)**

ignored **(1)** _____

admired **(1)** _____

studying **(1)** _____

dropped **(1)** _____

noticing **(1)** _____

wrestled **(1)** _____

Tanya dropped **(1)** _____ by my locker today.  She didn't know that Raul wrestled **(1)** _____ on the school team.  I told her not to feel bad if he ignored **(1)** _____ her in class.  He's too busy studying **(1)** _____ to be noticing **(1)** _____ anyone!  She said she really admired **(1)** _____ his hard work.

Name _____

# Words with *-ed* or *-ing*

A **base word** is a word to which endings can be added. When a base word ends with *e*, you usually drop the *e* when *-ed* or *-ing* is added. If a base word does not end with *e*, you usually add the ending *-ed* or *-ing* without a spelling change.

amuse + ing = amus**ing**          direct + ing = direct**ing**

When a one-syllable word ends with a vowel and a consonant, you usually double the consonant when adding *-ed* or *-ing*. When a two-syllable word ends with a vowel and a consonant, you often do not double the consonant when adding *-ed* or *-ing*.

plan + ed = plan**ned**          cover + ed = cover**ed**

▶ The spelling of *mixed* differs from the usual spelling pattern. Although *mix* is a one-syllable word, the final consonant is not doubled when *-ed* is added.

**Write each Spelling Word under the heading that shows what happens to the base word when *-ed* or *-ing* is added.**
Order of answers for each category may vary.

### Final *e* Dropped

amusing **(1 point)**

rising **(1)**

deserved **(1)**

squeezing **(1)**

decided **(1)**

### Final Consonant Doubled

bragging **(1)**

planned **(1)**

swimming **(1)**

spotted **(1)**

hitting **(1)**

### No Spelling Change

covered **(1)**

directing **(1)**

offered **(1)**

visiting **(1)**

mixed **(1)**

sheltered **(1)**

resulting **(1)**

suffering **(1)**

arrested **(1)**

ordered **(1)**

Assessment Tip: Total **20** Points

# Spelling Spree

**Ending Clues** **Write the Spelling Word that fits each clue.**

1. What *-ing* word is causing others to smile?
2. What *-ed* word was arranged ahead of time?
3. What *-ing* word is moving through water?
4. What *-ed* word was all stirred up?
5. What *-ing* word is pressing hard on something?
6. What *-ing* word is coming about as a consequence?
7. What *-ed* word was commanded?
8. What *-ing* word is striking?

1. amusing **(1 point)**
2. planned **(1)**
3. swimming **(1)**
4. mixed **(1)**
5. squeezing **(1)**
6. resulting **(1)**
7. ordered **(1)**
8. hitting **(1)**

**Finding Words** **Each word below is hidden in a Spelling Word.  Write the Spelling Word.**

9. serve — deserved **(1)**
10. rest — arrested **(1)**
11. over — covered **(1)**
12. off — offered **(1)**
13. pot — spotted **(1)**
14. rag — bragging **(1)**
15. she — sheltered **(1)**

### Spelling Words

1. covered
2. directing
3. bragging
4. amusing
5. offered
6. planned
7. rising
8. deserved
9. visiting
10. mixed*
11. swimming
12. sheltered
13. resulting
14. spotted
15. suffering
16. arrested
17. squeezing
18. ordered
19. decided
20. hitting

Theme 4: **Person to Person**   239
Assessment Tip: Total **15** Points

Name _____

# Proofreading and Writing

**Proofreading** Circle the five misspelled Spelling Words in this diary entry. Then write each word correctly.

**Spelling Words**

Dear Diary,

Well, I'm still (suffring) from shyness around Paul Eng. Today I spotted him in the hall, (visitting) with some other students. Although nervous, I (desided) to go say hello. I was only a few steps away when Paul saw me. Suddenly, I felt all my blood (riseing) to my face. I ended up (dirieckting) my eyes straight at the floor and walking right past Paul. Why on earth am I so afraid of him?

**Spelling Words**

1. covered
2. directing
3. bragging
4. amusing
5. offered
6. planned
7. rising
8. deserved
9. visiting
10. mixed*
11. swimming
12. sheltered
13. resulting
14. spotted
15. suffering
16. arrested
17. squeezing
18. ordered
19. decided
20. hitting

1. suffering **(1 point)**
2. visiting **(1)**
3. decided **(1)**
4. rising **(1)**
5. directing **(1)**

✏️→ **Write a Description** Have you ever wanted to have a secret admirer? What would that person look like? What qualities would he or she have? What interests would you have in common?

**On a separate sheet of paper, write a description of your ideal secret admirer. Use Spelling Words from the list.** Responses will vary. **(5)**

Name _____

# Pinpointing Prefixes

**Read the dictionary entries. Then in the sentences below, underline the word with a prefix. Write the definition of the word after the sentence.**

> *in-* or *im-* A prefix that means "not."
>
> *re-* A prefix that means "again" or "back."
>
> *un-* A prefix that means "not."

1. After waiting so long, the people were <u>impatient</u> for the play to begin. **(1)**
   restless; not patient **(2)**

2. My uncle likes to <u>refresh</u> himself with a nap before going out to
   dinner. **(1)** to make fresh again **(2)**

3. Nina thought it was <u>unfair</u> to have a science test the morning
   after the school concert. **(1)** not fair **(2)**

4. I wrote down the <u>incorrect</u> directions and got lost. **(1)**
   not correct; wrong **(2)**

5. The mayor used words we didn't understand, so we asked
   her to <u>rephrase</u> what she said. **(1)** to phrase again; restate **(2)**

6. When she feels <u>unhappy</u>, Brenda cheers herself up by
   playing soccer with her friends. **(1)** sad **(2)**

7. Jesse's visits to the doctor are <u>infrequent</u>, because
   he rarely gets sick. **(1)** not frequent **(2)**

8. When I'm in the city, I like to <u>revisit</u> my
   old neighborhood. to visit again **(2)**

Name _____

# Hey! Let's Play!

**Interjections** An *interjection* is a word or words that express strong feeling.
An interjection usually appears at the beginning of a sentence.
It can be followed by either a comma or an exclamation point, depending
on how strong a feeling is expressed.

> **Common Interjections**
>
> Well    Wow    Hey    Ouch    Whew    Oh, no    Oh

**Write an interjection and appropriate punctuation on each blank
line below.** Answers will vary.

1. _Hey! **(1 point)**_ Where is the music for our rehearsal?

2. _Oh, **(1)**_ here it is.

3. _Well, **(1)**_ let's start with the piece by Brubeck.

4. _Wow! **(1)**_ I have a long trumpet solo!

5. _Whew! **(1)**_ I made it all the way through without any big errors.

6. _Ah, **(1)**_ that was beautiful.

7. _Ouch, **(1)**_ I stubbed my toe on this chair.

8. _Oh, no, **(1)**_ we're going to practice the hardest part.

9. _Well, **(1)**_ let's get started.

10. _Wow! **(1)**_ We're good!

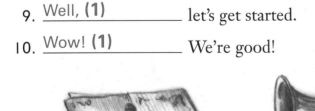

Assessment Tip: Total **10** Points

Name _____

# "What Kind of Music Do You Like?" I Asked

**Quotations** A *direct quotation* gives a speaker's exact words. Set off exact words with quotation marks. Begin each quotation with a capital letter. Place end punctuation inside quotation marks. Use commas to separate most quotations from the rest of the sentence. If a quotation is two sentences, use a period after the speaker's name.

Clara said, "I like to listen to all kinds of music."

"Yesterday," she said, "I heard a recording of Chinese opera."

"I liked it," said Clara. "Where can I see a performance?"

**Rewrite each quotation below, adding needed punctuation marks and capital letters.**

1. Sara asked what did the music of ancient Greece sound like

   Sara asked, "What did the music of ancient Greece sound like?" **(2 points)**

   _____

2. nobody really knows said Ms. Walter.

   "Nobody really knows," said Ms. Walter. **(2)**

3. Lacey said I like the new music from African musicians.

   Lacey said, "I like the new music from African musicians." **(2)**

   _____

4. Lacey, Ms. Walter asked, where can I hear new music from Africa?

   "Lacey," Ms. Walter asked, "where can I hear new music from Africa?" **(2)**

   _____

5. you can hear it on the radio said Lacey it's on a program called
   World Music Today

   "You can hear it on the radio," said Lacey. "It's on a program called

   World Music Today." **(2)**

Theme 4: **Person to Person**    243
Assessment Tip: Total **10** Points

Name _____

# Grandma said, "Yes."

**Punctuating Quotations** A good writer is careful to punctuate sentences correctly. An incorrectly punctuated sentence is easily misunderstood.

**Incorrect:** Mrs. Voss said Ana please help me.

**Corrected:** "Mrs. Voss," said Ana. "Please help me."

**Corrected:** Mrs. Voss said, "Ana, please help me."

**Megan is writing about a visit with her grandmother. She has included exactly what she said and exactly what her grandmother said. Proofread Megan's dialogue, correcting any mistakes in punctuating quotations. (1 point each)**

"Your great-grandfather was born in Ireland, Nana said.

I said Wow, I never knew that!"

His parents Nana said owned a small store where all the family

worked.

"Didn't my great-grandfather want to work in the store" I asked.

There were, Nana explained already two older sisters working in the

store, and there would not be enough work for him.

I asked "What did he do?

He had read so much about America that he decided he wanted to

see it for himself," Nana said The next time you visit, I'll tell you about

his first job in New York City."

Name _____

# Writing a How-To Paragraph

When you want to tell readers how to do something, write a **how-to paragraph.**

Use this page to plan and organize a how-to paragraph. First, choose a topic like how to wash dishes, how to make a pizza, or how to tie a certain knot or, prepare to explain something you know how to do. Next, list the materials that are needed. Then outline each step, giving details that readers need to know to do each one. Doing the activity yourself will help you outline each step.

How to **(1 point)** _____

Materials **(1)** _____

Step 1 **(2)** _____

_____

Step 2 **(2)** _____

_____

Step 3 **(2)** _____

_____

Step 4 **(2)** _____

_____

Step 5 **(2)** _____

_____

Using the information you recorded, write your how-to paragraph on a separate sheet of paper. In the first sentence, describe what skill will be taught. Then tell what materials are needed. Next, explain each step clearly and in order. Use sequence words such as *before, after,* and *now* to clarify the order. If necessary, include diagrams or pictures to help readers picture the process. When you finish, work with your classmates to create a class How-To-Do-It book. **(8)**

Name _____

# Using Order Words

A careful writer uses **order words** such as *first*, *next*, and *finally* in a how-to paragraph. Order words help readers understand a process and keep track of the sequence of steps.

**Read the following how-to paragraph written by Yingtao in *Yang the Second and Her Secret Admirers*. Then rewrite the paragraph on the lines, adding order words and phrases from the list to make the sequence of steps clearer and to help readers follow the process. Be sure to use correct capitalization and punctuation when you add order words and phrases or combine two sentences. (12 points)**

To clean chopsticks, you will need a big pan, hot water, and dishwashing liquid. Fill the pan with hot water. Add about a teaspoon of dishwashing liquid. Drop the dirty chopsticks in the hot, soapy water. Grab a handful of chopsticks and roll them together like a stack of pencils between your two hands. You hear a burrrr sound. This means the chopsticks are getting really clean! Rinse the chopsticks with clean water.

**Order Words**

until

next

then

finally

first

now

To clean chopsticks, you will need a big pan, hot water, and dishwashing liquid.

**First,** fill the pan with hot water. **Next,** add about a teaspoon of dishwashing liquid.

**Then** drop the dirty chopsticks in the hot, soapy water. **Now** grab a handful of

chopsticks and roll them like a stack of pencils between your two hands **until** you

hear a burrrr sound. This means the chopsticks are getting really clean! **Finally,**

rinse the chopsticks with clean water.

Name _____

# A Writer's Words

**Write each word from the box beside the phrase that describes it.**

1. very wonderful <u>splendid **(1 point)**</u>

2. writing that is not poetry <u>prose **(1)**</u>

3. a person who invades the privacy of others
   <u>snoop **(1)**</u>

4. a book not to be read by others without permission
   <u>diary **(1)**</u>

5. how you feel when you're not able to do something you've
   been wanting to do <u>disappointed **(1)**</u>

6. a thing that happens to you <u>experience **(1)**</u>

7. what you have done when you have given an article to a newspaper
   for publication <u>submitted **(1)**</u>

8. the opposite of *accepted* <u>rejected **(1)**</u>

9. knowing why things are the way they are <u>understanding **(1)**</u>

**Vocabulary**

diary
experience
understanding
prose
snoop
disappointed
submitted
splendid
rejected

**Now write three sentences about being a writer. Use at least one vocabulary word in each sentence.**

(3) _____

_____

_____

_____

_____

Name _____

# Reading Between the Lines

**Read the prompt in the first column. Use evidence from the story and your own experiences to make inferences about Leigh.**

Answers will vary. Samples are shown.

| | Evidence from the Story | Own Experiences | Inferences |
|---|---|---|---|
| • **What kind of person is Leigh?** | When the librarian tells him he still has time to enter a contest to meet a famous author, which he wants to do, he gets right to work. **(2 points)** | Someone who is willing to start a difficult task right away in order to achieve something is industrious. **(2)** | Leigh is industrious. **(2)** |
| • **How does Leigh feel about his house?** | He says he wasn't sure his friend would like coming to his house because it is small. **(2)** | People who worry that someone else won't like their house may feel ashamed of it, or they may just be worried that the other person will find some reason not to like them. **(2)** | Leigh might feel a little ashamed of his house, or he might just be worried that Barry might stop being his friend. **(2)** |

Assessment Tip: Total **12** Points

Name _____

# The "Write" Connection

**What relationship did each person have with Leigh in *Dear Mr. Henshaw*? Answer in complete sentences.**

**Miss Neely** She convinced Leigh to enter the writing contest. She handed out copies of the Yearbook, which had Leigh's description in it. She invited Leigh to meet Angela Badger after the first prize winner was disqualified. **(2 points)**

**Leigh's dad** He talked to Leigh on the phone. Leigh wrote about a time he took Leigh on a hauling job. Leigh worried about him getting married. **(2)**

**Barry** He came to Leigh's house for dinner and had a good time. Leigh was glad Barry was his friend. **(2)**

**Leigh's mom** She made a great dinner for Leigh and Barry. She and Leigh had a difficult discussion about Leigh's dad. She said she was proud of Leigh when he told her that Angela Badger had called him an author. **(2)**

**Angela Badger** She read and praised Leigh's description. She gave him advice and told him he was an author, which made him proud. **(2)**

Name _____

# Connecting Clues

**Read the diary entries. Then complete the activity on page 251.**

## Julia's Diary

*Monday, October 1*

Today was my first day at George Washington Elementary School. My old school's name was better: Woodside. I miss the stretch of woods nearby where my best friend Laura and I would go to skip stones in the creek and look for frogs. The area around this school is made out of concrete, even the playground. I sat by myself at lunch.

*Tuesday, October 2*

Today my teacher, Mrs. Langley, asked me to stand up in front of the class and tell one exciting fact about where I moved from. My face felt like it was on fire. I said I was from Illinois and on the license plate it says "Land of Lincoln." I thought I saw Mrs. Langley hide a laugh behind her sleeve, but I can't be sure. After that, I was glad I have a desk in the back of the room. When I got home, Mom asked me how school was. I gave her the same answer I'd given the day before, "Okay."

*Thursday, October 4*

Today at lunch they had chocolate pudding. I took two because chocolate pudding is my favorite. I was sitting alone (again) reading a book (again) when I heard someone say, "Julia?" It was Megan, the girl with the loud laugh, asking me to sit with her. Megan also had two servings of chocolate pudding. She told a story about her older brother that was so funny I almost choked on my broccoli. Today when Mom asked me how school was, I said, "Pretty good."

*Tuesday, October 9*

Today after school Megan and I took her puppy to the park. She showed me how to do a cartwheel in the grass. When Mom asked me how my day was, I said, "Fun." She looked happy.

Name _____

# Connecting Clues continued

**Answer each question about the passage on page 250. Below your answer, write the clues and what you know from your own experience that helped make the inference.** Sample answers shown.

1. How does Julia feel after the first day at her new school?

   Julia is unhappy after the first day. **(2 points)**

| Story Clues | | My Own Experience |
|---|---|---|
| She says she likes her old school's name better. She thinks the new school is not as attractive. She sits alone at lunch. **(2)** | **+** | It can be scary to start a new school. I might miss my friends and feel lonely without someone to sit with. I also like a grass playground better than a concrete one. **(2)** |

2. How does Julia feel about talking in front of the class?

   She is nervous and embarrassed. **(2)**

| Story Clues | | My Own Experience |
|---|---|---|
| Her face turns red. She is glad her desk is in the back. **(2)** | **+** | I know people blush when they are embarrassed. Some people sit in the back of the class so they won't be noticed. **(2)** |

3. How do Julia's feelings change after the first week of school?

   She starts to like her new school better after the first week. **(2)**

| Story Clues | | My Own Experience |
|---|---|---|
| At first she tells her Mom school is "okay," but by the second week she says it is "fun." She starts to do things with Megan. **(2)** | **+** | I know that people describe things differently as their feelings change. And I know that having a friend makes school more fun. **(2)** |

Name _____

# Thanks with Suffixes

**Read Leigh's thank-you letter to Angela Badger. In the underlined words, circle the suffixes *-ly*, *-ness*, *-ment*, *-ful*, and *-less*. (10 points)**

April 3

Dear Mrs. Badger,

I couldn't believe it when I heard the announcement that I could go to the writers' lunch today. It was wonderful to meet you. Before today, I felt hopeless about my fitness to be a writer. I was doubtful what I should write. My ideas mostly went nowhere. But you gave me encouragement. Now I feel fearless when I write. I think I'll be in the writing business for a long time.

Sincerely yours,
Leigh Botts

**Now, write each word with a suffix beside its correct definition.**

1. mostly **(1)** _____ : for the most part
2. hopeless **(1)** _____ : without hope
3. business **(1)** _____ : profession
4. sincerely **(1)** _____ : truly; honestly
5. announcement **(1)** _____ : message
6. wonderful **(1)** _____ : great
7. encouragement **(1)** _____ : a lift in confidence
8. fearless **(1)** _____ : without fear
9. fitness **(1)** _____ : suitability
10. doubtful **(1)** _____ : full of doubts

Assessment Tip: Total **20** Points

Name _____

# Words with Suffixes (-ly, -ness, -ment, -ful, -less)

A **suffix** is a word part added to the end of a base word. A suffix adds meaning to the word. The word parts *-ly, -ness, -ment, -ful* and *-less* are suffixes. The spelling of the base word is usually not changed when the suffix begins with a consonant.

safe + ly = saf**ely**

pale + ness = pale**ness**

enjoy + ment = enjoy**ment**

cheer + ful = cheer**ful**

speech + less = speech**less**

**Write each Spelling Word under its suffix.**

Order of answers for each category may vary.

<table>
<tr><td colspan="2">

**Spelling Words**

1. dreadful
2. enjoyment
3. safely
4. watchful
5. speechless
6. paleness
7. breathless
8. government
9. cheerful
10. actively
11. closeness
12. lately
13. goodness
14. retirement
15. forgetful
16. basement
17. softness
18. delightful
19. settlement
20. countless
</td></tr>
</table>

| *-ness* or *-ment* | *-ful* or *-less* |
|---|---|
| enjoyment **(1 point)** | dreadful **(1)** |
| paleness **(1)** | watchful **(1)** |
| government **(1)** | speechless **(1)** |
| closeness **(1)** | breathless **(1)** |
| goodness **(1)** | cheerful **(1)** |
| retirement **(1)** | forgetful **(1)** |
| basement **(1)** | delightful **(1)** |
| softness **(1)** | countless **(1)** |
| settlement **(1)** | |

| *-ly* | | |
|---|---|---|
| safely **(1)** | actively **(1)** | lately **(1)** |

Theme 4: **Person to Person**   253
Assessment Tip: Total **20** Points

Name _____

# Spelling Spree

**Adding Suffixes** **Write the Spelling Word that contains each base word below.**

1. soft    softness

2. retire    retirement

3. good    goodness

4. forget    forgetful

5. govern    government

6. breath    breathless

7. settle    settlement

**Contrast Clues** **The second part of each clue contrasts with the first part.  Write a Spelling Word for each clue.**

**Example:** not weak, but *powerful*

8. not long ago, but    lately

9. not talkative, but    speechless

10. not careless, but    watchful

11. not distance, but    closeness

12. not grouchy, but    cheerful

13. not wonderful, but    dreadful

14. not darkness, but    paleness

15. not few, but    countless

### Spelling Words

1. dreadful
2. enjoyment
3. safely
4. watchful
5. speechless
6. paleness
7. breathless
8. government
9. cheerful
10. actively
11. closeness
12. lately
13. goodness
14. retirement
15. forgetful
16. basement
17. softness
18. delightful
19. settlement
20. countless

254    Theme 4: **Person to Person**
Assessment Tip: Total **15** Points

Name _____

# Proofreading and Writing

**Proofreading** **Circle the five misspelled Spelling Words in the following newspaper article. Then write each word correctly.**

Spelling Words

**Young Writers Meet Famous Author**

The winners of the Young Writers' Yearbook contest had a delightfull lunch with Mrs. Angela Badger last week. Some students were speechless upon meeting the popular author, but others acttively sought her attention and talked easily with her. Mrs. Badger was impressed by the number of our students who read and write for their own injoyment. Everyone had a wonderful time, and our young writers returned safly to the school. If any students have not yet read the winning stories, copies of the yearbook are available in the supply room in the school basment.

1. dreadful
2. enjoyment
3. safely
4. watchful
5. speechless
6. paleness
7. breathless
8. government
9. cheerful
10. actively
11. closeness
12. lately
13. goodness
14. retirement
15. forgetful
16. basement
17. softness
18. delightful
19. settlement
20. countless

1. delightful **(1 point)**    4. safely **(1)**

2. actively **(1)**    5. basement **(1)**

3. enjoyment **(1)**

✏️ **Write an Opinion** Leigh was disappointed because his story received an honorable mention instead of a prize. In the end, though, it was his story that Mrs. Badger remembered. If you were in Leigh's position, would you rather have won the contest or received Mrs. Badger's praise?

**On a separate piece of paper, write a paragraph describing how you would have felt if you were in Leigh's place and why. Use Spelling Words from the list.** Responses will vary. **(5)**

Name _____

# That's Good or Bad?

A script for *Dear Mr. Henshaw* might contain a scene in which Leigh tells his mother about meeting Angela Badger. Rewrite each sentence first replacing the underlined word with a positive connotation. Then, write the sentence again replacing the word with a negative connotation. Choose your words from the list below.

| | | | |
|---|---|---|---|
| odd | aroma | chatted | notorious |
| famous | inventive | stink | jabbered |

1. "Mom, Mrs. Badger called my story <u>original</u>!"

   "Mom, Mrs. Badger called my story inventive!" **(2 points)**

   "Mom, Mrs. Badger called my story odd!" **(2)**

2. "She liked what I wrote about the <u>smell</u> of grapes in the sun."

   "She liked what I wrote about the aroma of grapes in the sun." **(2)**

   "She liked what I wrote about the stink of grapes in the sun." **(2)**

3. "We asked her what it felt like to be a <u>well-known</u> author."

   "We asked her what it felt like to be a famous author." **(2)**

   "We asked her what it felt like to be a notorious author." **(2)**

4. "The other kids <u>talked</u> with Mrs. Badger more than I did."

   "The other kids chatted with Mrs. Badger more than I did." **(2)**

   "The other kids jabbered with Mrs. Badger more than I did." **(2)**

256    Theme 4: **Person to Person**
Assessment Tip: Total **16** Points

Name _____

# Make It Shorter!

**Abbreviations** An **abbreviation** is a shortened form of a word. Most abbreviations begin with a capital letter and end with a period. Most abbreviations should only be used in special kinds of writing, such as in addresses and lists.

| Common Abbreviations | | | | | |
|---|---|---|---|---|---|
| Mr. | Mister | St. | Street | Co. | Company |
| Mrs. | married woman | Ave. | Avenue | Inc. | Incorporated |
| Ms. | any woman | Apt. | apartment | WV | West Virginia |
| Dr. | Doctor | P. O. | Post Office | TX | Texas |
| Jr. | Junior | Dec. | December | CA | California |
| Sr. | Senior | Mon. | Monday | ME | Maine |

**Rewrite each group of words using abbreviations where possible.**

1. Morgan Glass, Incorporated Morgan Glass, Inc. **(1 point)**

2. Mister David Kowalsky, Junior Mr. David Kowalsky, Jr. **(1)**

3. Wednesday, February 28, 2004 Wed., Feb. 28, 2004 **(1)**

4. 2557 Hastings Avenue, Apartment 4 2557 Hastings Ave., Apt. 4 **(1)**

5. Bangor, Maine Bangor, ME **(1)**

6. Post Office Box 1287 P. O. Box 1287 **(1)**

7. Star, West Virginia Star, WV **(1)**

8. 25 Westgate Road, Apartment 6
   25 Westgate Rd. Apt. 6 **(1)**

Name _____

# Titles, "Titles," and *More Titles*

**Titles** Capitalize the first, the last, and each important word in the titles of books, movies, or newspapers. Capitalize forms of the word *be*, including *is*, *are*, and *am*. Capitalize words like *and*, *in*, *of*, *to*, *a*, and *the* only when they are the first or last word in a title. Put titles in italic type or underline them. Titles of short works, such as short stories, poems, articles, songs, and chapters of books are enclosed in quotation marks.

**Newspaper:** My mother reads <u>The Wall Street Journal</u> every day.
**Book:** I read <u>Make Way for Ducklings</u> to my younger brother.
**Chapter:** The first chapter of this book is called "On the Beach."

**Each of the sentences below contains a title. Rewrite each title correctly.**

1. The book The cat in the hat was a childhood favorite of mine.
   <u>The Cat in the Hat</u> **(2 points)**

2. Lester read a book called the second floor mystery.
   <u>The Second Floor Mystery</u> **(2)**

3. The disappearance of the ladder is the name of the first chapter.
   "The Disappearance of the Ladder" **(2)**

4. Chris saw the old movie My friend flicka.
   <u>My Friend Flicka</u> **(2)**

5. Have you seen the review in The gladeview gazette, our school paper?
   <u>The Gladeview Gazette</u> **(2)**

6. Do you know the words to the song America?
   "America" **(2)**

7. Deer at dusk is one of my favorite poems
   "Deer at Dusk" **(2)**

Assessment Tip: Total **14** Points

Name _____

# Using Abbreviations

A good writer uses abbreviations only in special kinds of writing, such as lists and addresses. Marcus used abbreviations where he should have written out the entire word, and wrote out words that should be abbreviated.

**Rewrite and correct the address. Then proofread the body of the letter. Correct each error above the line.** (1 point for each correct response.)

Marcus Chester, Junior _Marcus Chester, Jr._____

218 Mulberry Street _218 Mulberry St._____

Bowen, California _Bowen, CA_____

                  **Mr.**
Dear Mister Vasquez:
                              **Saturday**

    I am a big fan of your work. Last Sat. I read your latest mystery. It was
                                                    **road**
exciting. When Randolph and Kildare chased Brad and Chris down the rd.,

I read as fast as I could to find out what would happen next.
                              **North Carolina**

    Have you ever thought of setting a story in NC? If you came here to
                              **apartment**
do research, I could help you. My family lives in an apt. in Charlotte, and we
                          **street**
would be happy to have you stay with us. Our st. has a big, dark old house
                                               **August**
you would like. My friends and I saw something mysterious there last Aug.

    Thanks for writing such great books.

                                Your fan,

                                *Marcus*

                                Marcus Chester

Name _____

# Writing a Journal Entry

Leigh Botts, the main character in *Dear Mr. Henshaw*, keeps a journal. A **journal** is a notebook, diary, folder, or file in which you can keep a record of your thoughts, ideas, and experiences.

**On the lines below, write a journal entry about a day in your own life. Follow these guidelines:**

▶ **Write the date at the beginning.  You might also want to include the location.**

▶ **Write in the first person, using the pronouns *I, me, my, mine, we,* and *our*.**

▶ **Narrate or describe the day's events or experiences.**

▶ **Include personal thoughts, feelings, reactions, questions, and ideas.**

▶ **Use details to describe what you saw or experienced.**

**(10 points)**

_____

_____

_____

_____

_____

_____

_____

_____

_____

_____

**When you finish your journal entry, you may want to share it with a friend or a classmate.**

Assessment Tip: Total **10** Points

Name _____

# Expanding Sentences with Adjectives

An **adjective** like *plump* or *icy* describes a noun or pronoun. Good writers use adjectives to create a clear, vivid picture of what they are describing or narrating.

**Read this journal entry that Leigh Botts might have written after a day of hiking. Then rewrite it on the lines, adding adjectives from the list to bring Leigh's description to life. Use as many adjectives as you can, joining related adjectives with *and* or a comma if appropriate.**

*Saturday, March 10*
*Today I took a hike through the woods. A cloud of monarch butterflies fluttered through the air. As I leaned quietly against the bark of a tree trunk, they landed in the leaves above. Soon the afternoon sun appeared like a coin against the hills. I knew it was time to go home for supper, but the gas station is so noisy compared with the silence of the forest.*

**Adjectives**

| | |
|---|---|
| dark | lonely |
| distant | orange |
| huge | green |
| delicate | short |
| scratchy | busy |
| golden | cool |
| crowded | small |
| shiny | |

Responses may vary. **(15 points)**

Today I took a **short** hike through the **lonely** woods. A **small** cloud of

monarch butterflies, **orange** and **delicate,** fluttered through the **cool** air.

As I leaned quietly against the **scratchy** bark of a tree trunk, they landed

in the **green** leaves above. Soon the afternoon sun, **golden** and **shiny,**

appeared like a **huge** coin against the **dark, distant** hills. I knew it was

time to go home for supper, but the gas station, **busy** and **crowded,** is so

noisy compared with the silence of the forest.

Name _____

# Vocabulary Items

Use the test-taking strategies and tips you have learned to help you answer vocabulary items. This practice will help you when you take this kind of test.

**Read each pair of sentences below. Then choose the word that correctly completes both sentences. Fill in the circle for your answer at the bottom of the page.**

1   The _____ led the class on a tour through the museum.
    The instructor will _____ us in doing the project.

    **A**   teacher              **C**   lead

    **B**   guide               **D**   instructor

2   Lee made her sandwich on the kitchen _____.
    Kevin put the last math _____ in his notebook.

    **F**   chair               **H**   table

    **G**   block               **J**   book

3   Our best runner was struck out at first _____.
    The _____ of the statue was cracked and uneven.

    **A**   floor               **C**   base

    **B**   arm                **D**   basket

4   The dogs played and _____ in the park.
    Which candidate _____ the best race?

    **F**   sat                **H**   won

    **G**   limped             **J**   ran

ANSWER ROWS   I Ⓐ **Ⓑ** Ⓒ Ⓓ **(5 points)**   3 Ⓐ Ⓑ **Ⓒ** Ⓓ **(5)**
                  2 Ⓕ Ⓖ **Ⓗ** Ⓙ **(5)**          4 Ⓕ Ⓖ Ⓗ **Ⓙ** **(5)**

Name _____

# Vocabulary Items continued

**5** Rita thought the math test was a _____.
The boy tightened the _____ so the saddle would not fall off the horse.

   **A** rope                   **C** girth

   **B** cinch                 **D** nightmare

**6** The girl wanted to find a pet that would _____ her.
Dad wore his blue _____ to the meeting.

   **F** suit                    **H** like

   **G** uniform             **J** comfort

**7** Grandpa taught me how to _____ my own problems.
Don't touch the _____ on the hot frying pan.

   **A** lid                     **C** handle

   **B** solve                 **D** understand

**8** Every person has to learn how to make _____ decisions.
The meat was too _____ to chew.

   **F** tender                **H** stringy

   **G** wise                  **J** tough

ANSWER ROWS   5 Ⓐ **Ⓑ** Ⓒ Ⓓ **(5 points)**   7 Ⓐ Ⓑ **Ⓒ** Ⓓ **(5)**
                       6 **Ⓕ** Ⓖ Ⓗ Ⓙ **(5)**   8 Ⓕ Ⓖ Ⓗ **Ⓙ** **(5)**

Assessment Tip: Total **40** Points

Name _____

# Spelling Review

**Write Spelling Words from the list on this page to answer the questions.** Order of answers in each category may vary.

1–9. Which nine words have the VCCCV pattern?

1. complain **(1 point)**

2. mischief **(1)**

3. countless **(1)**

4. laughter **(1)**

5. farther **(1)**

6. sandwich **(1)**

7. government **(1)**

8. improve **(1)**

9. address **(1)**

10–17. Which eight words have a VV pattern that makes two vowel sounds?

10. rodeo **(1)**

11. riot **(1)**

12. radio **(1)**

13. actual **(1)**

14. diary **(1)**

15. fuel **(1)**

16. cruel **(1)**

17. usual **(1)**

18–32. Which fifteen words have suffixes or end in *-ed* or *-ing*? Underline four words that also have the VCCCV pattern.

18. <u>countless</u> **(2)**

19. <u>delightful</u> **(2)**

20. actively **(1)**

21. lately **(1)**

22. <u>government</u> **(2)**

23. goodness **(1)**

24. <u>watchful</u> **(2)**

25. planned **(1)**

26. decided **(1)**

27. offered **(1)**

28. amusing **(1)**

29. hitting **(1)**

30. visiting **(1)**

31. covered **(1)**

32. ordered **(1)**

**Spelling Words**

1. complain
2. planned
3. mischief
4. countless
5. laughter
6. rodeo
7. decided
8. offered
9. delightful
10. farther
11. sandwich
12. actively
13. riot
14. amusing
15. radio
16. lately
17. government
18. actual
19. improve
20. goodness
21. hitting
22. diary
23. fuel
24. address
25. visiting
26. cruel
27. covered
28. watchful
29. usual
30. ordered

Theme 4: **Person to Person**    265
Assessment Tip: Total **36** Points

Name _____

# Spelling Spree

**Phrase Fillers** **Write the Spelling Word that best completes each phrase.**

1. loud _laughter_ **(1 point)** after a joke

2. working to _improve_ **(1)** my grades

3. music on the _radio_ **(1)**

4. a _countless_ **(1)** number of stars

5. running out of _fuel_ **(1)**

6. a cowboy starring in the _rodeo_ **(1)**

7. a ham and cheese _sandwich_ **(1)**

**Word Detective** **Use the following clues to figure out each Spelling Word. Write the word on the line.**

8. Not kind, but _cruel_ **(1)**

9. Not out of the ordinary _usual_ **(1)**

10. Tells where you live _address_ **(1)**

11. A disturbance of the peace _riot_ **(1)**

12. A daily written record _diary_ **(1)**

13. Funny _amusing_ **(1)**

14. The way a nation is ruled _government_ **(1)**

15. Real, true, and factual _actual_ **(1)**

## Spelling Words

1. sandwich
2. cruel
3. address
4. actual
5. countless
6. government
7. laughter
8. amusing
9. fuel
10. usual
11. riot
12. diary
13. improve
14. rodeo
15. radio

Assessment Tip: Total **15** Points

Name _____

# Proofreading and Writing

**Proofreading** Circle the six misspelled Spelling Words in this e-mail message. Then write each word correctly.

Dear Aunt Leslie and Uncle Alex,

My (goodnes!) I am excited about (visiding) you. Dad (orderd) me a new suitcase, so it has been hard (laitly) to wait until it is time to pack. I have been preparing (activly) for this vacation. I want to practice my pitching under Uncle Alex's (wachful) eye.

See you soon, Roy

1. ordered
2. complain
3. goodness
4. farther
5. visiting
6. offered
7. lately
8. decided
9. covered
10. delightful
11. hitting
12. planned
13. watchful
14. mischief
15. actively

1. goodness **(1 point)**
2. visiting **(1)**
3. ordered **(1)**
4. lately **(1)**
5. actively **(1)**
6. watchful **(1)**

**Finish the Entry** Complete the list by writing Spelling Words that make sense on the lines.

7. Uncle Alex offered **(1)** to help me with baseball.
8. We will practice hitting **(1)** baseballs.
9. Bring a gift for the party they have planned **(1)**.
10. I will be farther **(1)** from home than I've ever been.
11. Do not get into mischief **(1)**.
12. Bring my camera. Their beautiful garden will be covered **(1)** with flowers.
13. I have decided **(1)** to try fishing this year.
14. My aunt and uncle are delightful **(1)** people.
15. Don't complain **(1)** about anything.

✏➤ **Write a Letter** On a separate sheet of paper, write a letter to someone you would like to visit. Use the Spelling Review Words. Responses will vary. **(5)**

Name _____

# Setting Up a Scene

Think about a sequel for *The Case of the Runaway Appetite* in which Joe Giles visits Princess Veronica in her own country. What would be the new setting for the opening scene? Which new characters would you introduce? What new problem could the characters face? Fill in a description of the setting, the characters, and the problem in the chart below. Be as precise as you can. Answers will vary.

| Opening Scene | Description |
|---|---|
| Setting<br><br>  Time:<br>  Place: | (2 points) |
| Characters: | (4) |
| Problem: | (4) |

Name ─────────────────────────────────

# Comparing Productions

Think of a movie, play, or television show you have enjoyed. Compare it to *The Case of the Runaway Appetite.* Make sure to think about the characters, the setting, the plot, and other details. Write about each production in the Venn diagram below. Remember to use the intersecting part of the circles for the things that both productions have in common. Answers will vary. **(5 points** for each section of the diagram.)

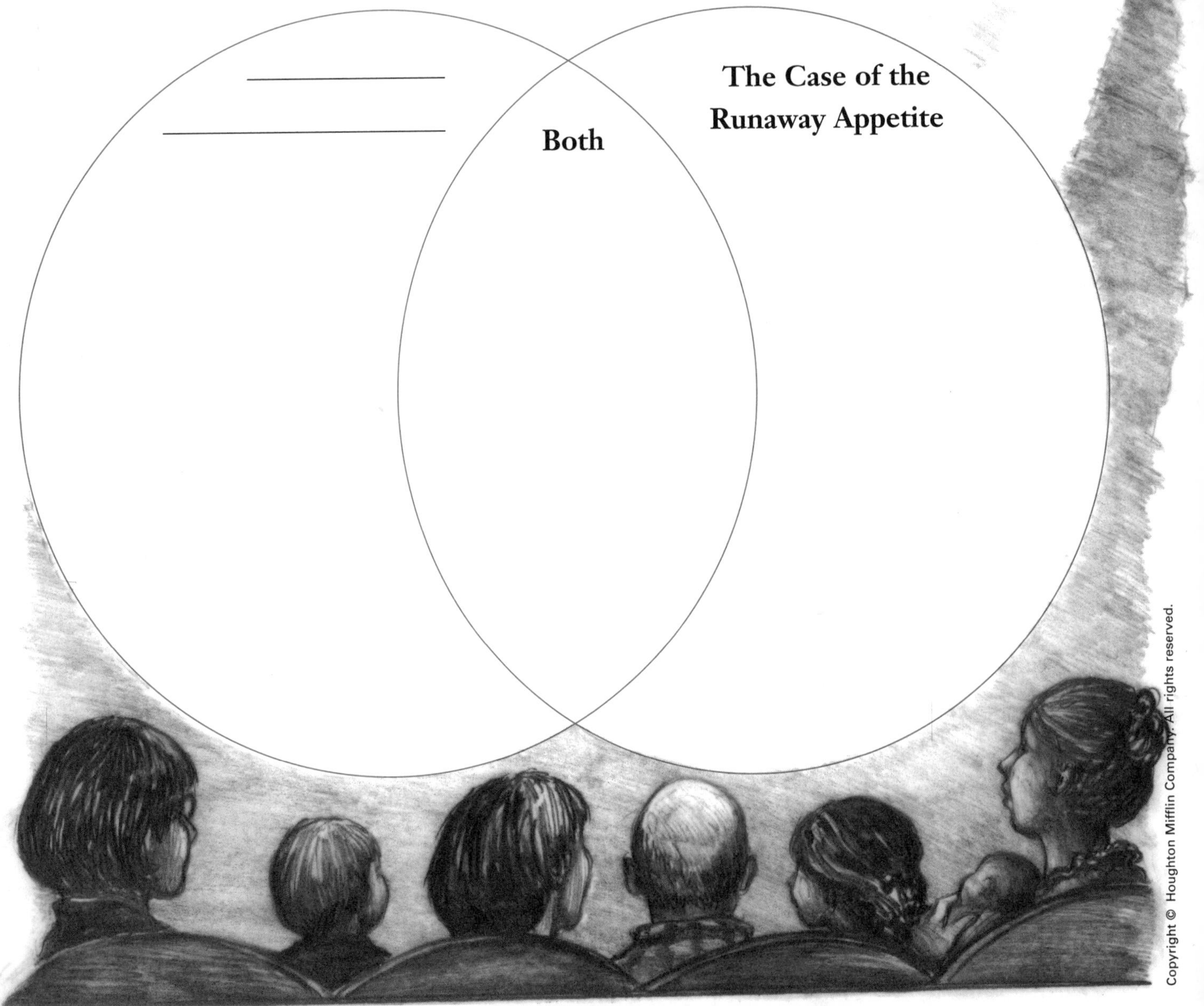

─────────────────

─────────────────

**Both**

**The Case of the Runaway Appetite**

Assessment Tip: Total **15** Points

Name _____

# One Land, Many Trails

After reading each selection, complete the chart to show what you learned about the people who lived on the American frontier long ago.

| | Pioneer Girl | A Boy Called Slow |
|---|---|---|
| **Tell who the main character in this selection is, and give one important fact about that person.** | The main character is Grace McCance. She was a young girl in a pioneer family that settled on the prairie. **(2.5 points)** | The main character is a boy named Slow. He was a member of the Lakota Sioux people, who lived on the Great Plains. **(2.5)** |
| **What special challenges did this person face in the selection?** | Grace faced harsh living conditions, fierce storms, prairie fires, and difficult chores. **(2.5)** | Slow had to earn a new name for himself by doing something brave or outstanding. **(2.5)** |
| **What traits helped this person successfully overcome the challenges?** | Grace was willing to do whatever was asked of her. She was brave in the face of dangers and made the best of her situation. **(2.5)** | Slow's determination helped him develop skills and strength. He showed courage and quick thinking in the battle that earned him the name Sitting Bull. **(2.5)** |
| **How did this person's efforts contribute to America's past?** | Grace and her family helped settle the Great Plains. **(2.5)** | Slow became a great leader of the Sioux. **(2.5)** |

Theme 5: **One Land, Many Trails** 271

Assessment Tip: Total **10** Points per selection and **2** points for the final question

Name _____

# One Land, Many Trails

|  | **Black Cowboy Wild Horses** | **Elena** |
|---|---|---|
| **Tell who the main character in this selection is, and give one important fact about that person.** | Bob Lemmons is the main character. He was an African American cowboy who was an expert at catching wild mustangs. **(2.5)** | Elena is the main character. She was born in Mexico and had to flee to the United States to escape a war. **(2.5)** |
| **What special challenges did this person face in the selection?** | Bob had the difficult job of catching wild mustangs. He had to find the mustangs by tracking them and then get the herds to follow him. **(2.5)** | Elena lost her husband at a young age. She had children to care for. She had to leave her home and make a new life in a new land. **(2.5)** |
| **What traits helped this person successfully overcome the challenges?** | Bob understood mustangs. He had the special talent of getting the horses to believe he was one of them. He was clever and brave. **(2.5)** | Elena was strong and steady. She knew what she needed to do and she did it. Her hard work helped her children thrive in America. **(2.5)** |
| **How did this person's efforts contribute to America's past?** | He helped other cowboys do their jobs by obtaining horses for them. **(2.5)** | She helped settle California and make that part of the country grow. **(2.5)** |

What have you learned about the contributions different people have made to America's culture and heritage?

Sample answer: I learned that people from many different cultural

backgrounds and from many different places contributed to America's

growth. I learned that our diverse culture began on the frontier.

Assessment Tip: Total **10** Points per selection and **2** points for the final question

Name _____

# Path of the Warrior

**Read the paragraph below. Use the words in the box to fill in the blanks.**

**Vocabulary**

customs
reputation
inherited
raid
extended
vision
determination
respect

Physical abilities are mostly <u>inherited **(1 point)**</u>
from parents and grandparents, but character is developed
through life experiences. How could a young brave earn a
<u>reputation **(1)**</u> as a courageous warrior?
One way was to lead a <u>raid **(1)**</u> against
an enemy camp. Another was to engage a rival group in battle
and touch their leader with a coup stick. Still another was to
show <u>determination **(1)**</u> in completing a difficult
mission. Earning the <u>respect **(1)**</u> of both
the <u>extended **(1)**</u> family and the tribal elders
was very important to young braves. This could only be done by
faithfully observing the traditions and <u>customs **(1)**</u>
of the people. One important tradition was going alone on a
wilderness journey to seek a <u>vision **(1)**</u>.
Sometimes this would provide the brave with a new name, one
that carried strength and power.

Name _____

# Conclusions Chart

| Story Clues | | | | Conclusions |
|---|---|---|---|---|
| **page 471** Returns Again and his wife give thanks when a son is born. **(2 points)** | + | Returns Again hopes his son will hunt for the people and protect them. **(2)** | = | The boy is born into a loving family who will help him grow up to be strong and brave. **(2)** |
| **pages 472–475** As Slow grows up, he is unhappy with his name. He wishes for a vision of bravery. **(2)** | + | Slow admires his father's courage, wisdom, and bravery. **(2)** | = | Slow probably has the makings of a good leader. |
| **pages 476–479** Slow wrestles and practices hunting. He becomes strong. He kills a buffalo at age ten. | + | Slow is careful and deliberate. People stop teasing him. He decides to join a battle against the Crow. | = | Slow has grown to be strong, confident, and skilled—maybe he is old enough to become a warrior. **(2)** |
| **pages 480–483** Slow announces that he will join the raid. Instead of waiting, he races ahead toward the Crow. | + | Slow touches a Crow warrior with his coup stick and knocks an arrow out of his hand. The Crow warriors flee. | = | Slow is daring and brave, and he shows skill as a warrior. **(2)** |

What predictions can you make about the kind of person Slow will grow up to be?

Answers will vary. **(2)**

_____

_____

Assessment Tip: Total **16** Points

Name _____

# Slow's Early Life in a Line

**The timeline below shows some important events in Sitting Bull's early life. Answer each question to tell about each event.**

1. **1831:**
   Who has a son?

2. **First Months of Life:**
   What name do Returns Again and his wife give their son? Why?

3. **Age Seven:**
   How does Slow feel about his name? What does he dream of?

4. **The Hunting Trip:**
   What happens when Returns Again goes hunting?

5. **Age Ten:**
   What big thing does Slow do? What else does he do to prepare himself for adulthood?

6. **Age Fourteen:**
   What does Slow decide to do? What happens as a result?

1. Returns Again's wife gives birth to a son. **(2 points)**

2. They name him Slow because he does everything slowly. **(2)**

3. Slow doesn't like his name. He dreams that a vision of bravery will come to him, a vision that would allow him to prove himself to his people. **(2)**

4. A big bull buffalo speaks four powerful names to Returns Again. **(2)**

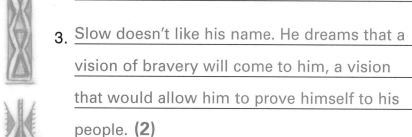

5. At the age of ten, Slow kills his first buffalo. He also hunts with his bow and arrows, races his gray pony, and wrestles with his friends. **(2)**

6. Slow goes with his father to fight the Crow. He leads the attack. The Crow warriors flee. Slow is a hero and he gets a new name: Sitting Bull. **(2)**

Name _____

# Why Do You Think . . . ?

**Read the following passage. Then complete the activity on page 277.**

## Sequoyah

When he was a child, few people would have guessed that Sequoyah would one day be hailed as a genius and a savior of the Cherokee nation. He was born around 1760 and grew up in Tennessee, following Cherokee customs and wearing the traditional dress of the Cherokee people. A childhood illness left him partially disabled, but he managed to acquire the skills of a silversmith and blacksmith.

Sequoyah never learned to speak, read, or write in English. However, he became fascinated with English writing. In fact, he believed that the secret of the white settlers' success was their written language.

Sequoyah figured out that each letter in the English alphabet represented a sound. In 1809 he set out to create a similar alphabet for the Cherokee language. On scraps of tree bark, he scratched symbols to stand for the sounds of Cherokee. His wife did not approve.

"Why are you wasting your time?" she complained. "You should be working, not drawing pictures!"

Sequoyah ignored her. He knew that his work could be important for the Cherokee people. Finally, after many years, he had created a set of eighty-five characters to represent all the sounds of the Cherokee language. When he showed the members of his tribe, however, they laughed at him.

"What do we need an alphabet for?" they said.

Sequoyah didn't lose faith, though. He traveled to Georgia to show his work to the top Cherokee chiefs. They were impressed. The alphabet was easy to learn, and it allowed people to communicate in writing. Soon, the Cherokee were publishing their own newspaper. Sequoyah was praised as a great man by both the Cherokee and the American government. He became a teacher and a highly respected leader of the Cherokee people.

Name _____

# Why Do You Think . . .? continued

**Answer these questions about the passage on page 276.**
Sample answers shown.

1. Why do you think Sequoyah was considered a genius?

   He created an entirely new alphabet even though he had had no

   formal education. **(2 points)**

2. In what ways might the Cherokee alphabet have helped to preserve

   Cherokee customs and ways of life?

   It allowed people to write about their customs and traditions

   so they wouldn't be forgotten. **(2)**

3. Why do you think Sequoyah continued working on the alphabet

   despite the fact that other members of his tribe did not approve?

   Maybe he knew the alphabet would be useful and important. **(2)**

4. Why do you think the Cherokee people changed their minds about

   the alphabet?

   Once they saw how useful the alphabet was they understood its

   importance. **(2)**

5. What character traits did Sequoyah possess?  Use details from the

   passage to help you answer.

   Examples: He was very smart because he created an alphabet; he

   was an independent thinker because he carried on despite the

   disapproval of others; he was persistent because he worked on the

   alphabet for many years. **(2)**

Name _____

# Word Parts Match

**Read each sentence. Match a prefix or suffix from the box on the left with a base word from the box on the right to form a word that completes the sentence. Write the word in the blank. (The prefixes and suffix may be used more than once.)**

| dis-  in-  -ion |
| re-  un- |

| accurate | agreed | aware | cooperate |
| direct | like | possess | turned |

1. As they grew older, many of the boys began to _dislike_ **(1 point)** their childhood names and wish for new ones.

2. Returns Again earned his name when he _returned_ **(1)** to protect his people from an enemy raid.

3. The low rumbling noise came from the _direction_ **(1)** of the trail.

4. Returns Again _disagreed_ **(1)** with the others, who wanted to take out their weapons.

5. Unlike Returns Again, the other men were _unaware_ **(1)** of what the big bull buffalo's sounds meant.

6. Slow struck the Crow warrior's arm with his coup stick to make his aim _inaccurate_ **(1)**.

7. After their victory, the Lakota Sioux warriors took _possession_ **(1)** of the enemy's horses and weapons.

8. Their spirit of _cooperation_ **(1)** helped the Lakota Sioux people provide for and protect each other.

Assessment Tip: Total **8** Points

Name _____

# Words with a Prefix or a Suffix (un-, dis-, in-, re-; -ion)

A **prefix** is a word part added to the beginning of a base word or a word root. It adds meaning to a word. Some of the Spelling Words above contain the prefixes *un-, dis-, in-,* or *re-.* To spell these words, find the prefix and the base word or the word root.

    Prefix + Base Word:    **un**able    **dis**cover

    Prefix + Word Root:    **re**port    **in**spect

A **suffix** is a word part added to the end of a base word. The suffix *-ion* can change verbs into nouns. When a verb ends with *e,* drop the *e* and add *-ion.* If a verb does not end with *e,* just add *-ion.*

    VERB: promote  react    NOUN: promot**ion**  react**ion**

**Write the Spelling Words. Underline the prefixes *un-, dis-, in-,* and *re-.* Circle the suffix *-ion.***

Order of responses for each category may vary.

| | |
|---|---|
| <u>un</u>able **(1)** | <u>re</u>act |
| <u>dis</u>cover **(1)** | <u>re</u>act⟨ion⟩ |
| <u>re</u>port **(1)** | tense |
| <u>dis</u>aster **(1)** | tens⟨ion⟩ |
| <u>un</u>aware **(1)** | correct |
| <u>re</u>mind **(1)** | correct⟨ion⟩ |
| televise **(1)** | promote |
| televis⟨ion⟩ **(1)** | promot⟨ion⟩ |
| <u>in</u>spect **(1)** | express |
| <u>in</u>spect⟨ion⟩ **(1)** | express⟨ion⟩ |

**Spelling Words**

1. unable
2. discover
3. report
4. disaster
5. unaware
6. remind
7. televise
8. television
9. inspect
10. inspection
11. react
12. reaction
13. tense
14. tension
15. correct
16. correction
17. promote
18. promotion
19. express
20. expression

Name _____

# Spelling Spree

**Meaning Match** Write the Spelling Word that has each meaning and word part below.

1. to examine + *ion*
2. *dis* + a container lid
3. to broadcast + *ion*
4. *re* + to do something
5. to make right + *ion*
6. *un* + capable of doing something
7. nervous + *ion*
8. to move to a higher position + *ion*

1. unable
2. discover
3. report
4. disaster
5. unaware
6. remind
7. televise
8. television
9. inspect
10. inspection
11. react
12. reaction
13. tense
14. tension
15. correct
16. correction
17. promote
18. promotion
19. express
20. expression

1. inspection **(1 point)**
2. discover **(1)**
3. television **(1)**
4. react **(1)**
5. correction **(1)**
6. unable **(1)**
7. tension **(1)**
8. promotion **(1)**

**Hidden Words** Write the Spelling Word that is hidden in each row of letters. Don't let the other words fool you!

9. c o r e a c t i o n c e
10. g l e e x p r e s s u r e
11. c h a i n s p e c t r i p
12. a r c o r r e c t a n g l e
13. h o t e l e v i s e n s e
14. d a m p r o m o t e a m
15. h a r d i s a s t e r n

9. reaction **(1)**
10. express **(1)**
11. inspect **(1)**
12. correct **(1)**
13. televise **(1)**
14. promote **(1)**
15. disaster **(1)**

Assessment Tip: Total **15** Points

Name _____

# Proofreading and Writing

**Circle the five misspelled Spelling Words in this part of a script for a class play. Then write each word correctly.**

Slow: How much longer will we have to be called by these
names?  Every time I hear mine, all it does is (remined)
me that the elders think of me as just a child.  These
days, whenever anyone calls my name, I get very (tens.)

Hungry Mouth: I know what you mean.  I have the same
reaction.  I'd like a name that's an (expresion) of something
more than the fact that I have a big appetite.  But what
can we do?  It's not like the elders are (unawear) of our
feelings.

Slow: That's true, but they're still waiting for us to do
something worthy of a new name.  The next time they
form a war party we should (repport) for duty.

1. remind **(1 point)**          4. unaware **(1)**

2. tense **(1)**                 5. report **(1)**

3. expression **(1)**

## Spelling Words

1. unable
2. discover
3. report
4. disaster
5. unaware
6. remind
7. televise
8. television
9. inspect
10. inspection
11. react
12. reaction
13. tense
14. tension
15. correct
16. correction
17. promote
18. promotion
19. express
20. expression

✏️ **Write a Summary** If a friend were to ask you what *A Boy Called Slow* is about, what would you say?  What happens in the story?  Who are the main characters?  What details are most important in understanding the events of the story?

**On a separate piece of paper, write a brief summary of the story. Use Spelling Words from the list.** Responses will vary. **(5)**

Name _____

# Slow Is to Boy as . . .

**Read each analogy. Write the word that best completes each analogy.**

1. *Share* is to *hoard* as *gain* is to __lose **(1)**__.
   collect    lose    heavy    surrender

2. *Inherited* is to *received* as *yelled* is to __shouted **(1)**__.
   hushed    anger    argued    shouted

3. *Son* is to *relative* as *pony* is to __animal **(1)**__.
   mane    saddle    animal    stirrups

4. *Courage* is to *warriors* as *wisdom* is to __elders **(1)**__.
   elders    infants    smart    college

5. *Retreat* is to *advance* as *speak* is to __listen **(1)**__.
   chatter    listen    silent    command

6. *Slow* is to *name* as *winter* is to __season **(1)**__.
   summer    frozen    snow    season

7. *Follow* is to *trail* as *protect* is to __guard **(1)**__.
   guard    warn    attack    watch

**Use any three of the words in the box to write an incomplete analogy on a separate piece of paper. Challenge a partner to complete it with one of the remaining words. Sample answer shown.**

| climb | deep | flat | mountains |
|-------|------|------|-----------|
| oceans | peaked | plains | swim |

8. *Plains* is to *flat* as *mountains* is to *peaked*. **(1)**

Assessment Tip: Total **8** Points

Name _____

# We Object to It

**Subject and Object Pronouns**  A pronoun is a word that replaces a noun.  *I, you, he, she, it, we,* and *they* are subject pronouns.  *Me, you, him, her, it, us,* and *them* are object pronouns.  Use a subject pronoun as the subject of a sentence or after forms of *be*.  Use an object pronoun as the object of an action verb or after words like *to, for,* or *with*.

**Underline the pronoun in parentheses that correctly completes each sentence.**

1. (I/me) have a nickname. **(1 point)**

2. My family gave (I/me) the nickname Skeeter. **(1)**

3. My brother Michael is called Apple because (he/him) has red cheeks. **(1)**

4. People give apples to (he/him) all the time. **(1)**

5. (They/Them) think Michael always wants an apple. **(1)**

6. My sister Cheryl is called Cookie by (we/us). **(1)**

7. Everyone gives cookies to (she/her). **(1)**

8. If anyone likes cookies, it is (she/her). **(1)**

9. Cheryl thanks (they/them). **(1)**

10. Michael and Cheryl share apples and cookies with (we/us). **(1)**

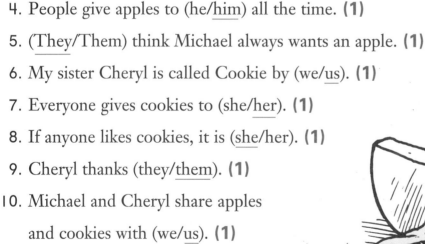

Name _____

# Should It Be *I* or *Me*?

**Using *I* and *Me*** Use *I* as the subject of a sentence and after forms of *be*. Use *me* after action verbs and after words like *to*, *in*, *for*, and *with*. When using the pronouns *I* and *me* with nouns or other pronouns, name yourself last.

| | |
|---|---|
| **Incorrect:** | **Jack and me** went to the movies. |
| **Incorrect:** | **I and Jack** went to the movies. |
| **Correct:** | **Jack and I** went to the movies. |

| | |
|---|---|
| **Incorrect:** | That was a treat for **Jack and I**. |
| **Incorrect:** | That was a treat for **me and Jack**. |
| **Correct:** | That was a treat for **Jack and me**. |

**Underline the words in parentheses that correctly complete each sentence. (1 point each)**

1. (Latisha and I/Latisha and me) found shiny, black arrowheads near the creek.
2. (She and I/Her and me) went to the library to learn about arrowheads.
3. The librarian told (Latisha and I/Latisha and me) that our arrowheads were made of obsidian, a kind of volcanic glass.
4. (You and I/You and me) should meet Latisha at the creek tomorrow.
5. Another discovery would be fun for (Latisha and I/Latisha and me).
6. If Latisha finds one, she will give it to (you and me/you and I).
7. (Her and I/She and I) have found broken arrowheads before.
8. But yesterday (I and she/she and I) found two perfect specimens!
9. The arrowhead collection gathered by (her and me/she and I) is growing.
10. Soon (she and I/her and me) will have the largest collection around.

Assessment Tip: Total **10** Points

Name _____

# We're Pronoun Pros

Good writers are careful to use a subject pronoun as the subject of a sentence or after a form of *be*. They use an object pronoun after an action verb and after a word like *to*, *for*, *with*, or *in*.

**Gloria is writing for the school newspaper. Proofread her draft. Cross out each incorrect pronoun or pronoun phrase and write the correct pronoun or phrase above it. (1 point each)**

Last Saturday, George, Nan, Kathy, and ~~me~~ [I] followed a trail

in the woods on Prospect Hill. Kathy and ~~me~~ [I] asked George and

Nan to lead us. The hiking club gave ~~he~~ [him] and ~~she~~ [her] trailblazing badges.

~~I and Kathy~~ [Kathy and I] knew they would keep us on the path. George knew a

special place at the end of the trail. It was ~~him~~ [he] who suggested the hike.

The trail was thick with brambles, but George and Nan kept us on

the right path. After half an hour of walking, ~~him~~ [he] and ~~her~~ [she] called out to

Kathy and ~~I~~ [me]. The sun shone brightly on wildflowers and bushes full of

fat, juicy blackberries. George picked four berries and washed ~~they~~ [them] with

water. Nan held out her hand and George gave one berry to ~~she~~ [her] and one

to each of us. Nothing has ever tasted so good. ~~Us~~ [We] will go back soon!

Assessment Tip: Total **12** Points

Name _____

# Writing a Speech

In *A Boy Called Slow*, a fourteen-year-old Lakota boy courageously protects his people from a Crow war party and earns himself a new name. His father, Returns Again, gives a very brief **speech** about Slow's bravery. Now you will write your own speech. Choose one of the topics listed below.

► Write a speech in which Returns Again describes his son's courage in the battle against the Crow and announces his son's new name.

► Write a speech about a current topic that you feel strongly about.

**Use the chart below to help you get started. First, identify the purpose of your speech — to entertain, to persuade, to thank, or to inform — and the audience to whom you will deliver it. Then jot down specific examples you might include to support your main idea. Before you begin writing, number your examples, beginning with *1*, to arrange the order in which you will present them.**

| Purpose | Audience | Examples |
|---------|----------|----------|
| (3 points) | (3) | (3) |
| | | |

**Write your speech on a separate sheet of paper. First, mention whom you are addressing and what the purpose of your speech is. Then present your ideas in a logical order. Be sure to use emotional words and powerful examples that help make your point. Finally, end with a conclusion that sums up or restates the purpose. When you finish, deliver your speech to the class. (6 points)**

Assessment Tip: Total **15** Points

Name _____

# Using Quotations

Good speechwriters make their speeches more lively and powerful by including **direct quotations** made by people who have something important to say about the topic. When you use a direct quotation in your own writing, make sure to do the following:

► Write the exact words the person said.
► Use quotation marks to separate the direct quotation from the rest of the sentence.
► Give the name of the person who is responsible for the quotation.
► Check that the spelling of the quoted person's name is correct.

**Carefully read these quotations by well-known Native Americans.**

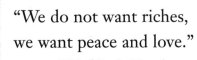

"We do not want riches, we want peace and love."
—*Chief Red Cloud*

"The earth and myself are of one mind."
—*Chief Joseph*

**Now proofread the speech excerpts in which these quotations are used. On the lines, rewrite each excerpt to correct the speechwriters' use of quotations. Use the guidelines listed above to help you.**

1. Scott Franklin will now share remarkable slides of his round-the-world camping trip. Mr. Franklin's experiment in living echoes Cheif Josef's belief that The earth and myself are of one mind.

   Scott Franklin will now share remarkable slides of his round-the-world

   camping trip. Mr. Franklin's experiment in living echoes **Chief**

   **Joseph's** belief that "The earth and myself are of one mind." **(4 points)**

2. Our neighborhood group opposes the proposed development because, as someone said, We do not want riches, we want peace and love.

   Our neighborhood group opposes the proposed development

   because, as **Chief Red Cloud** said, "We do not want riches, we want

   peace and love." **(4)**

Name _____

# Evaluating Your Research Report

**Reread your research report. What do you need to do to make it better? Use this page to help you decide. Put a checkmark in the box for each sentence that describes your research report.**

### Rings the Bell!

☐ I chose an interesting topic to research.

☐ I used different, reliable sources to find information on the topic.

☐ I took careful notes and used them to write my report.

☐ My paragraphs contain topic sentences and supporting facts.

☐ My pronoun references are clear.

☐ There are very few mistakes.

### Getting Stronger

☐ I could make the topic sound more interesting to the reader.

☐ More sources might help me make sure I have the facts right.

☐ I need to follow my notes more closely.

☐ Some of my pronoun references are unclear.

☐ There are quite a few errors that need to be fixed.

### Try Harder

☐ My topic isn't very interesting.

☐ I didn't use enough sources to find my facts.

☐ I didn't take careful notes on what I found out.

☐ Too many mistakes make the report hard to read.

Name _____

# Pronoun Reference

**Pronouns are words that replace nouns or other words. Write the word or words that the underlined pronoun refers to in each exercise.**

1. Gems are hard to find. <u>They</u> are usually embedded in ordinary-looking rocks.

2. Without impurities, gems would be colorless crystals. The color of a gem depends on the type of impurities <u>it</u> contains.

3. The metal chromium gives a green color to one kind of crystal, turning <u>it</u> into an emerald.

4. Gems can be harder than the rock that surrounds <u>them</u>.

5. Rock hunters often find gems in riverbeds. <u>They</u> look for places where the surrounding rock has been eroded away.

6. Sapphires are a fiery blue. <u>They</u> get their color from a mixture of titanium and iron.

7. Rubies have chromium as an impurity. It gives <u>them</u> a deep red color.

8. Once a gem is found, <u>it</u> must be cut by gem-cutters.

1. gems **(1 point)** _____

2. gem **(1)** _____

3. crystal **(1)** _____

4. gems **(1)** _____

5. rock hunters **(1)** _____

6. sapphires **(1)** _____

7. rubies **(1)** _____

8. gem **(1)** _____

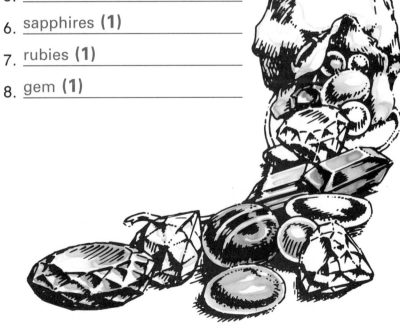

# Spelling Words

**Words Often Misspelled** Look for familiar spelling patterns to help you remember how to spell the Spelling Words on this page. Think carefully about the parts that you find hard to spell in each word.

**Write the missing letters in the Spelling Words below.**

1. __w__ __h__ ile **(1 point)**
2. __w__ __h__ ole **(1)**
3. __a__ __n__ __y__ way **(1)**
4. __a__ n __y__ one **(1)**
5. __a__ n __y__ thing **(1)**
6. favor __i__ __t__ __e__ **(1)**
7. on __c__ __e__ **(1)**
8. su __p__ __p__ ose **(1)**
9. ev __e__ __r__ __y__ body **(1)**
10. ev __e__ __r__ __y__ one **(1)**
11. r __e__ __a__ __l__ __l__ y **(1)**
12. m __o__ __r__ ning **(1)**
13. __a__ __l__ so **(1)**
14. __a__ __l__ ways **(1)**
15. f __i__ rst **(1)**

**Study List** **On a separate piece of paper, write each Spelling Word. Check your spelling against the words on the list.**

Order of words may vary.

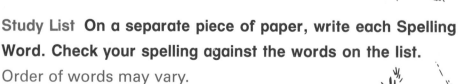

Assessment Tip: Total **15** Points

Name _____

# Spelling Spree

**Contrast Clues** The second part of each clue contrasts with the first part. Write a Spelling Word for each clue.

1. not evening, but _____
2. not lots of times, but _____
3. not never, but _____
4. not a fraction, but a _____
5. not a specific thing, but _____
6. not last, but _____

1. morning **(1 point)**
2. once **(1)**
3. always **(1)**
4. whole **(1)**
5. anything **(1)**
6. first **(1)**

**Hidden Words** Write the Spelling Word that is hidden in each row of letters. Don't let the other words fool you!

7. n e v e r y b o d y e s
8. c a t s u p p o s e a t
9. s t o r e a l l y i n g
10. t o w h i l e a r n
11. s i e v e r y o n e a r
12. m a n y w a y a k
13. m e a l s o u n d
14. a l f a l f a v o r i t e n t
15. c a n y o n e e d

7. everybody **(1)**
8. suppose **(1)**
9. really **(1)**
10. while **(1)**
11. everyone **(1)**
12. anyway **(1)**
13. also **(1)**
14. favorite **(1)**
15. anyone **(1)**

## Spelling Words

1. while
2. whole
3. anyway
4. anyone
5. anything
6. favorite
7. once
8. suppose
9. everybody
10. everyone
11. really
12. morning
13. also
14. always
15. first

Name _____

# Proofreading and Writing

**Proofreading** Circle the four misspelled Spelling Words in this song. Then write each word correctly.

The sun was burning bright this (mornning)

while I was working my field alone

I didn't have (anyon) to help me

My (favorit) dog had gone

I (realy) wish I had the money

to buy my ticket home.

1. while
2. whole
3. anyway
4. anyone
5. anything
6. favorite
7. once
8. suppose
9. everybody
10. everyone
11. really
12. morning
13. also
14. always
15. first

1. morning **(1 point)**     3. favorite **(1)**

2. anyone **(1)**     4. really **(1)**

✏️➤ **Write Tag-Team Poetry Pair up with a classmate. Then create a poem about the West by taking turns writing lines. Use Spelling Words from the list.** Responses will vary. **(6)**

Assessment Tip: Total **10** Points

Name _____

# Starting Anew

**Read the paragraph below.  Fill in each blank with a word from the box.  You will use one word twice.**

**Vocabulary**

homestead
claims
immigrants
sod
discouraged
convinced
heifer
fertile
prairie

During the second half of the nineteenth century many
___immigrants **(1 point)**___ from Europe traveled west
across America to begin new lives.  Families filed
___claims **(1)**___ on pieces of land.  There
they could establish a ___homestead **(1)**___ and
raise crops and livestock.  Advertisements paid for by the
railroads said that the flat, treeless ___prairie **(1)**___
had ___fertile **(1)**___ soil for growing crops.
These ads ___convinced **(1)**___ many families
that they would have success farming in the region.  Some did
succeed, but others became ___discouraged **(1)**___
and returned to the East.  Many who stayed built homes
from squares of prairie ___sod **(1)**___.
With a home built, crops growing, and a healthy
___heifer **(1)**___ grazing in a
___fertile **(1)**___ field nearby,
a family was off to a good start.

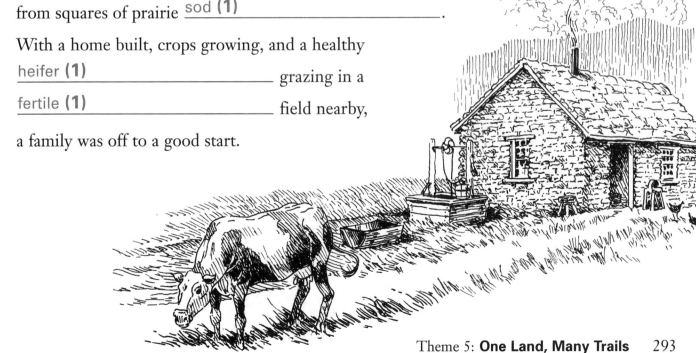

Theme 5: **One Land, Many Trails**   293
Assessment Tip: Total **10** Points

Name _____

# Pioneer Life

| What I **K**now | What I **W**ant to Know | What I **L**earned |
|---|---|---|
| Pioneers were people who journeyed to wilderness areas to start farms or ranches. **(2 points)**<br><br>Pioneer children had to do chores. **(2)** | When did pioneers settle in Nebraska? **(2)**<br><br>What kinds of work did pioneer children do? **(2)** | The McCance family took a claim in Nebraska in 1885. **(2)**<br><br>Three-year-olds chased birds out of fields and gathered chips for fuel. Four-year-olds ran errands, took water to field-workers, and gathered eggs. Five-year-olds broke up clods in fields, pulled weeds, fed the cookstove, milked cows, plowed, and herded cows. **(2)** |

Assessment Tip: Total **12** Points

Name ______________________________

# Across-the-Prairie Crossword

**Use these clues to complete the crossword puzzle about *Pioneer Girl*.**
(**1 point** for each correct answer)

1 prairie
2 backfire
3 immigrants
4 popcorn
5 calico
6 seconds
7 dash
8 tallgrass
9 gracie
10 seeds
11 herding
12 shortgrass
13 haystack
14 treeless
15 paper

## Across

3. Most homesteaders near the McCances were _____.
5. material for making dresses
8. prairie in the wetter eastern part of the Midwest
11. A common job for children was _____ cows.
12. prairie in the dry western part of the Midwest
14. Much of the Great Plains is bare and _____.
15. The McCances' Christmas "tree" was decorated with _____ chains.

## Down

1. grassy land
2. When a prairie fire approached, farmers set _____.
4. The McCances used this to decorate their Christmas "tree."
6. The hungry children had to wait for _____ table on holidays.
7. Grace made a mad _____ to escape from the heifer.
9. the real first name of "Pete"
10. Wild geese stole precious _____.
13. The cows made a cave in this.





Assessment Tip: Total **15** Points

Name _____

# Join Up!

**Read the following fliers, which are modeled on handbills from the 1870s. Use them to answer the questions on page 297.**

1

**Join the Grange Now!**
**All Your Neighbors Are!**
As a member, you benefit from cooperative prices on farm products and tools. Plus, you can take part in Grange social and educational events.

2

**Act Now!**
**Fight the Big City Bosses!**
The railroad bosses say they barely make a profit, but don't you believe it! While we struggle to make ends meet, they are all living lives of luxury in the big cities.

3

**Farmers Unite!**
**It Will Make Your Work Easier!**
The Grange is the farmer's friend. It is the one organization created by farmers to improve farmers' lives.

4

**Ulysses S. Grant Says,**
**"Join the Grange!"**
Do you listen to your President? You should! President Grant approves of the Grange.

5

**Fight the Railroads!**
**Jefferson and Jackson Would Have!**
Rise up, fellow farmers! Join the movement that feeds the great nation of Presidents Thomas Jefferson and Andrew Jackson.

Name _____

# Join Up! continued

**Answer each question about the fliers on page 296. Then fill in the blanks with the propaganda technique that each flier uses.**

## Propaganda Techniques

**Overgeneralization:** making general statements with no basis in fact

**Testimonial:** using the words of a famous person to support a cause

**Bandwagon:** persuading people to act because everyone else is

**Transfer:** associating a famous person with a product or cause

**Faulty cause and effect:** suggesting that this will make life better

1. How does the first flier persuade farmers to join the Grange?

   by saying that everyone else is **(1 point)**

   Propaganda Technique: Bandwagon **(1)**

2. What does the second flier say about all railroad bosses?

   They are all living lives of luxury in the big cities. **(1)**

   Propaganda Technique: Overgeneralization **(1)**

3. What does the third flier promise?

   that the Grange will make farmers' work easier and improve their

   lives **(1)**

   Propaganda Technique: Faulty cause and effect **(1)**

4. Why does the fourth flier quote President Grant?

   If people like the President, they might do what he says. **(1)**

   Propaganda Technique: Testimonial **(1)**

5. What association does the fifth flier make?

   It associates Presidents Jefferson and Jackson with the Grange

   movement. **(1)**

   Propaganda Technique: Transfer **(1)**

Name _____

# Stress That Syllable!

**Read each sentence. Say the underlined word several times, placing stress on a different syllable each time. Circle the choice that shows the correct stress for the underlined word. (The stressed syllable is shown in capital letters.)**

1. Grace and Florrie wore dresses made of calico.

   (CAL i co) **(1 point)**    cal I co                cal i CO

2. They sweetened their cereal with molasses.

   MO las ses         (mo LAS ses) **(1)**        mo las SES

3. The family's Christmas tree was decorated with paper chains.

   (DEC o rat ed) **(1)**  dec O rat ed        dec o RAT ed        dec o rat ED

4. Spring was their favorite time of year.

   (FA vor ite) **(1)**        fa VOR ite            fa vor ITE

5. Nebraska's population grew rapidly.

   POP u la tion        pop U la tion        (pop u LA tion) **(1)**  pop u la TION

6. Poppie was determined to make a success of the farm.

   DE ter mined         (de TER mined) **(1)**     de ter MINED

7. The homesteaders began making preparations for the long winter.

   PREP a ra tions    prep A ra tions      (prep a RA tions) **(1)**    prep a ra TIONS

8. The harsh weather did not discourage them.

   DIS cour age         (dis COUR age) **(1)**     dis cour AGE

Name _____

# Unstressed Syllables

To spell a two-syllable or three-syllable word, divide the word into syllables. Spell the word by syllables, noting carefully the spelling of the unstressed syllable or syllables.

**doz | en** /dŭz′ ən/    **dis | tance** /dĭs′ təns/

**de | stroy** /dĭ stroi′/

When you hear the final /ĭj/, /ĭv/, or /ĭs/ sounds, think of these patterns:

/ĭj/ *age* (voy**age**)    /ĭv/ *ive* (nat**ive**)    /ĭs/ *ice* (not**ice**)

► The /ĭj/ sound in *knowledge* is spelled *-edge*, and differs from the usual spelling pattern.

**Write each Spelling Word under the heading that shows which syllable is stressed. Underline the unstressed syllable or syllables.** Order of answers for each category may vary.

### Spelling Words

1. dozen
2. voyage
3. forbid
4. native
5. language
6. destroy
7. notice
8. distance
9. carrot
10. knowledge*
11. captive
12. spinach
13. solid
14. justice
15. ashamed
16. program
17. message
18. respond
19. service
20. relative

## First Syllable Stressed

doz<u>en</u> **(1 point)**    cap<u>tive</u> **(1)**

voy<u>age</u> **(1)**    spin<u>ach</u> **(1)**

na<u>tive</u> **(1)**    sol<u>id</u> **(1)**

lan<u>guage</u> **(1)**    jus<u>tice</u> **(1)**

no<u>tice</u> **(1)**    pro<u>gram</u> **(1)**

dis<u>tance</u> **(1)**    mes<u>sage</u> **(1)**

car<u>rot</u> **(1)**    ser<u>vice</u> **(1)**

knowl<u>edge</u> **(1)**    rel<u>ative</u> **(1)**

## Last Syllable Stressed

<u>for</u>bid **(1)**    <u>a</u>shamed **(1)**

<u>de</u>stroy **(1)**    <u>re</u>spond **(1)**

Theme 5: **One Land, Many Trails**    299

Assessment Tip: Total **20** Points

Name _____

# Spelling Spree

**Write a Spelling Word by combining the beginning of the first word with the ending of the second word.**

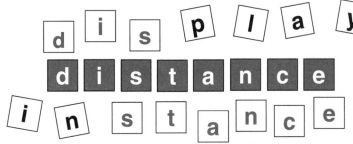

1. capture + olive
2. ashen + framed
3. knowing + pledge
4. nation + forgive
5. languish + passage

6. respect + fond
7. justify + practice
8. serving + office
9. spine + reach
10. progress + madam

1. captive **(1 point)**
2. ashamed **(1)**
3. knowledge **(1)**
4. native **(1)**
5. language **(1)**

6. respond **(1)**
7. justice **(1)**
8. service **(1)**
9. spinach **(1)**
10. program **(1)**

**Word Magic** **Write a Spelling Word to fit each clue.**

11. Add two letters to *relate* to write a word for a family member.
12. Replace two letters in *formed* to write a word meaning "to refuse to allow."
13. Insert one consonant into *doze* to write a word meaning "a set of twelve."
14. Replace one letter in *carry* with two to write a word for a root vegetable.
15. Change the ending of *voice* to write a synonym for *journey*.

11. relative **(1)**
12. forbid **(1)**
13. dozen **(1)**
14. carrot **(1)**
15. voyage **(1)**

**Spelling Words**

1. dozen
2. voyage
3. forbid
4. native
5. language
6. destroy
7. notice
8. distance
9. carrot
10. knowledge*
11. captive
12. spinach
13. solid
14. justice
15. ashamed
16. program
17. message
18. respond
19. service
20. relative

Assessment Tip: Total **15** Points

Name _____

# Proofreading and Writing

**Proofreading** Circle the five misspelled Spelling Words in this journal entry. Then write each word correctly.

*October 11, 1891*

*Every day I (notise) something new and different about this strange land, but I still do not know if I will like it here. There is certainly something beautiful about the way the earth and sky stretch into the (distence) as far as the eye can see. At the same time, you live with the knowledge that the land can (distroy) you at any moment. It makes you wish for something more (sollid) than a sod house to call home. The loneliness is hard too. It takes all day just to send a (mesage) to the next farm. I should not complain, though. Our lives are good, and I believe that they will only get better.*

1. notice **(1 point)**
2. distance **(1)**
3. destroy **(1)**
4. solid **(1)**
5. message **(1)**

**Spelling Words**

1. dozen
2. voyage
3. forbid
4. native
5. language
6. destroy
7. notice
8. distance
9. carrot
10. knowledge*
11. captive
12. spinach
13. solid
14. justice
15. ashamed
16. program
17. message
18. respond
19. service
20. relative

▬▬▶ **Write About a Photograph** The photographs used to illustrate the selection show scenes from life on the Great Plains in the 1800s. Choose one that you find interesting. Who are the people in the photograph? What do they seem to be doing? Based on what you read in the selection, what do you think their lives were like?

**On a separate piece of paper, write a brief paragraph describing the photograph. Use Spelling Words from the list.** Responses will vary. **(5)**

Name _____

# Sentences Using Suffixes

**Read the dictionary definition for each suffix. Combine each base word in the box with one of the suffixes and write a sentence using the new word. Use each suffix at least once.**

Sample answers shown.

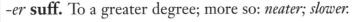

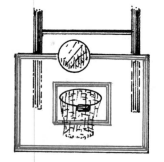

> *-er* **suff.** To a greater degree; more so: *neater; slower.*
>
> *-est* **suff.** To the most extreme degree; the most: *greatest; earliest.*
>
> *-ly* **suff.** In a specified manner: *gradually.*
>
> *-ment* **suff.** 1. Act, action, or process. 2. State of being acted upon.
>
> *-ness* **suff.** State, condition, or quality.

> ## Vocabulary
>
> constant
> encourage
> happy
> hard
> short
> usual

1. I usually shoot baskets in the school gym before I go home. **(2 points)**

2. My older brother needs encouragement to do his homework. **(2)**

3. The little girl is happiest in a room full of puppies. **(2)**

4. I don't like the shortness of winter days. **(2)**

5. Playing chess is harder than it looks. **(2)**

6. My parents are constantly driving me to soccer practice. **(2)**

Assessment Tip: Total **12** Points

Name _____

# Possessive Messages

**Possessive Pronouns** A **possessive pronoun** shows ownership. *My,*
*your, his, her, its, our,* and *their* appear before nouns that are subjects.
*Mine, yours, his, hers, its, ours,* and *theirs* stand alone and replace nouns in
sentences.

| Possessives Used with Nouns | | Possessives That Stand Alone | |
|---|---|---|---|
| **my** | This is **my** cup. | **mine** | This cup is **mine.** |
| **your** | **Your** cup is blue. | **yours** | **Yours** is blue. |
| **his** | **His** jacket is torn. | **his** | The torn jacket is **his.** |
| **her** | **Her** dress is new. | **hers** | **Hers** is the new dress. |
| **its** | **Its** food is in the trough. | **its** | The food in the trough is **its.** |
| **our** | Please visit **our** farm. | **ours** | The farm is **ours.** |
| **their** | We walk by **their** fields. | **theirs** | Those fields are **theirs.** |

**Underline the pronoun in parentheses that correctly completes
each sentence.**

1. (Their/Theirs) favorite place is the meadow. **(1 point)**
2. (My/Mine) is the apple orchard. **(1)**
3. (Our/Ours) is the orchard on Harrow Road. **(1)**
4. What is (your/yours) favorite place? **(1)**
5. Molly's favorite place is (her/hers) room. **(1)**
6. The books are (theirs/their). **(1)**
7. The yellow one is (my/mine). **(1)**
8. (Our/Ours) favorite place is nearby. **(1)**
9. (Her/Hers) is nearby too. **(1)**
10. Where is (your/yours)? **(1)**

Name _____

# Contraction Reactions

**Contractions with Pronouns** A **contraction** is a shortened form of two words. You can combine pronouns with the verbs *am, is, are, will, would, have, has,* and *had* to form **contractions**. Use an apostrophe in place of the dropped letter or letters.

| Contractions with Pronouns | | | |
|---|---|---|---|
| I am | I'm | I have | I've |
| he is | he's | he has | he's |
| it is | it's | it has | it's |
| you are | you're | you have | you've |
| they are | they're | they have | they've |
| I will | I'll | I had | I'd |
| you will | you'll | you had | you'd |
| we would | we'd | we had | we'd |

**Rewrite each sentence below, replacing the pronoun and verb with a contraction.**

1. It is fun to read about early settlers.

   It's fun to read about early settlers. **(1 point)**

2. I have read two books about pioneer life.

   I've read two books about pioneer life. **(1)**

3. You would like this story about settlers in Oklahoma.

   You'd like this story about settlers in Oklahoma. **(1)**

4. We will visit my grandfather in Oklahoma next summer.

   We'll visit my grandfather in Oklahoma next summer. **(1)**

5. He has lived there all his life.

   He's lived there all his life. **(1)**

Assessment Tip: Total **5** Points

Name _____

# It's a Great Invention!

**Using *Its* and *It's*** A good writer is careful not to confuse the possessive pronoun *its* with the contraction *it's*.

> The cat licked **its** paws.  **possessive**
> **It's** time for the cat's dinner.  **contraction**

**Jon wrote this page in his journal. Proofread the copy below and correct the places he has confused the possessive pronoun *its* with the contraction *it's*. Write the correction above each error.**

It's                                its

~~Its~~ hard to imagine living long ago.  Life must have had ~~it's~~ good

points, but it's hard not to think about what the pioneers didn't have.  I

                                       It's

don't know what I would do without a computer.  ~~Its~~ a modern invention

that connects me to the world.  The people on the prairie could never

          its

imagine ~~it's~~ usefulness.

It's                                       it's

~~Its~~ great for doing research.  All I have to do is make sure ~~its~~

                    its

plugged in and turn on ~~it's~~ monitor.  Then I can find out what pioneer

            It's                               it's

life was like.  ~~Its~~ not quite the same as living back then, but ~~its~~ the best I

            It's

can do.  ~~Its~~ a resource pioneers didn't have.  In fact, it's a resource even

my parents didn't have.

Name _____

# Writing a Problem-Solution Composition

A **problem-solution composition** outlines a problem and then gives details about the steps leading to its solution.

**Prepare to write a problem-solution composition. First, choose one of the topics listed below, or write about how you solved a problem of your own. Then fill in the chart, identifying the problem you will write about, the solution to the problem, details about the steps that led to the solution, and the outcome. The topics are how prairie settlers got water, how they got household supplies, and how they made a holiday festive when money and goods were scarce.**

| |
|---|
| **Problem**<br>**(2 points)** |
| **Solution**<br>**(2)** |
| **Steps toward the solution**<br>**(2)** |
| **Outcome**<br>**(2)** |

**On a separate sheet of paper, write a two- to three-paragraph problem-solution composition. Begin with an introductory sentence. Then state the problem in the first paragraph. In the following paragraphs, describe the solution to the problem and give details about it. Finally, end with a strong concluding sentence. (4)**

306    Theme 5: **One Land, Many Trails**
Assessment Tip: Total **12** Points

Name _____

# Combining Sentences

Good writers streamline their writing by combining short, choppy
sentences that have repeated pronouns or nouns into one sentence.

> The prairie **fire** raged all night long. **It** scorched the shortgrass.
> **It** burned down barns and homes. **It** injured some horses.
>
> Raging all night long, the prairie fire scorched the shortgrass,
> burned down barns and homes, and injured some horses.

**Read this friendly letter from Grace McCance. Then revise the body
of the letter by combining short, choppy sentences that have
repeated pronouns or nouns into one sentence. Write the revised
letter on the lines.** Responses may vary slightly.

> Dear Dora,
>
> How are you? I am still getting used to prairie life. We live in a
> one-room house made of "Nebraska marble." Poppie made the house
> himself. He cut blocks of tough prairie earth. He stacked the blocks to
> construct the walls. He also used a layer of sod for the roof. Our soddy is
> dark. It is warm in the winter. It is cool in the summer. It is definitely
> not waterproof, however! Yesterday in a rainstorm, rain leaked right
> through the roof. Sometimes I really miss Missouri. Write soon!
>
> Your friend,
> Grace

_____How are you? I am still getting used to prairie life. We live in a one-room house

made of "Nebraska marble." Poppie made the house himself by cutting blocks of

tough prairie earth, stacking the blocks to construct the walls, and using a layer of

sod for the roof. Our dark soddy is warm in the winter and cool in the summer, but

it is definitely not waterproof! Yesterday in a rainstorm, rain leaked right through

the roof. Sometimes I really miss Missouri. Write soon!

Name _____

# Tracking Wild Horses

**Read the labels below. Write each word from the box under the label that fits it.**

### Vocabulary

| mares | milled | herd |
| skittered | mustang | remorse |
| stallion | bluff | ravine |

## Kinds of Horses

mustang **(1 point)**     stallion **(1)**     mares **(1)**

## Landforms

ravine **(1)**     bluff **(1)**

## Actions of Horses

milled **(1)**     skittered **(1)**

## Feelings

remorse **(1)**

## Groups of Animals

herd **(1)**

**Use at least three words from the box to write directions for rounding up wild horses.**

Answers will vary. **(3)** _____

_____

_____

Name _____

# Judgments Chart
Sample answers shown.

| | Facts from the Selection | Own Values and Experience | Judgment |
|---|---|---|---|
| What kind of person is Bob Lemmons? | He treats his horse very kindly. **(1 point)** | People should be kind to animals. **(1)** | Bob Lemmons does the right thing by treating his horse kindly. **(1)** |
| What are some of his character traits? | He waits out a rainstorm on the plains. **(1)** | It is uncomfortable to stand outside in a rainstorm. **(1)** | Bob is a physically tough person who is also very patient. **(1)** |
| What are some more of his character traits? | He spends a whole day standing still and moving slowly to make the herd accept him. **(1)** | It is very hard to stand still for a long time. **(1)** | Bob is patient and has great self-control. **(1)** |
| What are some of Bob's values? | He lets the rattlesnake live. He says everything in nature has the right to protect itself. **(1)** | Most people who allow creatures to live that can be troublesome have great respect for nature. **(1)** | Bob has great respect for nature. **(1)** |
| What kind of person is Bob Lemmons? | He doesn't spend any time with the other cowboys. He rides off with his horse and talks to it. **(1)** | People who do not visit with the people they work with may not enjoy the company of other people. **(1)** | He is a loner. He prefers the companionship of his horse to that of people. **(1)** |

Name _____

# What's So Important About . . . ?

**Tell why each item listed was important in the story of how Bob Lemmons brought in the herd of wild mustangs.** Sample answers shown.

1. **tracks in the dirt** Bob read these, realized that a herd of mustangs was in the area, and figured out which way they were moving. **(2)**

2. **the lightning** It enabled Bob to see the herd of mustangs across the plains. **(2)**

3. **the rainstorm** It washed away the smells of civilization from Bob's clothing. **(2)**

4. **the river** Bob knew the wild horses would go there to drink, so he he waited nearby. Then, when they came to drink, he acted in a way that would make them comfortable with him. **(2)**

5. **the rattlesnake** It bit a colt and the colt died. In the confusion that followed, Bob moved to take over the herd. **(2)**

6. **the battle of the stallions** Bob guided Warrior to attack the stallion that was the leader of the herd of mustangs. Warrior defeated the stallion, enabling Bob to take control of the herd. **(2)**

7. **the corral** Bob led the mustangs back to the corral. When they reached the gate, Bob turned Warrior aside while the mustangs ran in. **(2)**

Assessment Tip: Total **14** Points

Name _____

# You Be the Judge

**Read the following passage. Then answer the questions on page 312.**

### Bill Pickett: Master Cowboy

One of the greatest cowboys who ever lived was an African American man named Bill Pickett. He was born in 1870 in west Texas, where he learned to rope and ride early in life. As a young man he worked as a ranch hand and then became a trick rider and rodeo star. He later joined Zack Miller's 101 Ranch Wild West Show—a touring cowboy act—and became the star performer. Miller called him "the greatest sweat and dirt cowhand that ever lived, bar none."

Pickett is credited with inventing the rodeo sport known as bulldogging, also known as steer wrestling. Legend has it that Pickett was herding cattle in 1903, when an ornery steer started tearing around the pasture, scattering the other cattle. Losing his patience, Pickett raced after the steer on his horse, leaped onto its back, and wrestled it to the ground. He later perfected this technique and made bulldogging a regular part of his rodeo act.

One of the most famous incidents involving Pickett occurred in New York's Madison Square Garden. There, Pickett was bulldogging with a young assistant, Will Rogers, who later became a show business star himself. Suddenly, a steer bolted out of the ring and charged into the grandstand. The terrified spectators panicked, but Pickett and Rogers stayed calm. They jumped into the stands and wrestled the giant steer back down to the ring. They not only saved lives that day but also put on a great show!

Name _____

# You Be the Judge continued

**Answer these questions about the passage on page 311.**

1. What judgment about Bill Pickett does the author make in
   the first paragraph?
   that he was one of the greatest cowboys who ever lived **(1 point)**

2. Do you agree with this judgment? Why or why not?
   Answers will vary. **(1)**
   _____

3. In the rodeo bull wrestling is done purely for sport. Do you think
   this is right? Give reasons for your judgment.
   Answers will vary. **(2)**
   _____

4. Circle each trait below that you think Bill Pickett possessed. Next to
   each trait you circle, tell why that trait applies to him.
   Sample answers shown.

| Traits | Reasons |
|--------|---------|
| (brave) | He did the dangerous work of a cowboy. **(2)** |
| kind | |
| (tough) | He wrestled steers for sport. **(2)** |
| (ambitious) | He went from being a cowhand in west Texas to being a rodeo star. **(2)** |

Name _____

# Saddle Up Those Syllables!

**Read each sentence. On the line below the sentence, divide the underlined word into syllables, using slashes between the syllables. Then write another sentence using the word. The first one is done for you.** Sample sentences shown.

> **Example:** Bob awoke as soon as the sun came over the <u>horizon</u>.
> ho/ri/zon  On the ocean, nothing blocks a view of the horizon.

1. At daybreak, Bob was <u>immediately</u> awake and ready to ride.
   im/me/di/ate/ly **(1 point)** My dog sits immediately after I give her
   the command. **(2)**

2. Bob Lemmons held his <u>shoulders</u> high as he rode Warrior.
   shoul/ders **(1)** The woman's shoulders ached after an hour of
   shoveling snow. **(2)**

3. A <u>rattlesnake</u> doesn't always give a warning before it strikes.
   rat/tle/snake **(1)** I once read about a rattlesnake with twelve rattles.
   **(2)**

4. Warrior neighed <u>triumphantly</u> after challenging the stallion.
   tri/um/phant/ly **(1)** The winning swimmer waved triumphantly as
   he accepted his medal. **(2)**

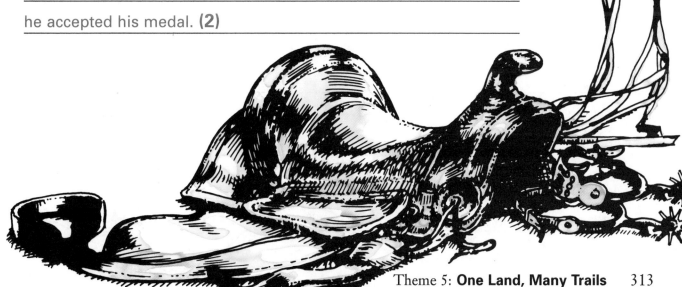

Name _____

# Final /n/ or /ən/, /chər/, /zhər/

Each of these words has the final /n/, /ən/, /chər/, or /zhər/ sounds. When you hear these final sounds, think of these patterns:

/n/ or /ən/ *ain* (capt**ain**)     /chər/ *ture* (cul**ture**)

/zhər/ *sure* (trea**sure**)

► The /ən/ sound in the starred words *surgeon* and *luncheon* is spelled *eon* and does not follow the usual spelling pattern.

**Write each Spelling Word under its final sound.**
Order of answers for each category may vary.

### Final /n/ or /ən/ Sound

mountain **(1 point)**     surgeon **(1)**

fountain **(1)**     curtain **(1)**

captain **(1)**     luncheon **(1)**

### Final /chər/ Sound

culture **(1)**     pasture **(1)**

creature **(1)**     vulture **(1)**

future **(1)**     feature **(1)**

adventure **(1)**     furniture **(1)**

moisture **(1)**     mixture **(1)**

lecture **(1)**

### Final /zhər/ Sound

treasure **(1)**     pleasure **(1)**

measure **(1)**

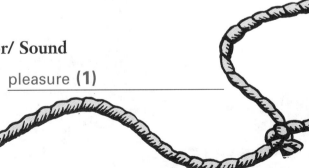

Assessment Tip: Total **20** Points

Name _____

# Spelling Spree

**Word Root Hunt** Write the Spelling Word that has the same root as each word below.

1. pleasing

2. collect

3. furnish

4. capital

5. cultivate

6. surgery

7. pastoral

1. pleasure **(1 point)**

2. lecture **(1)**

3. furniture **(1)**

4. captain **(1)**

5. culture **(1)**

6. surgeon **(1)**

7. pasture **(1)**

**Ending Match** Write Spelling Words by matching word parts and endings. Be sure to write each ending correctly.

&lt;a&gt; /n/ *or* /ən/    &lt;b&gt; /chər/    &lt;c&gt; /zhər/

8.  vul&lt;b&gt;

9.  fu&lt;b&gt;

10. trea&lt;c&gt;

11. curt&lt;a&gt;

12. mix&lt;b&gt;

13. mea&lt;c&gt;

14. lunch&lt;a&gt;

15. fount&lt;a&gt;

8. vulture **(1)**

9. future **(1)**

10. treasure **(1)**

11. curtain **(1)**

12. mixture **(1)**

13. measure **(1)**

14. luncheon **(1)**

15. fountain **(1)**

**Spelling Words**

1. mountain
2. treasure
3. culture
4. fountain
5. creature
6. captain
7. future
8. adventure
9. moisture
10. surgeon*
11. lecture
12. curtain
13. pasture
14. measure
15. vulture
16. feature
17. furniture
18. pleasure
19. mixture
20. luncheon*

Name _____

# Proofreading and Writing

**Proofreading** Circle the five misspelled Spelling Words in this travelogue. Then write each word correctly.

The corral sits at the foot of a rise—more than a hill, but not quite a (mountin.) The land doesn't get much (moisure,) and every living (creacher) is always on the lookout for its survival. It is here that Bob Lemmons lives and works. I had the pleasure of meeting Mr. Lemmons shortly after he had captured a herd of mustangs. He has a special way of getting his work done. The most remarkable (featur) of his method is that he gets the horses to accept him as one of them, rather than as a human being. It seemed like quite an (adveture) to me, but to Mr. Lemmons it was all in a day's work.

1. mountain
2. treasure
3. culture
4. fountain
5. creature
6. captain
7. future
8. adventure
9. moisture
10. surgeon*
11. lecture
12. curtain
13. pasture
14. measure
15. vulture
16. feature
17. furniture
18. pleasure
19. mixture
20. luncheon*

1. mountain **(1 point)**    4. feature **(1)**

2. moisture **(1)**    5. adventure **(1)**

3. creature **(1)**

✎ **Write a Character Sketch** Bob Lemmons was an unusual person who had a very special way of capturing wild mustangs. How would you describe his work? What was his relationship with Warrior like? What were his most outstanding qualities?

**On a separate piece of paper, write a character sketch about Bob Lemmons. Use Spelling Words from the list.** Responses will vary. **(5)**

316    Theme 5: **One Land, Many Trails**
Assessment Tip: Total **10** Points

Name _____

# Using Parts of Speech

**Read the dictionary entries. For each entry word, write two sentences, using the word as a different part of speech in each sentence.** Sample answers shown.

**clear** (klîr) *adj.* Free from clouds, mist, or haze. *v.* To make free of objects or obstructions.

**close** (klōs) *adj.* Near in space or time. *v.* (klōz) To move so that an opening or a passage is blocked; shut.

**faint** (fānt) *adj.* Lacking brightness or clarity; dim; indistinct. *v.* To lose consciousness for a short time.

**print** (prĭnt) *n.* A mark or an impression made in or on a surface by pressure. *v.* To write in block letters.

1. The sky was clear when the plane took off. **(2 points)**

   My chore is to clear the table after dinner. **(2)**

   _____

2. The farmhouse was close to the road. **(2)**

   Close the door on your way out! **(2)**

   _____

3. The man heard a faint call from the other side of the campground. **(2)**

   If you faint at the sight of blood, you shouldn't become a doctor. **(2)**

   _____

4. We knew deer had been in our yard because we saw their prints in the snow. **(2)**

   Please print your name clearly at the top of the page. **(2)**

   _____

Name _____

# Double Trouble

**Double Subjects**  Do not use a double subject, a noun and a pronoun, to name the same person, place, or thing. Use either the noun or the pronoun as the subject, but not both.

| | |
|---|---|
| **Incorrect:** | Lenny he is my brother. |
| **Correct:** | Lenny is my brother. |
| **Correct:** | He is my brother. |

**Each sentence below has a double subject.  Cross out one unneeded subject, and write your new sentence on the line.**

Answers will vary.

1. My aunt and uncle ~~they~~ have a cattle ranch.

   My aunt and uncle have a cattle ranch. **(1 point)**

2. My aunt ~~she~~ runs the business end of things.

   My aunt runs the business end of things. **(1)**

3. ~~The ranch~~ it is big.

   It is big. **(1)**

4. The animals ~~they~~ are taken care of by my uncle.

   The animals are taken care of by my uncle. **(1)**

5. Kurt ~~he~~ is my cousin.

   Kurt is my cousin. **(1)**

6. ~~The horse~~ she trusts Kurt.

   She trusts Kurt. **(1)**

7. Uncle Henry ~~he~~ trains horses.

   Uncle Henry trains horses. **(1)**

8. The stable ~~it~~ is home to six horses.

   The stable is home to six horses. **(1)**

Assessment Tip: Total **8** Points

Name _____

# We or Us?

**Using *We* and *Us* with Nouns** Sometimes a writer may need to use a pronoun before a noun to make clear who is being talked about. Use *we* with a noun subject or after a linking verb. Use *us* with a noun object, a noun that follows an action verb, or after words like *to, for, with, at,* or *in*.

> **subject: We boys** are going to pitch hay.
>
> **object:** The cows will be herded by **us girls.**

**Write either *we* or *us* in each blank to correctly complete each sentence.**

1. The ranch hands showed __us (1)__ kids how to rope a calf.

2. The best riders were __we (1)__ girls.

3. __We (1)__ cooks made big meals for the ranch hands.

4. It's a great outdoor life for __us (1)__ cowboys.

5. __We (1)__ boys went to the rodeo on Friday.

6. The owners held a square dance for __us (1)__ visitors.

7. __We (1)__ fiddlers need to tune up.

8. The caller shook hands with __us (1)__ greenhorns.

9. __We (1)__ dancers whirled and twirled.

10. Saying good-night was hard for __us (1)__ guests.

Name _____

# Who Is He?

**Writing Clearly with Pronouns** A good writer makes clear to whom each pronoun refers.

> **Unclear:** After Mel turned hard on the key in the lock, it broke.
>
> **What broke—the key or the lock?**
>
> **Clear:** After Mel turned hard on the key in the lock, the lock broke.
>
> **Clear:** After Mel turned hard on the key in the lock, the key broke.

**Shirley wrote the following messages to her friends. Rewrite each sentence with unclear pronoun references to make the references clear.**

1. Phil and Bill visited Philadelphia and Pittsburgh. He thinks it has an interesting history.

   Phil (or Bill) thinks Philadelphia (or Pittsburgh) has an interesting

   history. **(2 points)**

2. Julie and Karen joined us in Mississippi. She is my cousin, but I'd never met her before.

   Karen (or Julie) is my cousin, but I'd never met Julie (or Karen)

   before. **(2)**

3. This morning, I fixed breakfast. Then I saw a skunk! The skunk turned around, and I was able to eat it.

   The skunk turned around, and I was able to eat breakfast. **(2)**

   _____

Assessment Tip: Total **6** Points

Name _____

# Writing an Explanation

*Black Cowboy Wild Horses* explains who Bob Lemmons was and how he tracked animals. The purpose of an explanation is to explain one of the following:

► who or what something is
► what is or was important about something or someone
► how something works or worked
► the steps of a process
► why something happens or happened

**Prepare to write several paragraphs explaining how Bob Lemmons was able to capture an entire herd of wild horses by himself. To plan and organize your explanation, use the graphic organizer below. First, write the topic in the center box. Then list the steps Lemmons took and details about the process he used. If necessary, look back at the selection to recall how one step led to another.**

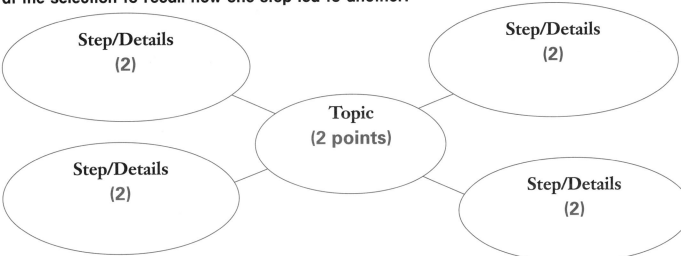

Step/Details (2)

Step/Details (2)

Topic (2 points)

Step/Details (2)

Step/Details (2)

**On a separate sheet of paper, write a two- to three-paragraph explanation, using the information you recorded. In the first sentence or paragraph, clearly state the topic. Then present the steps in a logical order, providing enough steps and clarifying details to help readers understand how this event happened. Be sure to define any special or technical terms the first time you use them. Finally, end with a conclusion. (5)**

Name _____

# Organizing Information

A good writer organizes ideas in a logical way so that readers understand his or her writing. You can organize ideas in your own writing by sequence of events, by causes and effects, or by main ideas and details.

**This explanation by an animal tracker like Bob Lemmons has been scrambled. Put the sentences in an order that makes sense. Then rewrite the explanation on the lines.**

### How to "Read" Animal Tracks

One way to locate an animal is by finding and studying its tracks. Once you identify what animal left a particular track, you can determine how long ago it passed by. To find tracks, try starting near water. A fresh, soft, sharply outlined track means an animal was recently in the area, but a hard, dry, less clearly defined track indicates that time has passed since the animal was there. After you've discovered a set of tracks, you can study their shape and size to figure out what kind of animal made them. Animals often leave tracks on the muddy banks of streams and ponds where they come to drink or hunt food.

One way to locate an animal is by finding and studying its tracks. To find tracks, try starting near water. Animals often leave tracks on the muddy banks of streams and ponds where they come to drink or hunt food. After you've discovered a set of tracks, you can study their shape and size to figure out what kind of animal made them. Once you identify what animal left a particular track, you can determine how long ago it passed by. A fresh, soft, sharply outlined track means an animal was recently in the area, but a hard, dry, less clearly defined track indicates that time has passed since the animal was there. **(12 points)**

Assessment Tip: Total **12** Points

Name _____

# Ride Those Riddles

**Write a word from the box to answer each riddle.**

**Vocabulary**

rugged
wounds
sombrero
urgently
notorious
condolences
dictator
transformed

1. Which word names a type of hat?
   sombrero **(1 point)**

2. Which word names injuries?
   wounds **(1)**

3. Which word means "completely changed"?
   transformed **(1)**

4. Which word describes someone who is well known for something bad? notorious **(1)**

5. Which word describes something rough, difficult, or uneven? rugged **(1)**

6. Which word means "expressions of sympathy"?
   condolences **(1)**

7. Which word means "without delay"?
   urgently **(1)**

8. Which word names a kind of ruler?
   dictator **(1)**

Theme 5: **One Land, Many Trails** 323
Assessment Tip: Total **8** Points

Name _____

# Story Map

Sample answers shown.

| **Characters** | |
|---|---|
| **The family:** Elena, Pablo, and their children: Rosa, the narrator, Luis, Esteban, and María **(1)** | **Other Characters:** the villagers, Pancho Villa and his followers, the Chinese fruit seller **(1)** |

| **Setting** | |
|---|---|
| **Where the story takes place:** rural Mexico; Ciudad Juárez; Santa Ana, California **(1)** | **When the story takes place:** in the early 1900s beginning in 1910 **(1)** |

| **Plot** |
|---|

**Problem:** Pablo dies in a riding accident just as the Mexican Revolution is beginning. Elena and the children must leave. **(1)**

**Events:**

1. At first Elena is crazy with grief but then grows quiet. **(1)**

2. One day Pancho Villa and his men arrive in the village, and Elena hides her eldest son and the horses in the kitchen. **(1)**

3. Elena gives Villa the last hat, and he has his men protect the house. **(1)**

4. Elena gathers money, clothing, and food, and takes her children on the train to Ciudad Juárez. **(1)**

5. Elena befriends a Chinese fruit seller who helps her get Esteban across the border. **(1)**

6. The family goes from San Francisco to Los Angeles, before settling in Santa Ana, where Elena runs a boardinghouse. The children also go to school, where they learn to be "real" Americans. **(1)**

**Resolution:** The children learn that their village in Mexico had been burned to the ground and many people had died during the war. **(1)**

Assessment Tip: Total **12** Points

Name _____

# A Portrait of Elena

**Complete the sentences below to show how Elena's feelings and character traits are revealed through her actions.  The first sentence has been completed for you.** Sample answers shown.

| In Mexico, in the family's home village | On the way to the United States | In California |
|---|---|---|
| **Example:** Elena shows her **deep love for her husband** when she strokes his hand and speaks gently to him while he is dying. | In the plaza, just before leaving the village, Elena shows **generosity** when she gives away all the goods from her shop. **(2)** | Elena shows she is **hard-working** when she runs a boarding-house to support her family. **(2)** |
| Elena shows **her grief** when she weeps, knocks down her flowerpots, and lets her pet birds go. **(2 points)** | In Ciudad Juárez, Elena shows **love for her son** Esteban when she figures out a way to get him across the border. **(2)** | Elena shows that she **values education** when she tells the children that school and home-work come first. **(2)** |
| Elena shows **cleverness** when she hides Esteban and the horses in the kitchen. **(2)** | | Elena shows she **wants her children to grow up "strong and full of hope"** when she does not tell them that their village in Mexico had been burned to the ground. **(2)** |
| Elena shows **courage** when she opens the door for Pancho Villa. **(2)** | | |

Name _____

# Mapping the Story

**Read the passage. Then complete the activity on page 327.**

## A Dangerous Journey

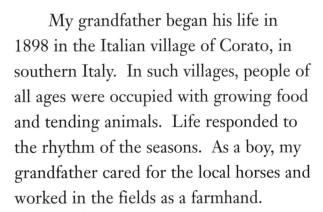

My grandfather began his life in 1898 in the Italian village of Corato, in southern Italy. In such villages, people of all ages were occupied with growing food and tending animals. Life responded to the rhythm of the seasons. As a boy, my grandfather cared for the local horses and worked in the fields as a farmhand.

By the time my grandfather was in his teens, World War I had broken out in Europe. One by one, the countries surrounding Italy entered the war. Italy managed to stay out of the fighting for nearly a year, but it was clearly only a matter of time before Italy, too, would be drawn into the conflict.

A powerful farm boy, my grandfather was a prime candidate for the Italian army. His mother, my great-grandmother, did not want to lose her son to war. She made what must have been one of the most difficult decisions of her life: she decided to send her son far away to America.

At that time, young men were being rounded up and forced to join the Italian army. My grandfather's family faced a daunting task—how to send my grandfather across Italy and onto a boat bound for America without the authorities finding out.

Very early one morning, well before dawn, a horse-drawn cart pulled up to my grandfather's house. The cart was filled with hay. To a casual observer, the cart was simply on its way from one farm to the next to deliver a load of hay. When the cart pulled away from the house, however, my grandfather lay hidden beneath the hay. In one hand he held a bundle that contained all his belongings. In the other, he held bread, fruit, and meat—enough food, his mother hoped, to last for at least part of the long journey that lay ahead.

The cart was bound for Bari, a seaport town on Italy's east coast. There my grandfather's family had arranged for a boat to take him on the first leg of the journey to America.

Name _____

# Mapping the Story  continued

**Answer these questions about the passage on page 326.**

1. What is the setting in which the events described in the passage take place? (Include both the time and place.)

   Italy at the beginning of World War I **(2 points)**

   _____

2. Who are the main characters in the passage?

   the narrator's grandfather and great-grandmother **(2)**

   _____

3. What problem is described in the passage?

   The narrator's grandfather must find a way to escape from Italy

   before he is forced to join the army. **(3)**

   _____

4. What is the solution to this problem?

   His family sneaks him out of the village in a cart full of hay, which

   takes him to Bari, a port town. There a boat will take him to

   America. **(4)**

   _____

5. Use the information above to write a brief summary of the passage.

   The narrator's grandfather was born in an Italian village in 1898.

   When he was a teenager, World War I broke out in Europe.

   Although Italy did not enter the war right away, it was only a

   matter of time before it would become involved. The narrator's

   grandfather's family did not want him to be forced to join the

   Italian army, so they hid him in a hay wagon and arranged for him

   to travel by boat to America. **(4)**

# I Spy the *Y*

**Read the letter from Rosa to a childhood friend in Mexico. Circle words in which a *y* changed to *i* before an ending or suffix was added.  Then, on the lines below the letter, write the base word and the ending or suffix for each circled word.**

**Endings
and Suffixes**

-ed

-er

-es

-est

-ful

Dear Maria,

    I wish you could see California.  It is (beautiful!) I will always love Mexico too, but I like it even better here.  We live in the (loveliest) valley!  And just think—there are no (flies!) We are so much (luckier) than the many (families) who were not able to escape the war in Mexico.  I know Mother (worried) about how she could make a life for us here.  But she has a good job, and we know the future is bright for all of us.

        Love,

        Rosa

(**1 point** for each circled word)

1. beauty **(1 point)** + -ful **(1)**
2. lovely **(1)** + -est **(1)**
3. fly **(1)** + -es **(1)**
4. lucky **(1)** + -er **(1)**
5. family **(1)** + -es **(1)**
6. worry **(1)** + -ed **(1)**

Name _____

# Changing Final *y* to *i*

Each Spelling Word has an ending or a suffix added to a base word. When a word ends with a consonant and *y*, change the *y* to *i* when adding *-es*, *-ed*, *-er*, *-est*, or *-ness*.

army + es = arm**ies**        spy + ed = sp**ied**

dirty + er = dirt**ier**        scary + est = scar**iest**

happy + ness = happ**iness**

**Write each Spelling Word. Underline the letter that replaced the final *y* when the ending or the suffix was added.**

Order of responses may vary.

### Final *y* changed to *i*

| | |
|---|---|
| liber**t**ies **(1 point)** | pit**i**ed **(1)** |
| victor**i**es **(1)** | lad**i**es **(1)** |
| countr**i**es **(1)** | bus**i**er **(1)** |
| sp**i**ed **(1)** | dut**i**es **(1)** |
| enem**i**es **(1)** | lil**i**es **(1)** |
| arm**i**es **(1)** | worth**i**ness **(1)** |
| scar**i**est **(1)** | tin**i**est **(1)** |
| dirt**i**er **(1)** | empt**i**ness **(1)** |
| happ**i**ness **(1)** | repl**i**es **(1)** |
| abilit**i**es **(1)** | dizz**i**ness **(1)** |

**Spelling Words**

1. liberties
2. victories
3. countries
4. spied
5. enemies
6. armies
7. scariest
8. dirtier
9. happiness
10. abilities
11. pitied
12. ladies
13. busier
14. duties
15. lilies
16. worthiness
17. tiniest
18. emptiness
19. replies
20. dizziness

Name _____

# Spelling Spree

**Adding Suffixes** Write a Spelling Word by adding the correct suffix to the word part in each phrase below.

1. a trip through seven countr_____
2. dirt_____ than a pigsty
3. the dut_____ of the president
4. lad_____ and gentlemen
5. the empt_____ of a beach in winter
6. to send repl_____ to letters
7. a beautiful bouquet of lil_____

| | |
|---|---|
| 1. liberties | |
| 2. victories | |
| 3. countries | |
| 4. spied | |
| 5. enemies | |
| 6. armies | |
| 7. scariest | |
| 8. dirtier | |
| 9. happiness | |
| 10. abilities | |
| 11. pitied | |
| 12. ladies | |
| 13. busier | |
| 14. duties | |
| 15. lilies | |
| 16. worthiness | |
| 17. tiniest | |
| 18. emptiness | |
| 19. replies | |
| 20. dizziness | |

1. countries **(1 point)**
2. dirtier **(1)**
3. duties **(1)**
4. ladies **(1)**
5. emptiness **(1)**
6. replies **(1)**
7. lilies **(1)**

**Word Clues** Write a Spelling Word to fit each clue.

8. another word for *freedoms*
9. having more work to do than another
10. watched sneakily
11. felt sorry for
12. a synonym for *joy*
13. the most frightening of all
14. the opposite of *friends*
15. a result of spinning around

8. liberties **(1)**
9. busier **(1)**
10. spied **(1)**
11. pitied **(1)**
12. happiness **(1)**
13. scariest **(1)**
14. enemies **(1)**
15. dizziness **(1)**

**Assessment Tip: Total 15 Points**

# Proofreading and Writing

**Proofreading** **Circle the five misspelled Spelling Words in this newspaper article. Then write each word correctly.**

Guadalajara—The situation in Mexico continues to grow more serious. The government has no control over large areas of the country, and the rebel (armys) are increasing in strength. Each one of their (victaries) brings more support to the revolution. It is feared that by 1911 Mexico will be in even worse shape.

    The rebels are hoping that the leaders of foreign countries will see the (worthyness) of their cause and send aid. Even the (tieniest) amount, they say, would be a great help. In the meantime, the Mexican people continue to suffer, while caring for their families to the best of their (ablities.)

**Spelling Words**

1. liberties
2. victories
3. countries
4. spied
5. enemies
6. armies
7. scariest
8. dirtier
9. happiness
10. abilities
11. pitied
12. ladies
13. busier
14. duties
15. lilies
16. worthiness
17. tiniest
18. emptiness
19. replies
20. dizziness

1. armies **(1 point)**
2. victories **(1)**
3. worthiness **(1)**
4. tiniest **(1)**
5. abilities **(1)**

✎ **Write a Screenplay** Suppose that *Elena* was being made into a movie. Think about the scene between Elena and Pablo just before Pablo dies. What do the characters say to each other during this scene? Are they sitting or standing while they talk? What tone of voice do they use? Do they look at each other while speaking?

**On a separate piece of paper, write a screenplay for the scene between Elena and Pablo. Be sure to indicate when each new speaker begins. Use Spelling Words from the list.** Responses will vary. **(5)**

Name _____

# Using Word Histories

**Read the dictionary entries. Then read the sentences. For each underlined word, write the word origin and its meaning. Then use the clues to think of other common English words that have the same origin.**

**conquer** 1. To defeat or subdue by force. 2. To gain control by overcoming difficulties. [Latin *com-*, intensive prefix + *quaerere*, to seek.]

**expect** To look forward to the probable occurrence or appearance of. [Latin *ex-*, off, away + *spectāre*, to look at.]

**memory** 1. The power or ability of remembering past experiences. 2. Something remembered. [Latin *memoria*, memory.]

1. Rosa had only a faint <u>memory</u> of her father.

   Word root: _memoria **(1 point)**_

   Meaning: _memory **(1)**_

   a monument or holiday that serves as a remembrance of a person or event _memorial **(1)**_

   to commit to memory; learn by heart _memorize **(1)**_

2. Elena did not <u>expect</u> that Pancho Villa would ask for a sombrero.

   Word root: _spectāre **(1)**_

   Meaning: _to look at **(1)**_

   an observer of an event _spectator **(1)**_

   a pair of eyeglasses _spectacles **(1)**_

3. Elena had <u>conquered</u> mathematics and valued education.

   Word root: _quaerere **(1)**_

   Meaning: _to seek **(1)**_

   to request information by asking questions _inquire **(1)**_

   to get; gain; obtain _acquire **(1)**_

Assessment Tip: Total **12** Points

Name _____

# How? When? Where?

**Adverbs**  An adverb tells *how*, *when*, or *where*.  Adverbs can describe verbs.  Many adverbs end in *-ly*.

| How | When | Where |
|-----|------|-------|
| fast | tomorrow | here |
| hard | later | inside |
| happily | again | north |
| quietly | first | forward |
| slowly | then | upstairs |

**Underline the adverb in each sentence below.  Then on the line write *how*, *when*, or *where* to show what the adverb tells.**

1. Elena and her family quickly left their home. <u>how **(1 point)**</u>

2. They left early in the morning. <u>when **(1)**</u>

3. The family traveled north. <u>where **(1)**</u>

4. Everyone worked hard. <u>how **(1)**</u>

5. The children greatly admired their mother. <u>how **(1)**</u>

6. Did you suddenly leave? <u>when **(1)**</u>

7. I stepped carefully over the ice. <u>how **(1)**</u>

8. She went inside. <u>where **(1)**</u>

9. Look closely at this picture. <u>how **(1)**</u>

10. Do you see now? <u>when **(1)**</u>

Theme 5: **One Land, Many Trails**   333
Assessment Tip: Total **10** Points

**Elena**

**Grammar Skill** Comparing with Adverbs

Name _____

# Prepare to Compare

**Comparing with Adverbs**  To compare two actions, add *-er* to most one-syllable adverbs; use *more* with adverbs of two or more syllables.  To compare three or more actions, add *-est* to most one-syllable adverbs; use *most* with adverbs of two or more syllables.

My little sister runs **fast**.          The weather here changes **quickly**.

My brother runs **faster** than her.    It changes **more quickly** at the shore.

My big sister runs **fastest** of all.   It changes **most quickly** in the mountains.

**Write the correct form of the adverb to complete each sentence.**

1. My alarm clock rings early.

2. My dad's alarm rings __earlier **(1 point)**__ than mine.

3. My brother's alarm rings __earliest **(1)**__ of all.

4. The retriever barks excitedly.

5. Our German shepherd barks __more excitedly **(1)**__.

6. Of all the dogs, however, the chihuahua barks
   __most excitedly **(1)**__.

7. Kim studies hard every evening.

8. Juan studies __harder **(1)**__ than Kim.

9. Sonya studies __hardest **(1)**__ of all.

10. Jim scored high on the test.

11. His brother scored __higher **(1)**__ than Jim.

12. Of everyone in the class, Celia scored
    the __highest **(1)**__.

13. I was exhausted.

14. Mom was __more exhausted **(1)**__ than me.

15. Dad was the __most exhausted **(1)**__ of all.

Assessment Tip: Total **10** Points

# Expand Your Description

**Expanding Sentences with Adverbs** A good writer expands sentences with adverbs to describe action more clearly.

Camille bakes bread.     Camille **cheerfully** bakes bread.

**Anna wants her pen-pal in Mexico to imagine what life is like in her house, but she has not used any adverbs. On a separate sheet of paper rewrite her letter, adding adverbs from the list above or those of your own choosing.**

slightly
suddenly
excitedly
noisily
happily
loudly
gracefully
still
carefully
peacefully
immediately
heartily

Hi Pen-pal!
    My family's dinner last night was unusual. We celebrated my good report card with a special dinner. Here is what happened:  We all pulled out our chairs.  My brother Todd remembered that the cat Clive was outside.  Todd jumped up, and his chair fell to the floor.  Everyone laughed. Mom carved the roast.  Without warning, Clive lept into the middle of the table.  Todd decided to put him back outside. We ate the rest of our dinner.

                    Your friend,
                    Anna

Sample answer: My family's dinner last night was <u>slightly</u> unusual. We <u>happily</u> celebrated my good report card with a special dinner. Here is what happened: We all <u>noisily</u> pulled out our chairs. My brother Todd <u>suddenly</u> remembered that the cat Clive was <u>still</u> outside. Todd jumped up <u>excitedly</u>, and his chair fell <u>loudly</u> to the floor. Everyone laughed <u>heartily</u>. Mom <u>carefully</u> carved the roast. Without warning, Clive <u>gracefully</u> lept into the middle of the table. Todd <u>immediately</u> decided to put him back outside. We <u>peacefully</u> ate the rest of our dinner.

Name _____

# Writing a Compare/ Contrast Paragraph

In *Elena*, you read about how the lives of Elena and her children changed as a result of the Mexican Revolution in the early 1900s. One way to explore how things are alike and different is by writing a **compare/contrast paragraph.** Comparing shows how things are alike, and contrasting shows how they are different. A good compare/contrast paragraph describes both the ways things are alike and the ways they are different.

**Use this Venn diagram to help you gather details about Elena's family's life in Mexico and about their life later in the United States.**

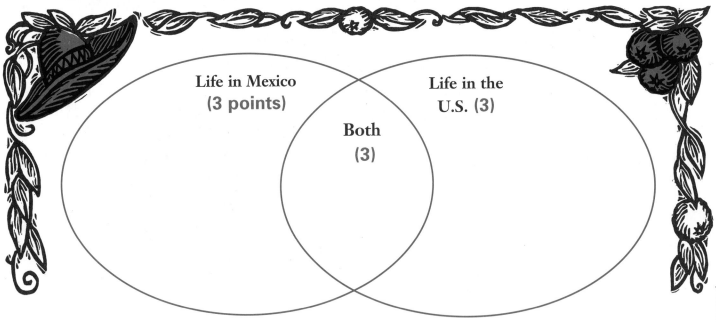

Life in Mexico
(3 points)

Life in the
U.S. (3)

Both
(3)

**On a separate sheet of paper, write a paragraph in which you use details from your Venn diagram to compare and contrast Elena's family's life in rural Mexico with their life in Santa Ana, California. In the opening sentence, clearly state the subject being compared and contrasted. In the supporting sentences, group details that compare and details that contrast in a clear manner. (6)**

Assessment Tip: Total **15** Points

Name _____

# Using Exact Adverbs

**Adverbs** such as *suddenly* and *wildly* clarify and enhance verbs or adjectives. A good writer uses exact adverbs to help sharpen the differences and similarities between things and to make details more vivid.

**Read the following advertisement for Pablo's sombreros. Then replace the inexact adverbs that have been underlined with more exact adverbs from the list. Write your revised ad on the lines. (2 points each)**

**Adverbs**
richly
drably
supremely
handsomely
exceptionally
exquisitely

Why dress <u>plainly</u> when you can dress <u>well</u> instead? Buy a <u>very</u> well-made sombrero by Pablo. Unlike other hat makers, Pablo fashions his famous hats with velvety soft, smooth felt and then trims them <u>nicely</u> with gleaming silver. From the shaped crown to the detailed brim, Pablo's hats are <u>certainly</u> crafted. Pancho Villa says, "I'd never wear another. Pablo's sombreros are the finest in all of Mexico." You will be <u>very</u> happy wearing a one-of-a-kind sombrero by Pablo!

Why dress **drably** when you can dress **handsomely** instead? Buy an

**exceptionally** well-made sombrero by Pablo. Unlike other hat makers,

Pablo fashions his famous hats with velvety soft, smooth felt and then

trims them **richly** with gleaming silver. From the shaped crown to the

detailed brim, Pablo's hats are **exquisitely** crafted. Pancho Villa says, "I'd

never wear another. Pablo's sombreros are the finest in all of Mexico." You

will be **supremely** happy wearing a one-of-a-kind sombrero by Pablo!

Name _____

# Writing an Answer to a Question

Use what you have learned about taking tests to help you write answers to questions about something you have read. This practice will help you when you take this kind of test.

**Read these paragraphs from the story *A Boy Called Slow*.**

> As Slow grew up, he was not happy with his name. Few boys were given names they wanted to keep. No one wanted to be known as "Hungry Mouth" or "Curly" or "Runny Nose" or "Slow" all of his life. But until a child earned a new name by having a powerful dream or by doing some brave or special deed, it could not be changed.
>
> Slow wished for this vision of bravery to come to him. He wished for a vision that would allow him to prove himself to his people.

**Now write your answer to each question.**

1. What kind of names were given to boys? How were these names different from the names they might get later? *(drawing conclusions)*

   Sample answer: Names like Slow and Hungry Mouth were given to them. These
   
   names weren't ones they earned, but ones they would be called until they did
   
   something to earn a different name. **(5 points)**

   _____

   _____

   _____

   _____

Name ______________________

# Writing an Answer to a Question continued

2. Why didn't Slow like his name? *(drawing conclusions)*

Sample answer: Slow was not a name that made him feel proud. This name did not allow Slow to prove anything to his people about what he could do. **(5)**

3. What are three ways that Slow could get his name changed? *(noting details)*

Sample answer: Slow could get his name changed by having a powerful dream or vision, by doing a brave deed, or by doing a special deed. **(5)**




Assessment Tip: Total **15** Points

Name _____

# Spelling Review

**Write Spelling Words from the list on this page to answer
the questions.** Order of answers in each category may vary.

1–8. Which eight words have the prefix *un-*, *dis-*, *in-*, or *re-*, or
the suffix *-ion*?

1. promotion **(1 point)**

2. unable **(1)**

3. tension **(1)**

4. discover **(1)**

5. react **(1)**

6. inspect **(1)**

7. correction **(1)**

8. respond **(1)**

9–15. Which seven words have the final /n/, /ən/, /chər/, or
/zhər/ sounds?

9. treasure **(1)**

10. vulture **(1)**

11. curtain **(1)**

12. furniture **(1)**

13. mountain **(1)**

14. pleasure **(1)**

15. adventure **(1)**

16–22. In which seven words was the final *y* changed to *i* before
an ending was added?

16. pitied **(1)**

17. countries **(1)**

18. spied **(1)**

19. happiness **(1)**

20. dirtier **(1)**

21. scariest **(1)**

22. busier **(1)**

23–30. Which nine words are partly spelled below? Write each
word. Then draw a line to divide each word into
syllables.

23. sol— sol | id **(2)**

24. —age voy | age **(2)**

25. spin— spin | ach **(2)**

26. no— no | tice **(2)**

27. —tance dis | tance **(2)**

28. de— de | stroy **(2)**

29. lan— lan | guage **(2)**

30. —tive na | tive **(2)**

**Spelling Words**

1. adventure
2. treasure
3. solid
4. promotion
5. vulture
6. busier
7. voyage
8. unable
9. spinach
10. tension
11. curtain
12. pitied
13. furniture
14. notice
15. discover
16. react
17. mountain
18. countries
19. pleasure
20. spied
21. happiness
22. inspect
23. distance
24. correction
25. destroy
26. dirtier
27. language
28. native
29. respond
30. scariest

Assessment Tip: Total **38** Points

Name _____

# Spelling Spree

**Sentence Fillers  Write the Spelling Word that best completes each sentence.**

1. A person born in France is a _native_ **(1 point)** of France.

2. People in France speak the French _language_ **(1)**.

3. You might see snow on a _mountain_ **(1)** peak.

4. Eating _spinach_ **(1)** will give you strong bones.

5. A cruise is a long sea _voyage_ **(1)**.

6. Lower the _curtain_ **(1)** when the play is over.

7. A pirate buried his _treasure_ **(1)** in the sand.

8. Mom's _promotion_ **(1)** at work makes her a manager.

9. We did not mean to _destroy_ **(1)** your flowers.

10. There was great _tension_ **(1)** between the two rivals.

**Spelling Words**

1. language
2. mountain
3. spinach
4. voyage
5. curtain
6. treasure
7. native
8. furniture
9. discover
10. promotion
11. destroy
12. tension
13. dirtier
14. happiness
15. pleasure

**Word Hunt  Each word below is hidden in a Spelling Word. Write the Spelling Word.**

11. cove _discover_ **(1)**

12. dirt _dirtier_ **(1)**

13. pine _happiness_ **(1)**

14. plea _pleasure_ **(1)**

15. urn _furniture_ **(1)**

Name _____

# Proofreading and Writing

**Proofreading** Circle the six misspelled Spelling Words in this letter. Then write each word correctly.

> Our new neighbors just moved here from Mexico. Traveling such a long (distence) must be an (aventure.) They have two (countrys) to call home! I was (unabel) to meet their son until school started. We were editing a (notise) about tryouts for the school play, and we both started to make the same (correcshun.)

1. distance **(1 point)**
2. adventure **(1)**
3. countries **(1)**
4. unable **(1)**
5. notice **(1)**
6. correction **(1)**

**Spelling Words**

1. distance
2. scariest
3. adventure
4. countries
5. notice
6. unable
7. correction
8. inspect
9. react
10. busier
11. respond
12. spied
13. pitied
14. solid
15. vulture

**Story Time** **Write a Spelling Word on each line to complete the story.**

Before starting the trip, our leader took time to 7._____ to our questions with expert advice. Then he had to carefully 8. _____ each wagon. He also tested each horse to see how it might 9. _____ to surprises on the trail. I 10. _____ the poor animals pulling the heavy wagons. As the departure neared, everybody was 11. _____ than ever. Even after two 12. _____ weeks of preparation, we still had plenty of work to do.

It was the leader's job to give a warning if he 13. _____ trouble. The first day out, a 14. _____ circled overhead and worried us. That, however, was not the 15. _____ moment of our trip.

7. respond **(1)**
8. inspect **(1)**
9. react **(1)**
10. pitied **(1)**
11. busier **(1)**
12. solid **(1)**
13. spied **(1)**
14. vulture **(1)**
15. scariest **(1)**

✏️➤ **Write a Diary Entry** **On a separate sheet of paper, finish the story above by writing about the scariest moment on the trip. Use the Spelling Review Words.** Responses will vary.

Assessment Tip: Total **15** Points

Name ______________________

# Life Experiences

**An autobiography helps you learn about other people's experiences. Complete the chart below by writing about an experience that was important to each author in *Focus on Autobiography.* What experience in your life has been important to you?** Sample answers shown.

| **Author** | **Important Experience** |
|---|---|
| **Eloise Greenfield** | Moving into Langston Terrace on her ninth birthday is an important event to Eloise Greenfield. She grows to love the community and thinks of it as "a good growing-up place." **(4 points)** |
| **Jane Goodall** | Jane Goodall's trip to Africa is an important experience because it leads to her meeting Louis Leakey and getting a job studying chimpanzees. **(4)** |
| **Bill Peet** | Bill Peet's experience at a Disney Studios job tryout is important to him. He is excited by being able to work on *Snow White,* the first full-length cartoon film. **(4)** |
| **Alex Rodriguez** | Alex Rodriguez's learning experience during his first two years in professional baseball is important to him. He learns how hard athletes need to work to play well. **(4)** |
| **me** | Answers will vary. **(4)** |




Assessment Tip: Total **20** Points

Name _____

# How I Was Then . . .

It's the future, and you are famous. A children's magazine has asked you to tell its readers about what was important to you while you were growing up. Write a list of people, places, events, and interests that might be important in your life. Answers will vary.

From My Childhood . . .

People: (4 points) _____

_____

_____

_____

_____

Places: (4) _____

_____

_____

_____

_____

Events: (4) _____

_____

_____

_____

_____

Interests: (4) _____

_____

_____

_____

Assessment Tip: Total **16** Points

Name _____

# Animal Encounters

The selections in this theme explore some special relationships between people and wild creatures. After reading each selection, fill in this chart to show what you learned.

|  | What kind of writing is the selection an example of? | What creature or creatures does the selection describe? |
|---|---|---|
| **Grizzly Bear Family Book** | first-person narrative nonfiction **(2.5 points)** | grizzly bears **(2.5)** |
| **The Golden Lion Tamarin Comes Home** | expository nonfiction **(2.5)** | golden lion tamarins **(2.5)** |
| **My Side of the Mountain** | fiction **(2.5)** | many small creatures of the forest, such as raccoons and a falcon **(2.5)** |

Name _____

# Animal Encounters

| | What is the purpose of the encounter between humans and animals? | What are the results of the encounter? |
|---|---|---|
| **Grizzly Bear Family Book** | Michio Hoshino wants to learn as much as he can about grizzly bears. He wants to photograph them. **(2.5)** | People learn more about grizzly bears and how they live. **(2.5)** |
| **The Golden Lion Tamarin Comes Home** | The people of the Golden Lion Tamarin Conservation Program want to return golden lion tamarins to the forests where they naturally live. **(2.5)** | The golden lion tamarin population increases in the rain forest of Brazil. The monkeys are protected in the preserve. **(2.5)** |
| **My Side of the Mountain** | Sam wants to experience the wilderness and be self-sufficient in it. He sees the animals as companions and even friends. **(2.5)** | Sam learns more about himself and about the creatures with whom he shares his woodland home. **(2.5)** |

What are some ways in which people can help wild animals? **(2)**

People can help wild animals in zoos learn to live in the wild again. People can

protect wild animals' natural habitats. People can teach others about wild animals

to try to get them to care about the animals and understand their needs.

346    Theme 6: **Animal Encounters**

Assessment Tip: Total **10** Points per selection and **2** points for the final question

Name _____

# Creatures of the Far North

**Answer each question with a word from the word box.**

1. Which word names a grazing animal that lives in the Arctic?
   caribou **(1 point)** _____

2. Which word names the frozen land near the Arctic Ocean?
   tundra **(1)** _____

3. Which word names land that has not been developed?
   wilderness **(1)** _____

4. Which word names the body of an animal that has died?
   carcass **(1)** _____

5. Which word is a synonym for *cautiousness*?
   wariness **(1)** _____

6. Which word names the region that a predator such as a bobcat or a grizzly bear ranges across to find food?
   territory **(1)** _____

7. Which word is an adjective that means "likely to attack"?
   aggressive **(1)** _____

8. Which word is an adjective that means "plentiful"?
   abundant **(1)** _____

9. Which word means "the state of controlling others"?
   dominance **(1)** _____

10. Which word means "the state of being willing to yield to others"? subservience **(1)** _____

**Vocabulary**

carcass
caribou
aggressive
dominance
subservience
tundra
wilderness
abundant
territory
wariness

Name _____

# Detective Work

**What generalizations does the author make about bears, about people, and about the wilderness in this selection? As you read, look for generalizations on the pages listed below. Use the clues to help you recognize them. Write each generalization you find.**

| Page | Clue | Generalization |
|------|------|----------------|
| 605 | how people see bears | People have a fearful image of bears. **(1)** |
| 607 | what all living things do | All living things, including humans, depend on each other for survival. **(1)** |
| 608 | how grizzlies act toward each other during most of the year | Grizzlies avoid contact with other bears during most of the year. **(1)** |
| 608 | which bears command the best fishing spots | Stronger, more aggressive males usually get the best fishing spots. **(1)** |
| 609 | the tolerance of mother bears | Mother bears are usually tolerant of the cubs of others. **(1)** |
| 610 | bears selecting salmon | Bears can probably smell the difference between male and female fish. **(1)** |
| 612 | bears and soapberries | Bears seem to like soapberries best. **(1)** |
| 614 | bears pursuing people | Very few bears are interested in pursuing people. **(1)** |
| 615 | how hunters kill bears | A high-powered rifle was fired from a distance. **(1)** |
| 616 | how people treat nature | People continue to tame and subjugate nature. **(1)** |

Assessment Tip: Total **10** Points

Name _____

# Bear Facts

**Write facts about bears in the web provided.  Try to use each word in the creek at least once.**

**how bears act with each other**
They play; some show dominance; others show subservience. **(2 points)**

**bears and humans**
Show wariness toward each other **(2)**

**how bears survive the winter**
They sleep in a den. **(2)**

**how mother bears act**
Show tenderness toward cubs; tolerant of other bears' cubs; nurse their young **(2)**

**what bears eat**
Salmon; sedges; soapberries; carcass **(2)**

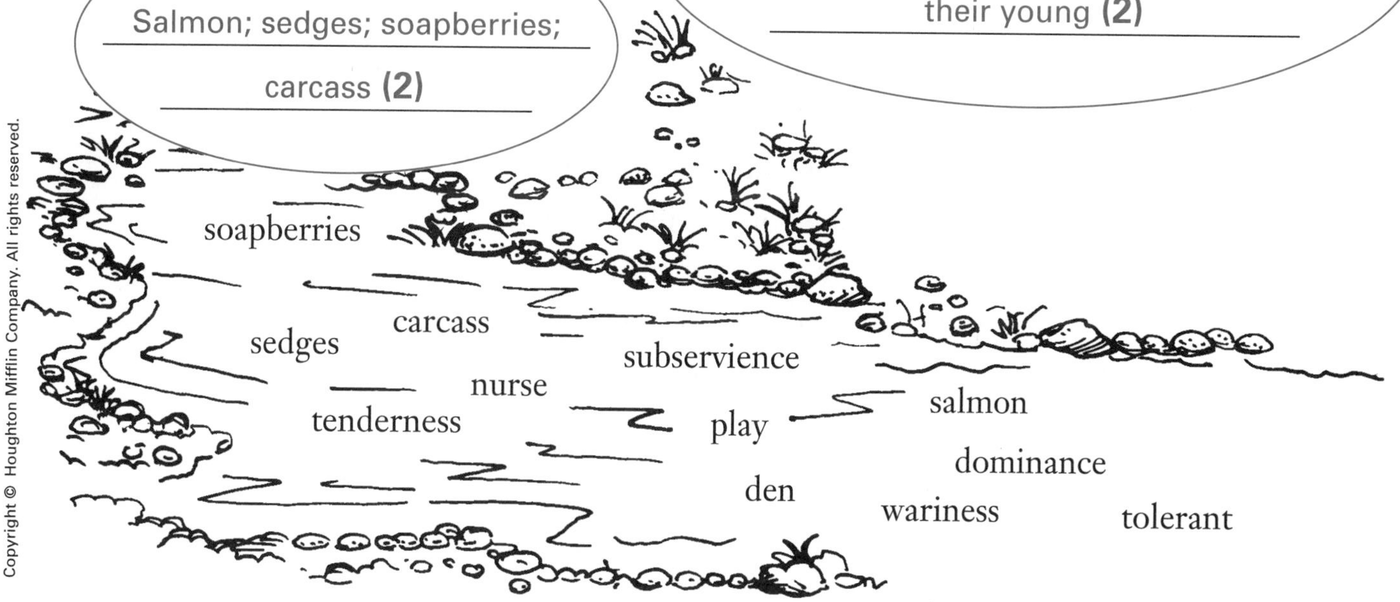

soapberries

sedges    carcass

nurse    subservience

tenderness    play    salmon

den    dominance

wariness    tolerant

Theme 6: **Animal Encounters**    349
Assessment Tip: Total **10** Points

Name _____

# Wolf Talk

**Read the passage. Then complete the activity on page 351.**

### Saved From Extinction:
### The Story of the Gray Wolf

Long ago, the gray wolf roamed through most of North America, from Canada to Mexico. Today, gray wolves are still common in Alaska and parts of Canada. South of Canada, however, only a few gray wolves survive.

People in the United States have always considered wolves to be evil and dangerous. Settlers shot them to protect their families. Ranchers shot them to protect their livestock. For decades the federal government paid hunters cash bounties for shooting wolves.

In the late 1960s, when the gray wolf was nearly extinct in the United States, public opinion began to change. Most people came to regard wolves as a valuable part of the natural environment. All who cared about the wilderness believed that wolves should be allowed to thrive in America's northern forests.

In 1995 federal agencies began a program to return the gray wolf to parts of its former range. They airlifted wolves from Canada into Yellowstone National Park. From there, the wolves have begun to reinhabit parts of Wyoming, Montana, and Idaho. But not everyone is pleased by the program's success. The ranchers in these states fear that wolves will destroy their livestock and have demanded an end to the program.

What will the gray wolf's fate be? No one can be sure. But wherever wolves and people share the land, conflicts are likely to occur.

Name _____

# Wolf Talk continued

**Answer these questions about the passage on page 350.**

1. What generalization does the author make in the second paragraph of the passage?

   People in the United States have always considered wolves to be evil and dangerous. **(2 points)**

2. Is this generalization valid or invalid? Why?

   Invalid. It's not true that all people in the United States have always considered wolves to be evil and dangerous. **(2)**

3. What two generalizations does the author make in the third paragraph?

   A. Most people came to see wolves as a valuable part of the natural environment. **(2)**

   B. All who cared about the wilderness believed that wolves should be protected and allowed to thrive. **(2)**

4. One of the generalizations in the third paragraph is invalid. Rewrite it to make it a valid statement.

   Many who cared about the wilderness believed that wolves should be protected and allowed to thrive. **(2)**

5. What generalization does the author make in the fourth paragraph?

   The ranchers in these states fear that wolves will destroy their livestock and have demanded an end to the program. **(2)**

6. Rewrite the generalization in the fourth paragraph to make it a valid statement.

   Many ranchers in these states fear that wolves will destroy their livestock and have demanded an end to the program. **(2)**

Name _____

# Prefix Prints

**The words in the box begin with the prefix *com-*, *con-*, *en-*, *ex-*, *pre-*, or *pro-*. Find the word that matches each clue and write it in the letter spaces. Then read the tinted letters to find a word that means "to keep from harm, attack, or injury."**

complete
continue
entrance
encourage
excited
predict
protest

1. bring to a finish     c   o   m   **p**   l   e   t   e   **(2 points)**

2. a door, for example     e   n   t   **r**   a   n   c   e   **(2)**

3. to fill with confidence     e   n   c   **o**   u   r   a   g   e   **(2)**

4. to keep on doing     c   o   n   **t**   i   n   u   e   **(2)**

5. to tell what will happen     p   r   **e**   d   i   c   t   **(2)**

6. thrilled     e   x   **c**   i   t   e   d   **(2)**

7. to complain about     p   r   o   **t**   e   s   t   **(2)**

**Write a sentence about grizzly bears, using a word from the box.**
Sample answer shown.
The grizzly bear continued to fish for salmon all afternoon. **(2)**

_____

Assessment Tip: Total **16** Points

# More Words with Prefixes

*Com-, con-, en-, ex-, pre-,* and *pro-* are prefixes. Because you know how to spell the prefix, pay special attention to the spelling of the base word or the word root. Spell the word by parts.

| | | |
|---|---|---|
| **com**pare | **con**vince | **en**force |
| **ex**cite | **pre**serve | **pro**pose |

**Write each Spelling Word under its prefix.**

Order of answers for each category may vary.

1. propose
2. convince
3. concern
4. enforce
5. compare
6. excuse
7. conduct
8. preserve
9. contain
10. excite
11. extend
12. prefix
13. engage
14. pronoun
15. consist
16. enclose
17. consent
18. proverb
19. complete
20. exchange

### *com-, con-*

convince **(1 point)**          contain **(1)**

concern **(1)**          consist **(1)**

compare **(1)**          consent **(1)**

conduct **(1)**          complete **(1)**

### *en-, ex-*

enforce **(1)**          engage **(1)**

excuse **(1)**          enclose **(1)**

excite **(1)**          exchange **(1)**

extend **(1)**

### *pre-, pro-*

propose **(1)**          pronoun **(1)**

preserve **(1)**          proverb **(1)**

prefix **(1)**

Theme 6: **Animal Encounters**     353
Assessment Tip: Total **20** Points

Name _____

# Spelling Spree

**Alphabet Puzzler** Write the Spelling Word that fits alphabetically between the two words in each group.

1. prong, _____, proof
2. company, _____, compass
3. enchant, _____, encore
4. contact, _____, contest
5. prefer, _____, preheat
6. convert, _____, convoy
7. consider, _____, consonant
8. express, _____, extinct

1. <u>pronoun</u> **(1 point)**
2. <u>compare</u> **(1)**
3. <u>enclose</u> **(1)**
4. <u>contain</u> **(1)**
5. <u>prefix</u> **(1)**
6. <u>convince</u> **(1)**
7. <u>consist</u> **(1)**
8. <u>extend</u> **(1)**

**The Third Word** Write the Spelling Word that belongs in each group.

9. trade, swap, _____
10. suggest, recommend, _____
11. agree, grant, _____
12. saying, phrase, _____
13. save, protect, _____
14. thrill, energize, _____
15. whole, total, _____

9. <u>exchange</u> **(1)**
10. <u>propose</u> **(1)**
11. <u>consent</u> **(1)**
12. <u>proverb</u> **(1)**
13. <u>preserve</u> **(1)**
14. <u>excite</u> **(1)**
15. <u>complete</u> **(1)**

## Spelling Words

1. propose
2. convince
3. concern
4. enforce
5. compare
6. excuse
7. conduct
8. preserve
9. contain
10. excite
11. extend
12. prefix
13. engage
14. pronoun
15. consist
16. enclose
17. consent
18. proverb
19. complete
20. exchange

I really (like, fancy, enjoy) books about bears!

Assessment Tip: Total **15** Points

Name _____

# Proofreading and Writing

**Proofreading** Circle the five misspelled words in these park rules. Then write each word correctly.

## PARK RULES

While in the park, please (condouct) yourself as follows:

1. If you see a bear, do not try to (ingage) it. Instead, leave it in peace. Trust us! You don't want a bear to (concirn) itself with you.

2. If you come across a bear, *never* turn and run. It will excite the bear, who will then run after you. There is no way to outrun a bear!

3. Do not feed any park animals. There is no (exscuse) for breaking this rule. We will (enforse) it strictly.

1. propose
2. convince
3. concern
4. enforce
5. compare
6. excuse
7. conduct
8. preserve
9. contain
10. excite
11. extend
12. prefix
13. engage
14. pronoun
15. consist
16. enclose
17. consent
18. proverb
19. complete
20. exchange

1. conduct **(1 point)**      4. excuse **(1)**

2. engage **(1)**      5. enforce **(1)**

3. concern **(1)**

✏️ **Write an Essay** The author of this selection knew and respected grizzlies, but he was killed by one. Does this change your thinking about bears?

**On a separate piece of paper, write a short essay stating your reaction to Michio Hoshino's fate. Use Spelling Words from the list.** Responses will vary. **(5)**

Name _____

# A Search for Meaning

**Read the passage. Then use context clues from the passage to figure out the underlined words. Write their meanings and the clues you used.**

Sample answers shown.

## The Rivals

Bridget saw the fight through her binoculars. It was really just a brief quarrel between two bears who were fishing. The younger bear was smaller but more aggressive, and he soon proved to be the <u>victor</u>. The older bear turned around and <u>retreated</u> to the riverbank. The entire group of bears in the river then began to fish. The former rivals, now <u>tolerant</u> of one another, fished almost side by side. But Bridget's own feeling of <u>wariness</u> kept her from going any closer.

| Word | Meaning | Clues from Context |
|---|---|---|
| victor | a winner of a contest **(1 point)** | The bears fought and the younger bear was more aggressive. **(2)** |
| retreated | went back **(1)** | The older bear turned around and went back to the riverbank. **(2)** |
| tolerant | accepting **(1)** | The former rivals now fished side by side. **(2)** |
| wariness | caution **(1)** | It was a feeling that kept her from going any closer. **(2)** |

Assessment Tip: Total **12** Points

Name _____

# Contraction Action

**Contractions with *not*** You can combine some verbs with the word *not* to make a **contraction**. An apostrophe takes the place of the letter or letters dropped to shorten the word.

**In sentences 1–5, underline the word combination with *not* that can be written as a contraction. Then write the contraction on the line. For sentences 6–10, underline the contraction. On the line, write the words that make up the contraction.**

| Common Contractions with a Verb and *not* | | | |
|---|---|---|---|
| do not | don't | have not | haven't |
| does not | doesn't | has not | hasn't |
| did not | didn't | had not | hadn't |
| is not | isn't | could not | couldn't |
| are not | aren't | would not | wouldn't |
| was not | wasn't | should not | shouldn't |
| were not | weren't | cannot | can't |
| will not | won't | must not | mustn't |

1. Bears are not found around here. aren't **(1 point)** _____

2. I had not seen a bear until last year. hadn't **(1)** _____

3. I could not visit Alaska. couldn't **(1)** _____

4. A bear will not show up in my backyard. won't **(1)** _____

5. I did not think I would ever see a bear. didn't **(1)** _____

6. "You haven't thought of going to the zoo!" said Dad. have not **(1)** _____

7. "It isn't the same as seeing wild bears," I said. is not **(1)** _____

8. He said, "The bears don't live in cages anymore." do not **(1)** _____

9. The new habitat hasn't been at the zoo long. has not **(1)** _____

10. You mustn't miss the bear cubs! must not **(1)** _____

Theme 6: **Animal Encounters**   357
Assessment Tip: Total **10** Points

Name _____

# No! Not Negatives!

**Negatives** Words that mean "no" or "not" are **negatives**. Do not use **double negatives**, two negative words in the same sentence.

> ### Negatives
> no    not    hardly    never    neither    none

There are often two ways to correct a double negative.

**Incorrect:** Fred **hasn't no** idea what Alaska is like.

**Correct:** Fred **hasn't any** idea what Alaska is like.

**Correct:** Fred **has no** idea what Alaska is like.

Alaska

**Rewrite each sentence to correct the double negative.**
Answers may vary.

1. Fred had not read nothing about Alaska.

   Fred had read nothing about Alaska. OR Fred had not read anything about

   Alaska. **(2 points)**

2. He didn't never plan to go there.

   He didn't plan to go there. OR He never planned to go there. **(2)**

   _____

3. He hadn't no curiosity about our forty-ninth state.

   He hadn't any curiosity about our forty-ninth state. OR He had no curiosity

   about our forty-ninth state. **(2)**

   _____

4. Since reading Michio's story, he can't never read enough about Alaska!

   Since reading Michio's story, he can never read enough about Alaska! OR

   Since reading Michio's story, he can't read enough about Alaska! **(2)**

5. Soon there won't be nobody who knows more about Alaska.

   Soon there won't be anybody who knows more about Alaska. or

   Soon there will be nobody who knows more about Alaska. **(2)**

Assessment Tip: Total **10** Points

Name _____

# Is That an Adverb, Herb?

**Adjective or Adverb?** A good writer is careful to use **adverbs**, not **adjectives**, to tell *how much* or to *what extent* about adjectives.

> **Incorrect:** The animal was **dreadful** hungry.

> **Correct:** The animal was **dreadfully** hungry.

**Sophie wrote to her friend June. In several places, Sophie used an adjective when she should have used an adverb. Proofread Sophie's letter, and make the corrections above the errors. (2 points each)**

Dear June,

      Last week, Mom and I saw a baby raccoon in our yard! It
    really                       completely
was ~~real~~ tiny. We knew that it should not be ~~complete~~ alone.
                           terribly
After waiting for its mother for a ~~terrible~~ long time, Mom called

the Wildlife Rescue Center. They sent an expert to help. She was
awfully
~~awful~~ kind. She said we should never touch a wild animal. She

put it in a special cage so it wouldn't get hurt. The Rescue Center
      extremely
will take ~~extreme~~ good care of the baby. I wish you could have seen it.
    Your friend,
    Sophie

Name _____

# Writing a Paragraph of Opinion

An **opinion** is a belief that may or may not be supported by facts.  Some opinions, such as those offered by Michio Hoshino in *The Grizzly Bear Family Book*, are highly personal.  For example, he says, "No matter how many books you read, no matter how much television you watch, there is no substitute for experiencing nature firsthand."

**As you read *The Grizzly Bear Family Book*, consider the following question:**

▶ *Do you think grizzlies should be kept in zoos?  Why or why not?*

**Then use this diagram to record your opinion and to write facts and examples that support it. (2 points each)**

```
                    ⟮  Opinion  ⟯


 ┌──────────────────┐  ┌──────────────────┐  ┌──────────────────┐
 │ Facts and Examples│  │ Facts and Examples│  │ Facts and Examples│
 │                  │  │                  │  │                  │
 │                  │  │                  │  │                  │
 │                  │  │                  │  │                  │
 └──────────────────┘  └──────────────────┘  └──────────────────┘
```

**Using the information you recorded in the diagram, write a paragraph of opinion on a separate sheet of paper. In the first sentence, state your opinion in response to the question above. In the body of the paragraph, write two to three reasons why you think and feel the way you do. Support your opinion with facts and examples. Then end your paragraph with a concluding sentence that restates your opinion. (4)**

Assessment Tip: Total **12** Points

Name _____

# Avoiding Double Negatives

The words *no, not, none,* and *nothing* are called **negatives.** A careful writer does not use two negatives within a single phrase. You can eliminate double negatives in your own writing by removing one of the negatives or by changing either one of the negatives to a positive.

Hunters do **not** have **no** right to shoot grizzlies in Alaska. (incorrect)

Hunters have **no** right to shoot grizzlies in Alaska. (corrected) or

Hunters do **not** have **any** right to shoot grizzlies in Alaska. (corrected)

**Read the following letter to the editor of the *Alaskan Argus*. Use the proofreaders' delete mark ( ✂ ) to remove double negatives. You may replace some negatives with positive words such as *any* or *anything*. Write the positive word above the negative one you replace. (2 points each)**

To the Editor:

I am concerned about a recent proposal to extend the hunting season in Alaska. In my opinion, the hunting season is long enough. Hunters from the lower United States and Europe do not need ~~no~~ *any* more time to hunt.

Most wildlife cannot compete against ~~no~~ high-powered rifles. As a result of more opportunities for hunting animals, there might not be ~~none~~ *any* left for the public to enjoy. Tourists will not come to the Alaskan wilderness if there is ~~not~~ nothing to observe there.

A longer hunting season increases the risk that people will be injured. I feel that if more trophy hunters are encouraged to come to Alaska, then we will not be able to do ~~nothing~~ *anything* to avoid the tragic consequences.

I strongly support keeping the hunting season the way it is now.

Sincerely,

Chris Morrow

Name _____

# Evaluating Your Persuasive Essay

**Reread your persuasive essay. What do you need to make it better?**
**Put a checkmark in each box that describes your persuasive essay.**

### Rings the Bell!

☐ My essay has a beginning that will capture my readers' attention.

☐ My goal is stated clearly at the beginning of the essay.

☐ I stated my reasons for my point of view and answered objections.

☐ I used facts and details to support my opinion.

☐ The essay is interesting to read and convincing.

### Getting Stronger

☐ I could make the beginning more attention grabbing.

☐ I could state my goal more clearly.

☐ I could answer more objections people might raise.

☐ I need to add more facts and details to support my point of view.

☐ There are some run-on sentences I need to fix.

☐ There are a few other mistakes.

### Try Harder

☐ I need a better beginning.

☐ I didn't state my goals or reasons for my opinion.

☐ I didn't answer any objections people might have.

☐ I need to add facts and details.

☐ This isn't very convincing.

☐ There are a lot of mistakes.

Name _____

# Correcting Run-On Sentences

Answers will vary.
Sample answers given.

**Correct each run-on sentence on the lines provided.**

1. **Run-On:** Wolves are ranked in a pack it is called a hierarchy.

   **Corrected:** Wolves are ranked in a pack. It is called a hierarchy. **(2 points)**

   _____

2. **Run-On:** Lower-ranked wolves are submissive to higher-ranked wolves alpha wolves have dominance over the other wolves in the pack.

   **Corrected:** Lower-ranked wolves are submissive to higher-ranked wolves, so alpha wolves have dominance over the other wolves in the pack. **(2)**

3. **Run-On:** Wolves survive in different climates they are adaptable.

   **Corrected:** Wolves survive in different climates because they are adaptable. **(2)**

4. **Run-On:** Wolves hunt in packs they catch larger prey such as moose or elk.

   **Corrected:** Wolves hunt in packs, and they catch larger prey such as moose or elk. **(2)**

5. **Run-On:** Wolves and dogs share many of the same traits they are both smart.

   **Corrected:** Wolves and dogs share many of the same traits. They are both smart. **(2)**

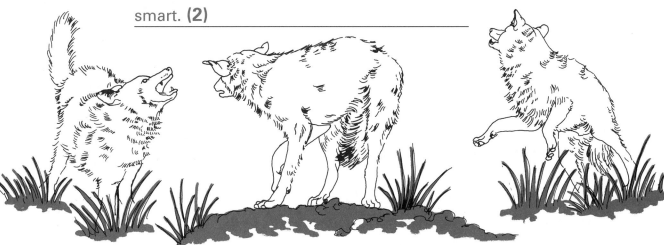

Name _____

# Spelling Words

**Words Often Misspelled** Look for familiar spelling patterns to help you remember how to spell the Spelling Words on this page. Think carefully about the parts that you find hard to spell in each word.

**Write the missing letters and apostrophes in the Spelling Words below.**

**Spelling Words**

1. heard
2. your
3. you're
4. field
5. buy
6. friend
7. guess
8. cousin
9. build
10. family
11. can't
12. cannot
13. didn't
14. haven't
15. don't

1. h _e_ _a_ _r_ d **(1 point)**
2. y _o_ _u_ _r_ **(1)**
3. you _'_ _r_ _e_ **(1)**
4. f _i_ _e_ _l_ d **(1)**
5. b _u_ y **(1)**
6. fr _i_ _e_ nd **(1)**
7. _g_ _u_ ess **(1)**
8. c _o_ _u_ _s_ _i_ n **(1)**
9. b _u_ _i_ ld **(1)**
10. fam _i_ ly **(1)**
11. ca _n_ _'_ _t_ **(1)**
12. ca _n_ _n_ _o_ _at_ **(1)**
13. did _n_ _'_ _t_ **(1)**
14. hav _e_ _n_ _'_ _t_ **(1)**
15. do _n_ _'_ _t_ **(1)**

**Study List** **On a separate piece of paper, write each Spelling Word. Check your spelling against the words on the list.**

Order of words may vary. **(5)**

Assessment Tip: Total **20** Points

Name _____

# Spelling Spree

**Alphabet Puzzler** Write the Spelling Word that fits alphabetically between the two words in each group.

1. fried, _____, frighten
2. head, _____, heart
3. donation, _____, doom
4. familiar, _____, famous
5. guard, _____, guest
6. fiddle, _____, filed
7. button, _____, buzz
8. court, _____, cover

1. friend **(1 point)**
2. heard **(1)**
3. don't **(1)**
4. family **(1)**
5. guess **(1)**
6. field **(1)**
7. buy **(1)**
8. cousin **(1)**

**Spelling Words**

1. heard
2. your
3. you're
4. field
5. buy
6. friend
7. guess
8. cousin
9. build
10. family
11. can't
12. cannot
13. didn't
14. haven't
15. don't

**Letter Math** Add and subtract letters from the words below to make Spelling Words. Write the new words.

9. carrot + nn − rr =
10. having − ing + en't =
11. sour − s + y =
12. want + ' − w + c =
13. guild − g + b =
14. they're + you − they =
15. hadn't + di −ha =

9. cannot **(1)**
10. haven't **(1)**
11. your **(1)**
12. can't **(1)**
13. build **(1)**
14. you're **(1)**
15. didn't **(1)**

Theme 6: **Animal Encounters** 365
Assessment Tip: Total **15** Points

# Proofreading and Writing

**Proofreading** Circle the five misspelled Spelling Words in this wanted poster. Then write each word correctly.

**Spelling Words**

1. heard
2. your
3. you're
4. field
5. buy
6. friend
7. guess
8. cousin
9. build
10. family
11. can't
12. cannot
13. didn't
14. haven't
15. don't

### HAVE YOU SEEN THIS CAT?

You may have (herd) about the escape of this mountain lion from the county zoo. We have been searching for the past week, but we (have'nt) been able to track her down. Our best (gess) is that she is keeping to wooded areas, but we can't say for sure. As a result, we are asking that you be extremely careful when outdoors, and that you keep an eye on (youre) children and pets. Above all, if you see the cat, (dont) approach her. Instead, call the police, or call us at the zoo at 555-7372.

1. heard **(1 point)**

2. haven't **(1)**

3. guess **(1)**

4. your **(1)**

5. don't **(1)**

✏️ **Animal Riddles** On a separate piece of paper, write three riddles about animals. Include a Spelling Word in each riddle. Then trade riddles with a classmate and try to guess each other's answers.
Responses will vary. **(5)**

**Assessment Tip: Total 10 Points**

Name _____

# Saving a Species

**Complete each statement with a word from the word box.**

1. If you are in the highest branches of the tallest trees in the rain forest, you are in the _canopy **(1 point)**_____ .

2. If the air has a lot of moisture in it, the weather is _humid **(1)**_____ .

3. If you release animals into a wild area in which their ancestors once lived, you are helping with the _reintroduction **(1)**_____ of a species.

4. If you study the region in which a wild creature lives, you study its _habitat **(1)**_____ .

5. If you are faced with a problem that seems to have no good solution, you are faced with a _dilemma **(1)**_____ .

6. If you study the material that determines the characteristics of a plant or animal, you study its _genes **(1)**_____ .

7. If no members of a species remain alive, that species has suffered _extinction **(1)**_____ .

8. If you are being held prisoner, you are a _captive **(1)**_____ .

9. If an animal is being watched, it is under _observation **(1)**_____ .

10. If an animal hunts other animals for food, it is a _predator **(1)**_____ .

## Vocabulary

dilemma

extinction

predator

observation

canopy

reintroduction

habitat

captive

humid

genes

Assessment Tip: Total **10** Points

Name _____

# Get the Idea?

**What are the main ideas of this selection? As you read, find the main ideas on the pages listed below. Then fill in the chart with the main idea and the details that support each main idea.** Entries will vary. Samples are shown.

| |
|---|
| **Topic:** The conservation of golden lion tamarins. |
| **(Page 630) Main Idea:** The native habitat of the tamarins is a diverse, colorful environment. **(1)** |
| **Details:** Birds sing, insects buzz, cicadas chirp; tangled vines and leaves; orange-gold flash; speckles of sunlight. **(1)** |
| **(Pages 632–633) Main Idea:** Captive-born tamarins need special training before being reintroduced into the wild. **(1)** |
| **Details:** **(1)** |
| **(Pages 634–637) Main Idea:** The observers prepare thoroughly before bringing the tamarins into the wild. **(1)** |
| **Details:** **(1)** |
| **(Page 638) Main Idea:** The observers carefully follow certain steps when releasing the tamarins. **(1)** |
| **Details:** **(1)** |
| **(Pages 640–641) Main Idea:** The observers gradually give less assistance as the tamarins adapt to their environment. **(1)** |
| **Details:** **(1)** |

Assessment Tip: Total **10** Points

Name _____

# The Lion Speaks

**Fill in the blanks below with information from the story.**

1. "I am a <u>golden lion tamarin</u>. My native home is in
   the rain forest of <u>Brazil</u>." **(2 points)**

2. "Unfortunately, humans have <u>cut</u> down many trees and
   <u>burned</u> much of the forest for their own use. Today I
   am in danger of <u>extinction</u>." **(2)**

3. "That is why biologists have established a protected
   <u>habitat</u> for us in the rain forest. Because many of
   us are bred in <u>zoos</u>, however, we must learn new
   <u>skills</u> before we go into the wild." **(2)**

4. "We are trained at the <u>National</u> Zoo in
   <u>Washington, D.C.</u>. Then we are shipped to our native
   country, <u>Brazil</u>. There a team of <u>observers</u>
   first releases us into <u>cages</u> within the rain forest." **(2)**

5. "When we are ready, they let us out. They <u>watch</u> us
   carefully and take detailed <u>notes</u> describing our behavior.
   They also give us <u>food</u> and <u>water</u> until we
   learn to find these things on our own." **(2)**

6. "The <u>juveniles</u> among us adapt the fastest. Today only
   about <u>30</u> percent of us survive more than <u>two years</u>
   in the wild. The <u>Golden Lion Tamarin</u> Conservation
   Program hopes to have <u>2,000</u> of us living in the wild by the
   year <u>2025</u>." **(2)**

Name _____

# Mind the Main Idea

**Read the passage. Then complete the activity on page 371.**

### The Decline of the Tiger

Once, many different types of tiger roamed throughout Asia. These were the Indian, Indochinese, Chinese, Siberian, Sumatran, Caspian, Javan, and Balinese tigers. Today, three of these eight types are extinct and several of the others are rare. Wild tigers can still be found only in some parts of Southeast Asia and Siberia.

Two main factors have caused the decline of tiger populations. One factor is the destruction of tigers' habitats. In central Asia, for example, farmers burned wooded areas along waterways to clear the land for farming. Thousands of acres of forest were also set on fire. As a result, much of the tigers' natural prey disappeared. Without enough food to support their roughly four-hundred-pound bodies, the tigers have disappeared as well.

Hunting is the second factor that has caused the decline of tiger populations. With the loss of their habitats and natural prey, tigers began to hunt closer to people. Farmers shot them to protect their livestock. Others hunted them for sport or for their fur.

Today, efforts are being made in many regions to protect wild tigers. India and Nepal have set aside reserves for them. Many countries have outlawed the import or sale of tiger skins. Successful captive breeding programs in zoos are also helping to ensure that the survival of these great cats continues.

Name _____

# Mind the Main Idea continued

**Answer the questions below. Use information from the passage on page 370.** Sample answers are shown.

1. What is the topic of the passage? <u>tigers **(3 points)**</u>

2. Write the main idea or supporting details of the following paragraphs below.

| | | |
|---|---|---|
| **First Paragraph** | Main Idea:<br><br>Supporting Details: | Today, tiger populations are in decline.<br>Indian, Indochinese, Chinese, Siberian, Sumatran, Caspian, Javan, and Balinese tigers once roamed through Asia. Today three of these eight types are extinct and several of the others are rare. Wild tigers remain only in parts of Southeast Asia and Siberia. **(4)** |
| **Second and Third Paragraphs** | Main Idea:<br><br>Supporting Details: | Two main factors caused the decline of tigers: destruction of their habitats and hunting.<br>The burning of waterway areas and forests caused the loss of tigers' food sources.<br>Tigers were hunted to protect livestock, for sport, and for their fur. **(4)** |
| **Fourth Paragraph** | Main Idea:<br><br>Supporting Details: | Today efforts are being made to save tigers. **(4)**<br>India and Nepal have set aside tiger reserves. Many countries outlawed importing or selling tiger fur. Zoos breed captive tigers to help more tigers survive. |

Name _____

# Syllable Sensations

**Read the sentences. Then circle the correct way to divide the
syllables of the underlined word. Check the syllable pattern
that applies to the word.**

| | VCV | VCCV |
|---|---|---|
| 1. | ✔ (1) | |
| 2. | ✔ (1) | |
| 3. | | ✔ (1) |
| 4. | | ✔ (1) |
| 5. | | ✔ (1) |
| 6. | ✔ (1) | |
| 7. | ✔ (1) | |

1. In zoos, ropes are hung to <u>simulate</u> vines for the tamarins.

si/mul/ate          (sim/u/late) **(1 point)**

2. Nesting boxes are made for the tamarins from <u>modified</u>
picnic coolers.

mod/if/ied          (mod/i/fied) **(1)**

3. After returning to the rain forest, the tamarins grow
<u>accustomed</u> to their new surroundings.

(ac/cus/tomed) **(1)**          acc/ust/omed

4. As <u>immigrants</u>, the newly arrived tamarins have a great deal
to learn.

imm/ig/rants          (im/mi/grants) **(1)**

5. Human <u>observers</u> watch and record everything the
tamarins do.

(ob/ser/vers) **(1)**          obs/erv/ers

6. Bit by bit, the tamarins become <u>familiar</u> with the rain forest.

(fa/mil/iar) **(1)**          fam/i/liar

7. Older tamarins must unlearn behaviors that were <u>adequate</u>
for zoo life but are useless in the forest.

a/deq/uate          (ad/e/quate) **(1)**

**Assessment Tip:** Total **14** Points

# Three-Syllable Words

A three-syllable word has one stressed syllable and two syllables with less stress. To help you spell the word, divide it into its syllables. Note the spelling of the syllables that have less stress.

**va | ca | tion**  /vā **kā′** shən/

**ed | u | cate**  /**ĕj′** ə kāt′/

**Write each Spelling Word under the heading that names its stressed syllable.** Order of answers for each category may vary.

**Spelling Words**

1. dangerous
2. history
3. vacation
4. popular
5. favorite
6. memory
7. personal
8. educate
9. regular
10. continue
11. potato
12. natural
13. sensitive
14. energy
15. emotion
16. period
17. property
18. condition
19. imagine
20. attention

## Stressed First Syllable

dangerous **(1 point)**

history **(1)**

popular **(1)**

favorite **(1)**

memory **(1)**

personal **(1)**

educate **(1)**

regular **(1)**

natural **(1)**

sensitive **(1)**

energy **(1)**

period **(1)**

property **(1)**

## Stressed Second Syllable

vacation **(1)**

continue **(1)**

potato **(1)**

emotion **(1)**

condition **(1)**

imagine **(1)**

attention **(1)**

Assessment Tip: Total **20** Points

Name _____

# Spelling Spree

**Syllable Scramble** Rearrange the syllables to write a
Spelling Word. One syllable in each item is extra.

1. ue con gel tin

2. gy ro en er

3. po to tion ta

4. at tion men ten

5. let vor fa ite

6. sen ring tive si

7. u ed gan cate

1. continue **(1 point)**

2. energy **(1)**

3. potato **(1)**

4. attention **(1)**

5. favorite **(1)**

6. sensitive **(1)**

7. educate **(1)**

1. dangerous
2. history
3. vacation
4. popular
5. favorite
6. memory
7. personal
8. educate
9. regular
10. continue
11. potato
12. natural
13. sensitive
14. energy
15. emotion
16. period
17. property
18. condition
19. imagine
20. attention

**Word Maze** Begin at the arrow and follow the Word Maze
to find eight Spelling Words. Write the words in order.

8. regular **(1)**

9. imagine **(1)**

10. emotion **(1)**

11. dangerous **(1)**

12. personal **(1)**

13. popular **(1)**

14. memory **(1)**

15. vacation **(1)**

Assessment Tip: Total **15** Points

Name _____

# Proofreading and Writing

**Proofreading** Circle the five misspelled Spelling Words in this brochure. Then write each word correctly.

The golden lion tamarin has a sad (histrey.) Over a (perriod) of years, much of Brazil's rain forest was cut down. The tamarin, therefore, was driven out of its (naturel) habitat. Most of the forest was turned into private (propety.) Brazil's government has now set aside some of the remaining forest as a wildlife refuge. Since then, the tamarins' (condishun) has improved. There is still much to be done, however. Won't you help us continue our work?

**Spelling Words**

1. dangerous
2. history
3. vacation
4. popular
5. favorite
6. memory
7. personal
8. educate
9. regular
10. continue
11. potato
12. natural
13. sensitive
14. energy
15. emotion
16. period
17. property
18. condition
19. imagine
20. attention

1. history **(1 point)**

2. period **(1)**

3. natural **(1)**

4. property **(1)**

5. condition **(1)**

✏️ **Write an Opinion** Only three out of every ten reintroduced tamarins survive for more than two years in the wild. Do you think the time and money spent in this effort is worth it? Why or why not?

**On a separate piece of paper, write your opinion of the Golden Lion Tamarin Conservation Program. Use Spelling Words from the list.** Responses will vary. **(5)**

Name _____

# A Pronounced Difference!

**Read the dictionary entries, paying special attention to the pronunciations. Then answer the questions below.**

gum
jam
pie
seen
sheen
sit

**different** /dĭf/ər/ənt/ or /dĭf/rənt/ *adj.* Unlike in form, quality, or nature.

**diversity** /dĭv/ûr/sĭ/tē/ or /dī/vûr/sĭ/tē/ *n.* 1. Difference. 2. Variety.

**program** /prō/grăm/ or /prō/grəm/ *n.* A public performance or presentation.

**species** /spē/shēz/ or /spē/sēz/ *n.* A group of similar animals or plants that are of the same kind and are able to produce fertile offspring.

**water** /wô/tər/ or /wŏt/ər/ *n.* A compound of hydrogen and oxygen occurring as a liquid.

1. How does the number of syllables change in the two pronunciations of *different*?

   The first pronunciation has three syllables, and the second has two. **(3 points)**

2. *Diversity* differs in pronunciation only in the first **(2)**

   two syllables. Which two words from the box above have the same vowel

   sounds as the pronunciations of its first syllable? sit, pie **(2)**

3. *Program* differs in pronunciation in the second or last **(2)**

   syllable. Which two words from the box have the same vowel sounds

   as the pronunciations of that syllable? jam, gum **(2)**

4. Which word from the box has the same consonant and vowel sounds as

   the second syllable in the first pronunciation of *species*? sheen **(2)**

5. If you use the first pronunciation of *water*, are you saying

   WAHtur or (WAWtur?) (Circle the correct answer.) **(2)**

Assessment Tip: Total **15** Points

Name _____

# Prepositions Give Positions

**Prepositions** A **preposition** relates the noun or pronoun that follows it to another word in the sentence. The **object of the proposition** is the noun or pronoun that follows the **preposition**.

---

**Common Prepositions**

| | | | | | | |
|---|---|---|---|---|---|---|
| about | around | beside | for | near | outside | under |
| above | at | by | from | of | over | until |
| across | before | down | in | off | past | up |
| after | behind | during | inside | on | through | with |
| along | below | except | into | out | to | without |

---

**Underline each preposition and circle the object of each preposition.**

1. Sandy visited the rain forest <u>with</u> other (tourists.) **(2 points)**

2. Moisture dripped <u>from</u> the (leaves.) **(2)**

3. The tourists heard bird squawks <u>in</u> the (distance.) **(2)**

4. Sandy took pictures <u>of</u> exotic (orchids,) **(2)**

5. The world would be a poorer place <u>without</u> these (forests.) **(2)**

6. <u>Above</u> our (heads,) we saw howler monkeys. **(2)**

7. Jaguars roam the forest <u>during</u> the (night.) **(2)**

8. We traveled <u>up</u> a (river) <u>to</u> a small (village.) **(2)**

9. The people there made fantastic animal carvings <u>in</u> (wood.) **(2)**

10. I bought a toucan carving <u>from</u> one (artist.) **(2)**

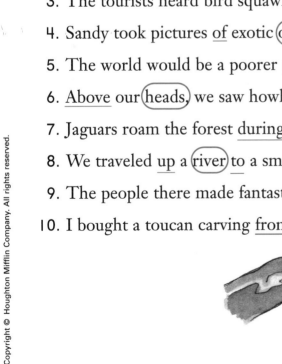

Name _____

# Prepositional Phrases Don't Faze Us

**Prepositional Phrases** A **prepositional phrase** is made up of a preposition, the object of the preposition, and all the words in between.

**Write each prepositional phrase on the line.**

1. My friend Molly watches birds in her backyard.

   in her backyard **(1 point)** _____

2. Molly's family lives far from town.

   from town **(1)** _____

3. In the field wildflowers grow.

   in the field **(1)** _____

4. Animals leave tracks by the pond.

   by the pond **(1)** _____

5. The hoots of an owl fill the air.

   of an owl **(1)** _____

6. Sometimes we camp out in the yard.

   in the yard **(1)** _____

7. At night stars twinkle in the sky.

   At night, in the sky **(1)** _____

8. We make out constellations above our heads.

   above our heads **(1)** _____

9. We tell ghost stories inside the tent.

   inside the tent **(1)** _____

10. We can hardly sleep during the night.

    during the night **(1)** _____

Assessment Tip: Total **10** Points

Name _____

# Expanding Isn't Demanding

**Expanding Sentences with Prepositional Phrases** A good writer can make sentences say more by adding prepositional phrases.

I took a walk.

**Expanded:** I took a walk along the path through the woods.

**Read Charlie's paragraph. Add details to his description by adding prepositional phrases in the blanks. Ask yourself, Where? When? How? What? Use your imagination!**

Answers will vary. Sample answers shown.

I walked through the woods in the morning **(1 point)** _____.

As I walked, I looked at the trees **(1)** _____. I hoped to see birds, but they must have been hiding behind the leaves **(1)** _____. I continued my walk toward a hill **(1)** _____. I saw tracks of an unknown animal **(1)** _____. I followed them to a stream **(1)** _____.

At the stream **(1)** _____ I found the owner of the tracks.

It stared at me **(1)** _____. Not wanting to frighten it, I stood quietly in the bushes **(1)** _____. Then it disappeared.

Was it a dream, or did I really see a unicorn in the woods **(1)** _____?

Name _____

# Writing a Compare/ Contrast Essay

In *The Golden Lion Tamarin Comes Home*, you read about similarities and differences between captive-born golden lion tamarins and those born in the wild. Both eat fruit, for example, but golden lion tamarins born in zoos do not know how to hunt or forage for food. One way to explain similarities and differences is by writing a **compare/contrast essay**. Comparing shows how things are alike, and contrasting shows how they are different.

**Using the Venn diagram, gather and organize details that compare and contrast grizzly bears with golden lion tamarins. Jot down facts about the two species, including their habitats, their diets, and threats to their survival.**

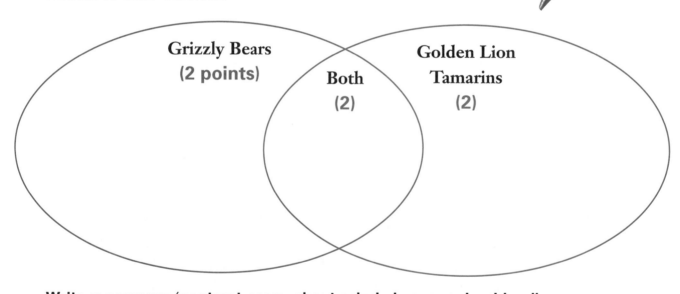

**Grizzly Bears (2 points)**  **Both (2)**  **Golden Lion Tamarins (2)**

**Write a compare/contrast essay about grizzly bears and golden lion tamarins on a separate sheet of paper. In the opening paragraph, clearly state the subject being compared and contrasted. In the following paragraphs, present details from your Venn diagram. Group details that compare and details that contrast in a clear manner. Use clue words such as *both* or *same* to help readers identify likenesses and *in contrast* or *although* to help them identify differences. (4)**

Assessment Tip: Total **10** Points

Name _____

# Combining Sentences

Good writers are always looking for ways to improve their writing. One method to streamline your writing is to combine short sentences that have a repeated subject but differing prepositional phrases into a single sentence with consecutive prepositional phrases.

The biologist was **in a tropical rain forest.** He stood **beneath some tall trees.** He peered **into the green vines.** He spotted a few golden lion tamarins **above him.**

Standing **beneath some tall trees in a tropical rain forest,** the biologist peered **into the green vines above him** and spotted a few golden lion tamarins.

**Revise these field notes. Combine short sentences that have a repeated subject but differing prepositional phrases into a single sentence. Write the revised notes on the lines.** (12 points)

Thursday, 10:20 A.M.

My tamarin family, which I call the green team, peeks out. The monkeys look out from a hole. The hole is in the top chamber. The chamber is part of a nesting box. One by one, the tamarins leave the box. Hungrily, the adults poke into the feeder. They probe the feeder with their long fingers and nails. The golden lion tamarins also eat some partly peeled bananas. The bananas are left on the branches. The branches hang near the nesting box.

My tamarin family, which I call the green team, peeks out from a hole in the top

chamber of a nesting box. One by one, the tamarins leave the box. Hungrily, the

adults poke into the feeder, probing with their long fingers and nails. The golden lion

tamarins also eat some partly peeled bananas left on the branches near the nesting box.

Name _____

# Late Autumn in the Woods

**Complete the paragraph below with words from the word box.**

The leaves have turned colors and fallen from the trees. Most birds have made their _migration_ **(1 point)** south to warmer lands. Farmers have finished _harvesting_ **(1)** the last of the wheat and rye, and they have filled crates with apples and have placed them in a cool _storehouse_ **(1)**. Each squirrel is busy adding a few more nuts to its _cache_ **(1)** of food for winter. Bears gorge themselves on one last meal of berries, for they need to have a thick layer of fat to ensure _survival_ **(1)** through the long winter. The few settlers who have come to the wild lands late in the season hurry to _fashion_ **(1)** shelter that will protect them from the _harsh_ **(1)** weather soon to arrive.

**Write three more sentences using words from the box to continue the paragraph.**

**(3)** _____

_____

_____

_____

_____

_____

Assessment Tip: Total **10** Points

Name _____

# Use the Clues

Read the story clues and conclusions provided in the boxes below.
Fill in the missing information with text from the selection.

| Story Clues | | | | Conclusions |
|---|---|---|---|---|
| **pages 652–653** Mice, squirrels, and chipmunks collected seeds and nuts. | + | Sam gathers various roots and smokes fish and rabbit. | = | On the wooded mountain where Sam is living, food is scarce in the winter. |
| **pages 654–655** The animals are growing thick coats of fur and making warm shelters for winter. **(2 points)** | + | Sam realizes he needs to build a small fireplace to warm his shelter. **(2)** | = | Sam's clothing and his current shelter aren't enough to protect him from the cold of winter. |
| **pages 656–658** Sam playfully chases the Baron Weasel up the mountain. | + | Sam runs after Frightful because he is warned the falcon has left him. | = | Sam relies on the animals to keep him from feeling too lonely. **(2)** |
| **pages 660–665** The Baron comes to get food from Sam, but doesn't let him get too close. **(2)** | + | The raccoons make a mess of Sam's food supply. **(2)** | = | Even though Sam enjoys the animals' company, he must remain alert around these wild creatures. |

Theme 6: **Animal Encounters**    383
Assessment Tip: Total **10** Points

Name _____

# Autumn Adventures

**The adventures Sam has that are recounted in this story begin in September and end just after Halloween. Use the sequence chart below to write the most important events in the order in which they occurred.**

### September

Sam watches the coming of autumn. He
gathers roots and tubers and smokes fish and rabbit. **(2 points)**

### October 15

The weasel's winter coat, the raccoon's rolls of fat, and the other animals' winter preparations make Sam realize that
he must figure out a way to stay warm in the winter. **(2)**

### The next three days

Sam brings clay back to his tree and fashions a chimney. He then
tries several different ways to keep the smoke from going into his home. **(2)**

### October 31

After the Baron visits, Sam realizes that it is Halloween. He decides
to put out food so the animals will come to a Halloween party. **(2)**

### November 1

The animals finally show up and there is a wild party in which Sam learns that he
must always show the animals that he is the strongest. **(2)**

Assessment Tip: Total **10** Points

Name —————————————————————————

# Gather the Clues

**Read the passage. Then answer the questions on page 386.**

### Taking Stock

It was nearing dusk when I got back to camp. The crickets were just launching into their evening serenade. I set my backpack down on the slab of granite I used as my table and began to unpack the treasures of the day.

I pulled out the sack of miner's lettuce that I'd gathered near the waterfall. Next, I lifted out a pouch of wild blackberries packed in a soft cushion of moss. From the bottom of the pack I drew handfuls of walnuts. The berries I'd expected to find, but the walnuts were an unexpected luxury, from a walnut tree I'd discovered in a grove of tan oaks. I carefully laid the food out on the stone. I had smoked two small trout the day before; these I had wrapped in paper and stored in a tree, away from hungry bears. The trout, nuts, and lettuce, with the berries as dessert, would make a feast indeed.

I then turned my attention to building a fire. The day had been a hot one, but I knew how fast the temperature would drop when the sun went down. After I had the campfire crackling cheerfully, I sat down to take stock.

Some things had gone better than I'd expected. Staying warm and dry had been easy. Even the rainstorm on the second night didn't soak any of my belongings. Other things, like finding enough to eat, had proved harder than I'd expected. An hour of picking lettuce resulted in a very small pile of greens. Overall, though, I couldn't complain. I thought about my two-way radio inside the tent. I hadn't had to use it yet. With luck, I wouldn't need to unpack it at all.

Name _____

# Gather the Clues

**Answer these questions about the passage on page 385.**

1. Where is the narrator? How do you know?

   She is in a wilderness area where there are mountains. I can tell because she

   gathers food in the wilderness and camps near a waterfall. **(3 points)**

   _____

2. Is the narrator stranded or did she choose to be there?
   How can you tell?

   She chose to be there. She seems confident and well-prepared. She talks about

   her expectations, so she thought about the trip beforehand. **(3)**

   _____

3. What time of year do you think it is? Why?

   It is summer or close to summer. There are crickets at night, the days are hot,

   and there are fresh berries, nuts, and lettuce. **(3)**

   _____

4. What do you think the two-way radio might be used for?
   Why do you think this?

   I think it might be used to call for help in an emergency. The narrator says she

   hasn't had to use it yet and hopes that she won't have to. **(3)**

   _____

5. Do you think the narrator has had other experiences in the
   wilderness? Why or why not?

   Yes. She knows how to gather food in the wilderness, catch and smoke fish,

   build a fire, and protect her food from bears. **(3)**

   _____

Assessment Tip: Total **15** Points

Name _____

# Significant Suffixes

| -able, -ible | -ant, -ent |
|---|---|
| edible | defiant |
| irresistible | hesitant |
| climbable | observant |
| indestructible | tolerant |

**You are writing a description of *My Side of the Mountain* for your school's Book Week. You need to liven up your description. Use the words from the box above to complete the sentences.**

Even when he's angry at them, Sam finds the animals on the mountain <u>irresistible **(2 point)**</u> for the funny things they do. Except for Frightful, he is <u>hesitant **(2)**</u> to get too close to them. Sam tries to be <u>tolerant **(2)**</u> of their bad behavior. But when the Baron Weasel gets that <u>defiant **(2)**</u> look in his eye, watch out!

Sam must prepare a winter shelter that is <u>indestructible **(2)**</u>, even in the worst storm. When out walking, Sam must always be <u>observant **(2)**</u> in order to find <u>edible **(2)**</u> food. He looks for trees that are <u>climbable **(2)**</u> so that he can pick the fruit from their high branches.

Name _____

# Words with *-ent, -ant;* *-able, -ible*

The suffixes *-ent* and *-ant* and the suffixes *-able* and *-ible* sound alike but are spelled differently. You have to remember the spellings of these suffixes because they begin with a schwa sound.

/ənt/　　　stud**ent**, merch**ant**

/əbəl/　　suit**able**, poss**ible**

**Write each Spelling Word under its suffix.**
Order of answers for each category may vary.

**-ent**

different **(1 point)**

student **(1)**

resident **(1)**

absent **(1)**

accident **(1)**

**-ant**

merchant **(1)**

vacant **(1)**

servant **(1)**

**-able**

fashionable **(1)**

comfortable **(1)**

suitable **(1)**

profitable **(1)**

valuable **(1)**

honorable **(1)**

reasonable **(1)**

remarkable **(1)**

laughable **(1)**

**-ible**

possible **(1)**

terrible **(1)**

horrible **(1)**

Assessment Tip: Total **20** Points

Name _____

**My Side of the Mountain**

Spelling Words with *-ent, -ant; -able, -ible*

# Spelling Spree

**Finding Words** Each word below is hidden in a Spelling Word. Write the Spelling Word.

1. chant _merchant_ **(1 point)**

2. sent _absent_ **(1)**

3. fit _profitable_ **(1)**

4. side _resident_ **(1)**

5. rent _different_ **(1)**

6. suit _suitable_ **(1)**

7. fort _comfortable_ **(1)**

**Crack the Code** Some Spelling Words have been written in the code below. Use the code to figure out each word. Then write the words correctly.

8. DHAKHIAP

9. URLLSIAP

10. BHMUSRFHIAP

11. WPLLSIAP

12. MWKOPFW

13. MPLDHFW

14. URFRLHIAP

15. YRMMSIAP

8. _valuable_ **(1)**

9. _horrible_ **(1)**

10. _fashionable_ **(1)**

11. _terrible_ **(1)**

12. _student_ **(1)**

13. _servant_ **(1)**

14. _honorable_ **(1)**

15. _possible_ **(1)**

**Spelling Words**

1. fashionable
2. comfortable
3. different
4. suitable
5. merchant
6. profitable
7. student
8. possible
9. resident
10. terrible
11. absent
12. vacant
13. servant
14. valuable
15. accident
16. horrible
17. honorable
18. reasonable
19. remarkable
20. laughable

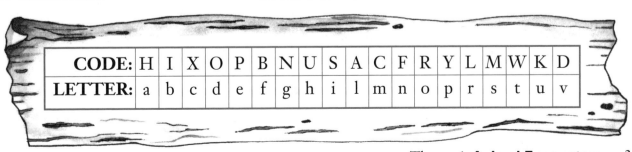

| CODE:   | H | I | X | O | P | B | N | U | S | A | C | F | R | Y | L | M | W | K | D |
|---------|---|---|---|---|---|---|---|---|---|---|---|---|---|---|---|---|---|---|---|
| LETTER: | a | b | c | d | e | f | g | h | i | l | m | n | o | p | r | s | t | u | v |

Theme 6: **Animal Encounters**    389
Assessment Tip: Total **15** Points

Name _____

# Proofreading and Writing

**Proofreading** Circle the five misspelled Spelling Words in this news report. Then write each word correctly.

**Spelling Words**

Finally tonight, (remarkabel) stories continue to filter in. We have learned of a wild boy living on a nearby mountain. Most of the sightings have been near a (vaccant) farm lot. Town leaders are dismissing the claims as (laughible.) Still, as one resident put it, "I don't think it's an (accidant) that these sightings keep coming in. If that many people say they've seen him, there's a (reasenable) chance he's out there."

**Spelling Words**

1. fashionable
2. comfortable
3. different
4. suitable
5. merchant
6. profitable
7. student
8. possible
9. resident
10. terrible
11. absent
12. vacant
13. servant
14. valuable
15. accident
16. horrible
17. honorable
18. reasonable
19. remarkable
20. laughable

1. remarkable **(1 point)**
2. vacant **(1)**
3. laughable **(1)**
4. accident **(1)**
5. reasonable **(1)**

✏️▸ **Write a Character Sketch** Sam Gribley finds food and shelter in the wilderness. He also makes friends with wild animals. What do you think this says about him?

**On a separate piece of paper, write a brief character sketch of Sam. Use Spelling Words from the list.** Responses will vary. **(5)**

Assessment Tip: Total **10** Points

Name _____

# Dictionary Division

**Read the dictionary entries and sentences. On the line after each sentence, write if the underlined part of the sentence is an idiom or run-on entry. If it is an idiom, also write what it means. If it is a run-on entry, also write its part of speech and the main entry word it belongs with.**

> **bold** *adj*. Having no fear; brave. –**boldly** *adv*. –**boldness** *n*.
>
> **clear** *adj*. Free from anything that obscures; transparent. –*idioms*. **clear out**. To leave a place, often quickly. **in the clear**. Free from dangers. –**clearly** *adv*. –**clearness** *n*.
>
> **eye** *n*. An organ of the body through which an animal sees. –*idioms*. **eye to eye**. In agreement. **lay (one's) eyes on**. To see.
>
> **furious** *adj*. 1. Raging. 2. Fierce; violent. –**furiously** *adv*. –**furiousness** *n*.
>
> **soft** *adj*. Smooth or fine to the touch. –**softly** *adv*. –**softness** *n*.
>
> **take** *v*. To carry to another place. –*idioms*. **take care**. To be careful. **take off**. To rise in flight.

1. Sam was sure that Frightful had <u>taken off</u> on a fall migration.
   idiom; risen in flight **(2 points)**

2. In the <u>clearness</u> of the stream Sam could see fish flashing by.
   run-on entry; noun, clear **(2)**

3. As soon as the skunk <u>laid its eyes on</u> Sam, it sprayed.
   idiom; saw **(2)**

4. The squirrels were <u>furiously</u> harvesting nuts.
   run-on entry; adverb, furious **(2)**

5. When Sam shouted, the animals <u>cleared out</u> of his house.
   idiom; left quickly **(2)**

6. Sam kneaded and rubbed the rabbit hides to <u>softness</u>.
   run-on entry; noun, soft **(2)**

Name _____

# I Don't Object to Objects

**Object Pronouns in Prepositional Phrases** Use **object pronouns** as objects in prepositional phrases.

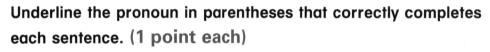

**Object Pronouns**

| Singular | Plural |
|----------|--------|
| me | us |
| you | you |
| him, her, it | them |

**Underline the pronoun in parentheses that correctly completes each sentence. (1 point each)**

1. Randy and his dog Maggie came with (I/<u>me</u>) on my walk up Mt. Hunter.

2. It seemed to (he/<u>him</u>) that we had found an old farmhouse.

3. We imagined the people who once lived here and told stories about (they/<u>them</u>).

4. For (we/<u>us</u>), the old farm was a window into the past.

5. Maggie barked, and we walked toward (she/<u>her</u>).

6. A squirrel in a tree chittered, and Maggie barked at (<u>him</u>/he).

7. More squirrels chattered, and we looked up at (<u>them</u>/they).

8. I guess to (they/<u>them</u>), we were enemies.

9. To (I/<u>me</u>), however, the squirrels were a surprise.

10. We went home. The day had been a success for (we/<u>us</u>).

Assessment Tip: Total **10** Points

Name _____

# Pronoun Pronouncements

**Pronouns in Prepositional Phrases with Compound Objects** Use an object pronoun in a compound object of a preposition. To see whether a pronoun is correct, say the sentence aloud without the other part of the compound.

**Underline the pronoun in parentheses that correctly completes each sentence. (1 point each)**

1. Lois gave a book about bats to Marjorie and (I/<u>me</u>).

2. We called for Todd and then looked for (he/<u>him</u>) and Adam.

3. Todd stood behind Adam and (I/<u>me</u>) as we looked for bats under the eaves.

4. Lois gave a flashlight to Adam and (we/<u>us</u>).

5. Suddenly, a bat flew in the direction of Adam and (she/<u>her</u>)!

6. Would it fly near Todd and (we/<u>us</u>) too?

7. Marjorie wasn't afraid since she had read the book Lois gave to (she/<u>her</u>) and me.

8. I knew that the bat did not care about Todd or (we/<u>us</u>).

9. Lois did not know that the bat would not fly at the boys or (she/<u>her</u>).

10. The bat flew away, and I gave the book to Todd and (she/<u>her</u>).

Theme 6: **Animal Encounters** 393
Assessment Tip: Total **10** Points

Name _____

# Pronouns in Compounds

**Using the Correct Pronoun in a Compound Structure**  Good writers are careful to use subject pronouns in compound subjects. They are also careful to use object pronouns in compound objects of a preposition.

**Underline incorrect compound subjects and objects in the record below. Then on the lines, write each underlined compound correctly.**

June 3, Monday, 4:30 P.M.

    Elizabeth and I walked Princess and Sherlock.  Ann arrived to help us.  <u>Her and Elizabeth</u> took Sherlock, while I took Princess.  Then we met Rick. <u>Him and Ann</u> threw a ball for the dogs.

    We also took care of Lanford the parrot.  Elizabeth asked about <u>he and Jackie</u> the parakeet.  <u>Elizabeth and me</u> are the bird experts.  The birds always have something to say to <u>Elizabeth and I</u>.  Today they squawked, "Feathers not fur! Feathers not fur!"

1. She and Elizabeth **(2 points)**
2. He and Ann **(2)**
3. him and Jackie **(2)**
4. Elizabeth and I **(2)**
5. Elizabeth and me **(2)**

Assessment Tip: Total **10** Points

Name _____

# Essay Question

An **essay question** is a test question that asks for a written answer of one or more paragraphs. You may write about an experience, give a personal opinion about an issue and back it up with reasons and examples, explain a process, or persuade readers to do or think something.

**Circle an essay question that you would like to write about.**

  A. Explain how Sam Gribley built a fireplace inside a tree by trial-and-error and how he learned from his mistakes in the process.

  B. Explain how golden lion tamarins raised in zoos are reintroduced into a wild habitat.

  C. Describe an experience you have had in the wilderness or outdoors in which you learned something about yourself.

**Organize your answer by filling in the planning chart. First, read the essay question carefully, identifying key words that tell you what kind of answer is needed. Next, jot down main ideas and details you might include. Finally, number your ideas, beginning with *1*, to arrange the order in which you will present them.**

| | |
|---|---|
| **Key Words** | A. explain how (give steps or reasons) |
| | B. explain how |
| | C. describe (give details) **(3 points)** |
| **Main Ideas (3)** | |
| **Details (3)** | |

**On a separate sheet of paper, write your answer to the essay question you chose. Begin by restating the question. Then write your main ideas and details in a logical order. (6)**

Name _____

# Placing Prepositional Phrases Correctly

Careful writers check the placement of prepositional phrases in their writing. If prepositional phrases appear in the wrong places in a sentence, they can make a sentence unclear. To avoid confusion, place prepositional phrases as close as possible to the words or phrases that they describe.

**On a boulder** Sam Gribley dried apple slices **in the sun**.

Sam Gribley dried apple slices **on a boulder in the sun**.

**Revise the sentences from Sam Gribley's notes. Make the meaning of each sentence clearer by moving one prepositional phrase as close as possible to the word that it describes. Circle the misplaced prepositional phrase, and then draw an arrow to show where it should go. (2 points each)**

1. I steered my raft down the creek with a long stick to deep pools.

2. In the icy water I drifted with my line for an hour.

3. Suddenly the line jerked from my hand behind the raft. Dinner!

4. I pulled a fish onto the dry logs from the blue water of my raft.

5. Then I pushed near my home the raft to the muddy banks.

6. I sprinkled dried herbs on the fresh fish from a leather pouch.

7. Over a fire I grilled the fish outside my tree for a delicious meal.

Assessment Tip: Total **14** Points

Name _____

# Writing an Opinion Essay

Use what you have learned about taking tests to write an essay that gives your opinion about a topic. This practice will help you when you take this kind of test.

**Many animals in the world are endangered. In *The Golden Lion Tamarin Comes Home*, you learned about the Golden Lion Tamarin Conservation Program and how this animal has been reintroduced to its natural habitat. Write an essay explaining what you think of the efforts of human beings to save endangered animals. Are these efforts important? Is it our responsibility to help these animals?**

ENDANGERED

Answers will vary. **(15 points)**

_____

_____

_____

_____

_____

_____

_____

_____

_____

_____

_____

_____

_____

_____

_____

Name _____

# Writing an Opinion Essay

**continued**

**Read your essay. Check to be sure that**

- each paragraph has a topic sentence that tells the main idea
- your reasons are strong and are supported with details
- your writing sounds like you
- the end of your essay sums up the important points
- there are few mistakes in capitalization, punctuation, grammar, or spelling

**Now pick one way to improve your essay. Make your changes below.**

Answers will vary. **(5)**

_____

_____

_____

_____

_____

_____

_____

_____

_____

_____

_____

_____

_____

_____

_____

**Assessment Tip: Total 20 Points**

Name _____

# Spelling Review

**Write Spelling Words from the list on this page to answer the questions.** Order of answers in each category may vary.

1–12. Which twelve words have the prefix *com-, con-, en-, ex-, pre-,* or *pro-?*

1. enforce **(1 point)**
2. prefix **(1)**
3. condition **(1)**
4. excite **(1)**
5. consist **(1)**
6. enclose **(1)**
7. proverb **(1)**
8. preserve **(1)**
9. complete **(1)**
10. concern **(1)**
11. propose **(1)**
12. continue **(1)**

13–22. Which ten words have the suffixes *-ent, -ant, -able,* or *-ible?*

13. remarkable **(1)**
14. accident **(1)**
15. suitable **(1)**
16. vacant **(1)**
17. fashionable **(1)**
18. resident **(1)**
19. possible **(1)**
20. merchant **(1)**
21. terrible **(1)**
22. laughable **(1)**

23–30. Which eight words have letters missing below? Write each word.

23. emo—— emotion **(1)**
24. sensi—— sensitive **(1)**
25. pota—— potato **(1)**
26. ——ural natural **(1)**
27. ima—— imagine **(1)**
28. ——ous dangerous **(1)**
29. ——ation vacation **(1)**
30. reg—— regular **(1)**

## Spelling Words

1. remarkable
2. emotion
3. accident
4. sensitive
5. enforce
6. potato
7. suitable
8. prefix
9. vacant
10. condition
11. excite
12. consist
13. fashionable
14. enclose
15. natural
16. proverb
17. resident
18. possible
19. imagine
20. preserve
21. complete
22. merchant
23. dangerous
24. concern
25. terrible
26. propose
27. laughable
28. vacation
29. regular
30. continue

Assessment Tip: Total **30** Points

Name _____

# Spelling Spree

**Hint and Hunt** **Write the Spelling Word that best answers each question.**

1. What word could describe lions and mountain climbing?
   dangerous **(1 point)**

2. What word refers to nature? natural **(1)**

3. What vegetable grows in the ground? potato **(1)**

4. What is a short saying that states an idea or truth?
   proverb **(1)**

5. What do you call a person who dresses in the latest styles?
   fashionable **(1)**

6. What do police officers and principals do with rules?
   enforce **(1)** them

7. What word means "strong feeling"?
   emotion **(1)**

8. What is the word for a person who buys and sells things?
   merchant **(1)**

**Contrast Clues** **Write the Spelling Word that means the opposite of the following words.**

9. not *to bore*, but to excite **(1)**

10. not *to destroy*, but to preserve **(1)**

11. not a *suffix*, but a prefix **(1)**

12. not *impossible*, but possible **(1)**

13. not *ordinary*, but remarkable **(1)**

14. not *wonderful*, but terrible **(1)**

15. not *to stop*, but to continue **(1)**

Assessment Tip: Total **15** Points

# Proofreading and Writing

**Proofreading** Circle the six misspelled Spelling Words in this paragraph. Then write each word correctly.

Before we went on (vacashion,) I tried to (imajine) what animals we might see. First we saw a small bird who was a (residunt) of the rain forest. It lived in a (vakant) hollow tree trunk. We thought it might be (sensative) to noise, so we watched quietly. It was (laffable) how it tried to catch a fly.

1. vacation **(1 point)**
2. imagine **(1)**
3. resident **(1)**
4. vacant **(1)**
5. sensitive **(1)**
6. laughable **(1)**

**Spelling Words**

1. imagine
2. vacation
3. resident
4. vacant
5. sensitive
6. laughable
7. consist
8. complete
9. enclose
10. concern
11. propose
12. regular
13. suitable
14. accident
15. condition

**Half Notes** Write Spelling Words to complete these notes.

What does a spider web consist **(1)** of?

If I write down everything I see, my notes will be complete **(1)**.

Should it concern **(1)** me that a snake is sleeping in my tent?

I propose **(1)** that we wake at dawn each day.

At home my regular **(1)** breakfast is cereal, but here I eat powdered eggs. Yuck!

A cold northern region is a suitable **(1)** habitat for a polar bear.

I can't follow the tracks because the condition **(1)** of the footprints is poor.

I squashed a bug by accident **(1)** !

If I can enclose **(1)** these insects in a cage, I can study them.

**Write Ideas** On a separate sheet of paper, write about an animal you would like to study in the wild. Use the Spelling Review Words.

Responses will vary. **(5)**

# Student Handbook

# Contents

# How to Study a Word

## 1. LOOK at the word.
➤ What does the word mean?
➤ What letters are in the word?
➤ Name and touch each letter.

## 2. SAY the word.
➤ Listen for the consonant sounds.
➤ Listen for the vowel sounds.

## 3. THINK about the word.
➤ How is each sound spelled?
➤ Close your eyes and picture the word.
➤ What familiar spelling patterns do you see?
➤ Did you see any prefixes, suffixes, or other word parts?

## 4. WRITE the word.
➤ Think about the sounds and the letters.
➤ Form the letters correctly.

## 5. CHECK the spelling.
➤ Did you spell the word the same way it is spelled in your word list?
➤ If you did not spell the word correctly, write the word again.

# Words Often Misspelled

| | | | | |
|---|---|---|---|---|
| accept | buy | friend | | |
| ache | by | goes | | |
| again | calendar | going | ninth | tried |
| all right | cannot | grammar | often | tries |
| almost | can't | guard | once | truly |
| already | careful | guess | other | two |
| although | catch | guide | people | unknown |
| always | caught | half | principal | until |
| angel | chief | haven't | quiet | unusual |
| angle | children | hear | quit | wasn't |
| | | | | |
| answer | choose | heard | quite | wear |
| argue | chose | heavy | really | weather |
| asked | color | height | receive | Wednesday |
| aunt | cough | here | rhythm | weird |
| author | cousin | hers | right | we'll |
| awful | decide | hole | Saturday | we're |
| babies | divide | hoping | stretch | weren't |
| been | does | hour | surely | we've |
| believe | don't | its | their | where |
| bother | early | it's | theirs | which |
| | | | | |
| bought | enough | January | there | whole |
| break | every | let's | they're | witch |
| breakfast | exact | listen | they've | won't |
| breathe | except | loose | those | wouldn't |
| broken | excite | lose | though | write |
| brother | expect | minute | thought | writing |
| brought | February | muscle | through | written |
| bruise | finally | neighbor | tied | you're |
| build | forty | nickel | tired | yours |
| business | fourth | ninety | to | |
| busy | Friday | ninety-nine | too | |

## Eye of the Storm

**The /ā/, /ē/, and /ī/ Sounds**
- /ā/ → male, claim, stray
- /ē/ → leaf, fleet
- /ī/ → strike, thigh, sign

### Spelling Words
1. speech
2. claim
3. strike
4. stray
5. fade
6. sign
7. leaf
8. thigh
9. thief
10. height
11. mild
12. waist
13. sway
14. beast
15. stain
16. fleet
17. stride
18. praise
19. slight
20. niece

### Challenge Words
1. campaign
2. describe
3. cease
4. sacrifice
5. plight

**My Study List**
Add your own spelling words on the back. →

## Nature's Fury Reading-Writing Workshop

**Look for familiar spelling patterns in these words to help you remember their spellings.**

### Spelling Words
1. enough
2. caught
3. brought
4. thought
5. every
6. ninety
7. their
8. they're
9. there
10. there's
11. know
12. knew
13. o'clock
14. we're
15. people

### Challenge Words
1. decent
2. stationery
3. stationary
4. correspond
5. reversible

**My Study List**
Add your own spelling words on the back. →

## Earthquake Terror

**Short Vowels**
- /ă/ → staff
- /ĕ/ → slept
- /ĭ/ → mist
- /ŏ/ → dock
- /ŭ/ → bunk

### Spelling Words
1. bunk
2. staff
3. dock
4. slept
5. mist
6. bunch
7. swift
8. stuck
9. breath
10. tough
11. fond
12. crush
13. grasp
14. dwell
15. fund
16. ditch
17. split
18. swept
19. deaf
20. rough

### Challenge Words
1. trek
2. frantic
3. summit
4. rustic
5. mascot

**My Study List**
Add your own spelling words on the back. →

## Take-Home Word List

Name _____

 **My Study List**

1. _____
2. _____
3. _____
4. _____
5. _____
6. _____
7. _____
8. _____
9. _____
10. _____

### Review Words

1. trunk
2. skill
3. track
4. fresh
5. odd

### How to Study a Word

**Look** at the word.
**Say** the word.
**Think** about the word.
**Write** the word.
**Check** the spelling.

## Take-Home Word List

Name _____

**My Study List**

1. _____
2. _____
3. _____
4. _____
5. _____
6. _____
7. _____
8. _____
9. _____
10. _____

### How to Study a Word

**Look** at the word.
**Say** the word.
**Think** about the word.
**Write** the word.
**Check** the spelling.

## Take-Home Word List

Name _____

**My Study List**

1. _____
2. _____
3. _____
4. _____
5. _____
6. _____
7. _____
8. _____
9. _____
10. _____

### Review Words

1. free
2. twice
3. gray
4. least
5. safe

### How to Study a Word

**Look** at the word.
**Say** the word.
**Think** about the word.
**Write** the word.
**Check** the spelling.

### Michelle Kwan: Heart of a Champion

**Compound Words**

**wheel + chair =**
  wheelchair

**up + to + date =**
  up-to-date

**first + aid =** first aid

### Spelling Words

1. basketball
2. wheelchair
3. cheerleader
4. newscast
5. weekend
6. everybody
7. up-to-date
8. grandparent
9. first aid
10. wildlife
11. highway
12. daytime
13. whoever
14. test tube
15. turnpike
16. shipyard
17. homemade
18. household
19. salesperson
20. brother-in-law

### Challenge Words

1. extraordinary
2. self-assured
3. quick-witted
4. limelight
5. junior high school

### Nature's Fury Spelling Review

### Spelling Words

1. slept
2. split
3. staff
4. fade
5. praise
6. slope
7. claim
8. stroll
9. mood
10. beast
11. crush
12. fond
13. dwell
14. strike
15. clue
16. boast
17. flute
18. sway
19. cruise
20. mild
21. grasp
22. swift
23. bunk
24. slight
25. thrown
26. stole
27. fleet
28. dew
29. youth
30. thigh

### See the back for Challenge Words.

### Volcanoes

**The /ō/, /o͞o/, and /yo͞o/ Sounds**

/ō/ → stole, boast, thrown, stroll

/o͞o/ or → rule, clue,
/yo͞o/ dew, mood, cruise, route

### Spelling Words

1. thrown
2. stole
3. clue
4. dew
5. choose
6. rule
7. boast
8. cruise
9. stroll
10. route
11. mood
12. loaf
13. growth
14. youth
15. slope
16. bruise
17. loose
18. rude
19. flow
20. flute

### Challenge Words

1. subdue
2. pursuit
3. molten
4. reproach
5. presume

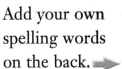

**My Study List**
Add your own spelling words on the back. ➡

**My Study List**
Add your own spelling words on the back. ➡

**My Study List**
Add your own spelling words on the back. ➡

Name _____

 **My Study List**

1. _____
2. _____
3. _____
4. _____
5. _____
6. _____
7. _____
8. _____
9. _____
10. _____

### Review Words

1. group
2. goal
3. fruit
4. blew
5. broke

### How to Study a Word

**Look** at the word.
**Say** the word.
**Think** about the word.
**Write** the word.
**Check** the spelling.

---

Name _____

 **My Study List**

1. _____
2. _____
3. _____
4. _____
5. _____
6. _____
7. _____
8. _____
9. _____
10. _____

### Challenge Words

| | |
|---|---|
| 1. frantic | 6. rustic |
| 2. trek | 7. describe |
| 3. cease | 8. campaign |
| 4. molten | 9. subdue |
| 5. pursuit | 10. reproach |

### How to Study a Word

**Look** at the word.
**Say** the word.
**Think** about the word.
**Write** the word.
**Check** the spelling.

---

Name _____

 **My Study List**

1. _____
2. _____
3. _____
4. _____
5. _____
6. _____
7. _____
8. _____
9. _____
10. _____

### Review Words

1. afternoon
2. ninety-nine
3. everywhere
4. all right
5. breakfast

### How to Study a Word

**Look** at the word.
**Say** the word.
**Think** about the word.
**Write** the word.
**Check** the spelling.

## The Fear Place

The /ôr/, /âr/, and /är/ Sounds

/ôr/ ➡ torch, soar, sore
/âr/ ➡ hare, flair
/är/ ➡ scar

### Spelling Words

1. hare
2. scar
3. torch
4. soar
5. harsh
6. sore
7. lord
8. flair
9. warn
10. floor
11. tore
12. lair
13. snare
14. carve
15. bore
16. fare
17. gorge
18. barge
19. flare
20. rare

### Challenge Words

1. folklore
2. unicorn
3. ordinary
4. marvelous
5. hoard

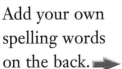

**My Study List**
Add your own spelling words on the back. ➡

## La Bamba

The /ou/, /ô/, and /oi/ Sounds

/ou/ ➡ ounce, tower
/ô/ ➡ claw, pause, bald
/oi/ ➡ moist, loyal

### Spelling Words

1. hawk
2. claw
3. bald
4. tower
5. halt
6. prowl
7. loyal
8. pause
9. moist
10. ounce
11. launch
12. royal
13. scowl
14. haunt
15. noisy
16. coward
17. fawn
18. thousand
19. drown
20. fault

### Challenge Words

1. announce
2. poise
3. loiter
4. somersault
5. awkward

**My Study List**
Add your own spelling words on the back. ➡

## Give It All You've Got!
### Reading-Writing Workshop

Look for familiar spelling patterns in these words to help you remember their spellings.

### Spelling Words

1. would
2. wouldn't
3. clothes
4. happened
5. someone
6. sometimes
7. different
8. another
9. weird
10. eighth
11. coming
12. getting
13. going
14. stopped
15. here

### Challenge Words

1. irresponsible
2. affectionate
3. brilliance
4. audible
5. menace

**My Study List**
Add your own spelling words on the back. ➡

Name _____

 **My Study List**

I. _____
2. _____
3. _____
4. _____
5. _____
6. _____
7. _____
8. _____
9. _____
10. _____

### How to Study a Word

**Look** at the word.
**Say** the word.
**Think** about the word.
**Write** the word.
**Check** the spelling.

412

---

Name _____

 **My Study List**

I. _____
2. _____
3. _____
4. _____
5. _____
6. _____
7. _____
8. _____
9. _____
10. _____

### Review Words

1. proud
2. dawn
3. false
4. cause
5. howl

### How to Study a Word

**Look** at the word.
**Say** the word.
**Think** about the word.
**Write** the word.
**Check** the spelling.

412

---

Name _____

**My Study List**

I. _____
2. _____
3. _____
4. _____
5. _____
6. _____
7. _____
8. _____
9. _____
10. _____

### Review Words

1. horse
2. sharp
3. square
4. stairs
5. board

### How to Study a Word

**Look** at the word.
**Say** the word.
**Think** about the word.
**Write** the word.
**Check** the spelling.

412

## And Then What Happened, Paul Revere?

**Final /ər/**

/ər/ ➝ ang**er**, act**or**
pill**ar**

### Spelling Words

1. theater
2. actor
3. mirror
4. powder
5. humor
6. anger
7. banner
8. pillar
9. major
10. thunder
11. flavor
12. finger
13. mayor
14. polar
15. clover
16. burglar
17. tractor
18. matter
19. lunar
20. quarter

### Challenge Words

1. oyster
2. clamor
3. tremor
4. scholar
5. chamber

**My Study List**
Add your own spelling words on the back. ➡

## Give It All You've Got! Spelling Review

### Spelling Words

1. weekend
2. hawk
3. flair
4. stir
5. first aid
6. halt
7. royal
8. carve
9. worth
10. hurl
11. up-to-date
12. noisy
13. soar
14. barge
15. steer
16. wildlife
17. coward
18. gorge
19. return
20. smear
21. brother-in-law
22. thousand
23. tore
24. early
25. pearl
26. test tube
27. launch
28. snare
29. perch
30. wheelchair

### See the back for Challenge Words.

**My Study List**
Add your own spelling words on the back. ➡

## Mae Jemison

**The /ûr/ and /îr/ Sounds**

/ûr/ ➝ ge**r**m, st**ir**, ret**ur**n, **ear**ly, wo**r**th

/îr/ ➝ p**eer**, sm**ear**

### Spelling Words

1. smear
2. germ
3. return
4. peer
5. stir
6. squirm
7. nerve
8. early
9. worth
10. pier
11. thirst
12. burnt
13. rear
14. term
15. steer
16. pearl
17. squirt
18. perch
19. hurl
20. worse

### Challenge Words

1. interpret
2. yearn
3. emergency
4. dreary
5. career

**My Study List**
Add your own spelling words on the back. ➡

Name _____

 **My Study List**

1. _____
2. _____
3. _____
4. _____
5. _____
6. _____
7. _____
8. _____
9. _____
10. _____

### Review Words

1. learn
2. curve
3. world
4. firm
5. year

### How to Study a Word

**Look** at the word.
**Say** the word.
**Think** about the word.
**Write** the word.
**Check** the spelling.

---

Name _____

 **My Study List**

1. _____
2. _____
3. _____
4. _____
5. _____
6. _____
7. _____
8. _____
9. _____
10. _____

### Challenge Words

1. extra-ordinary
2. announce
3. loiter
4. marvelous
5. yearn
6. self-assured
7. somersault
8. ordinary
9. emergency
10. dreary

### How to Study a Word

**Look** at the word.
**Say** the word.
**Think** about the word.
**Write** the word.
**Check** the spelling.

---

Name _____

 **My Study List**

1. _____
2. _____
3. _____
4. _____
5. _____
6. _____
7. _____
8. _____
9. _____
10. _____

### Review Words

1. enter
2. honor
3. answer
4. collar
5. doctor

### How to Study a Word

**Look** at the word.
**Say** the word.
**Think** about the word.
**Write** the word.
**Check** the spelling.

## Take-Home Word List

### James Forten

**Final /l/ or /əl/**

/l/ or ➡ spar**kle**,
/əl/      jewel, le**gal**

#### Spelling Words

1. jewel
2. sparkle
3. angle
4. shovel
5. single
6. normal
7. angel
8. legal
9. whistle
10. fossil
11. puzzle
12. bushel
13. mortal
14. gentle
15. level
16. label
17. pedal
18. ankle
19. needle
20. devil

#### Challenge Words

1. mineral
2. influential
3. vital
4. neutral
5. kernel

**My Study List**
Add your own spelling words on the back. ➡

## Take-Home Word List

### Katie's Trunk

**VCCV and VCV Patterns**

| VC\|CV | VC\|V | V\|CV |
|--------|-------|-------|
| ar\|rive | val\|ue | tu\|lip |
| par\|lor | clos\|et | a\|ware |
|  |  | be\|have |

#### Spelling Words

1. equal
2. parlor
3. collect
4. closet
5. perhaps
6. wedding
7. rapid
8. value
9. arrive
10. behave
11. shoulder
12. novel
13. tulip
14. sorrow
15. vanish
16. essay
17. publish
18. aware
19. subject
20. prefer

#### Challenge Words

1. device
2. skittish
3. logic
4. sincere
5. nuisance

**My Study List**
Add your own spelling words on the back. ➡

## Take-Home Word List

### Voices of the Revolution
### Reading-Writing Workshop

Look for familiar spelling patterns in these words to help you remember their spellings.

#### Spelling Words

1. happily
2. minute
3. beautiful
4. usually
5. instead
6. stretch
7. lying
8. excite
9. millimeter
10. divide
11. until
12. writing
13. tried
14. before
15. Saturday

#### Challenge Words

1. fatigue
2. antique
3. accumulate
4. camouflage
5. tongue

**My Study List**
Add your own spelling words on the back. ➡

## Take-Home Word List

Name _____

 **My Study List**

1. _____
2. _____
3. _____
4. _____
5. _____
6. _____
7. _____
8. _____
9. _____
10. _____

### How to Study a Word

**Look** at the word.
**Say** the word.
**Think** about the word.
**Write** the word.
**Check** the spelling.

## Take-Home Word List

Name _____

 **My Study List**

1. _____
2. _____
3. _____
4. _____
5. _____
6. _____
7. _____
8. _____
9. _____
10. _____

### Review Words

1. person
2. mistake
3. human
4. bottom
5. stomach

### How to Study a Word

**Look** at the word.
**Say** the word.
**Think** about the word.
**Write** the word.
**Check** the spelling.

## Take-Home Word List

Name _____

 **My Study List**

1. _____
2. _____
3. _____
4. _____
5. _____
6. _____
7. _____
8. _____
9. _____
10. _____

### Review Words

1. simple
2. special
3. metal
4. nickel
5. double

### How to Study a Word

**Look** at the word.
**Say** the word.
**Think** about the word.
**Write** the word.
**Check** the spelling.

### Person to Person
### Reading-Writing
### Workshop

**Look for familiar spelling patterns in these words to help you remember their spellings.**

#### Spelling Words

1. a lot
2. because
3. school
4. its
5. it's
6. tonight
7. might
8. right
9. write
10. again
11. to
12. too
13. two
14. they
15. that's

#### Challenge Words

1. opposite
2. scenery
3. questionnaire
4. excellence
5. pennant

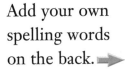

**My Study List**
Add your own spelling words on the back. ➡

### Mariah Keeps Cool

> **VCCCV Pattern**
> VCC|CV:   **laugh|ter**
> VC|CCV:   **com|plain**

#### Spelling Words

1. district
2. address
3. complain
4. explain
5. improve
6. farther
7. simply
8. hundred
9. although
10. laughter
11. mischief
12. complex
13. partner
14. orphan
15. constant
16. dolphin
17. employ
18. sandwich
19. monster
20. orchard

#### Challenge Words

1. control
2. abstain
3. conscience
4. function
5. extreme

**My Study List**
Add your own spelling words on the back. ➡

### Voices of the Revolution
### Spelling Review

#### Spelling Words

1. powder
2. burglar
3. rapid
4. value
5. bushel
6. actor
7. equal
8. publish
9. tractor
10. pedal
11. polar
12. aware
13. matter
14. single
15. sparkle
16. humor
17. behave
18. quarter
19. whistle
20. needle
21. mayor
22. sorrow
23. parlor
24. mortal
25. gentle
26. lunar
27. shoulder
28. jewel
29. legal
30. wedding

**See the back for Challenge Words.**

**My Study List**
Add your own spelling words on the back. ➡

## Take-Home Word List

Name _____

 **My Study List**

1. _____
2. _____
3. _____
4. _____
5. _____
6. _____
7. _____
8. _____
9. _____
10. _____

### Challenge Words

1. oyster    6. device
2. skittish    7. mineral
3. influential    8. vital
4. kernel    9. sincere
5. clamor    10. scholar

### How to Study a Word

**Look** at the word.
**Say** the word.
**Think** about the word.
**Write** the word.
**Check** the spelling.

418

---

# Take-Home Word List

Name _____

 **My Study List**

1. _____
2. _____
3. _____
4. _____
5. _____
6. _____
7. _____
8. _____
9. _____
10. _____

### Review Words

1. empty
2. hungry
3. handsome
4. quickly
5. illness

### How to Study a Word

**Look** at the word.
**Say** the word.
**Think** about the word.
**Write** the word.
**Check** the spelling.

418

---

# Take-Home Word List

Name _____

 **My Study List**

1. _____
2. _____
3. _____
4. _____
5. _____
6. _____
7. _____
8. _____
9. _____
10. _____

### How to Study a Word

**Look** at the word.
**Say** the word.
**Think** about the word.
**Write** the word.
**Check** the spelling.

418

### Dear Mr. Henshaw

**Words with Suffixes**

| | | |
|---|---|---|
| safe + ly | = | safe**ly** |
| pale + ness | = | pale**ness** |
| enjoy + ment | = | enjoy**ment** |
| cheer + ful | = | cheer**ful** |
| speech + less | = | speech**less** |

**Spelling Words**

1. dreadful
2. enjoyment
3. safely
4. watchful
5. speechless
6. paleness
7. breathless
8. government
9. cheerful
10. actively
11. closeness
12. lately
13. goodness
14. retirement
15. forgetful
16. basement
17. softness
18. delightful
19. settlement
20. countless

**Challenge Words**

1. suspenseful
2. suspiciously
3. defenseless
4. seriousness
5. contentment

**My Study List**
Add your own spelling words on the back. ➡

### Yang the Second and Her Secret Admirers

**Words with *-ed* or *-ing***

| | | |
|---|---|---|
| deserve + ed | = | deserv**ed** |
| offer + ed | = | offer**ed** |
| rise + ing | = | ris**ing** |
| direct + ing | = | direct**ing** |

**Spelling Words**

1. covered
2. directing
3. bragging
4. amusing
5. offered
6. planned
7. rising
8. deserved
9. visiting
10. mixed
11. swimming
12. sheltered
13. resulting
14. spotted
15. suffering
16. arrested
17. squeezing
18. ordered
19. decided
20. hitting

**Challenge Words**

1. rehearsing
2. shredded
3. anticipated
4. scalloped
5. entertaining

**My Study List**
Add your own spelling words on the back. ➡

### Mom's Best Friend

**VV Pattern**

V | V
**po | em**
**cre | ate**

**Spelling Words**

1. poem
2. idea
3. create
4. diary
5. area
6. giant
7. usual
8. radio
9. cruel
10. quiet
11. diet
12. liar
13. fuel
14. riot
15. actual
16. lion
17. ruin
18. trial
19. rodeo
20. science

**Challenge Words**

1. appreciate
2. variety
3. enthusiastic
4. realize
5. eventually

**My Study List**
Add your own spelling words on the back. ➡

Name _____

 **My Study List**

1. _____
2. _____
3. _____
4. _____
5. _____
6. _____
7. _____
8. _____
9. _____
10. _____

**Review Words**

1. title
2. listen
3. wrote
4. finish
5. music

**How to Study a Word**

**Look** at the word.
**Say** the word.
**Think** about the word.
**Write** the word.
**Check** the spelling.

Name _____

 **My Study List**

1. _____
2. _____
3. _____
4. _____
5. _____
6. _____
7. _____
8. _____
9. _____
10. _____

**Review Words**

1. dancing
2. flipped
3. dared
4. checking
5. rubbing

**How to Study a Word**

**Look** at the word.
**Say** the word.
**Think** about the word.
**Write** the word.
**Check** the spelling.

Name _____

 **My Study List**

1. _____
2. _____
3. _____
4. _____
5. _____
6. _____
7. _____
8. _____
9. _____
10. _____

**Review Words**

1. fearful
2. movement
3. careless
4. lonely
5. powerful

**How to Study a Word**

**Look** at the word.
**Say** the word.
**Think** about the word.
**Write** the word.
**Check** the spelling.

## One Land, Many Trails
### Reading-Writing Workshop

**Look for familiar spelling patterns in these words to help you remember their spellings.**

### Spelling Words

1. while
2. whole
3. anyway
4. anyone
5. anything
6. favorite
7. once
8. suppose
9. everybody
10. everyone
11. really
12. morning
13. also
14. always
15. first

### Challenge Words

1. embarrass
2. recommend
3. confidence
4. regretted
5. laboratory

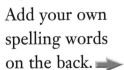

**My Study List**
Add your own spelling words on the back. ➡

---

## A Boy Called Slow

> **Words with a Prefix or a Suffix**
> PREFIX + BASE WORD:
>   **un**able, **dis**cover
> PREFIX + WORD ROOT:
>   **in**spect, **re**port
> VERB + *-ion* = NOUN:
>   react, react**ion**
>   promot**e**, promot**ion**
>   express, express**ion**

### Spelling Words

1. unable
2. discover
3. report
4. disaster
5. unaware
6. remind
7. televise
8. television
9. inspect
10. inspection
11. react
12. reaction
13. tense
14. tension
15. correct
16. correction
17. promote
18. promotion
19. express
20. expression

### Challenge Words

1. inquiry
2. unnecessary
3. responsible
4. except
5. exception

**My Study List**
Add your own spelling words on the back. ➡

---

## Person to Person
### Spelling Review

### Spelling Words

1. laughter
2. sandwich
3. mischief
4. actual
5. offered
6. watchful
7. cruel
8. planned
9. lately
10. countless
11. complain
12. address
13. usual
14. riot
15. amusing
16. ordered
17. diary
18. covered
19. visiting
20. govern- ment
21. improve
22. farther
23. radio
24. fuel
25. hitting
26. goodness
27. decided
28. actively
29. delightful
30. rodeo

**See the back for Challenge Words.**

**My Study List**
Add your own spelling words on the back. ➡

## Take-Home Word List

Name _____

 **My Study List**

1. _____
2. _____
3. _____
4. _____
5. _____
6. _____
7. _____
8. _____
9. _____
10. _____

### Challenge Words

1. control        6. conscience
2. extreme        7. enthusiastic
3. rehearsing     8. suspenseful
4. anticipated    9. entertaining
5. defenseless   10. realize

### How to Study a Word

**Look** at the word.
**Say** the word.
**Think** about the word.
**Write** the word.
**Check** the spelling.

## Take-Home Word List

Name _____

 **My Study List**

1. _____
2. _____
3. _____
4. _____
5. _____
6. _____
7. _____
8. _____
9. _____
10. _____

### Review Words

1. unsure
2. dislike
3. repaint
4. disorder
5. uneven

### How to Study a Word

**Look** at the word.
**Say** the word.
**Think** about the word.
**Write** the word.
**Check** the spelling.

## Take-Home Word List

Name _____

 **My Study List**

1. _____
2. _____
3. _____
4. _____
5. _____
6. _____
7. _____
8. _____
9. _____
10. _____

### How to Study a Word

**Look** at the word.
**Say** the word.
**Think** about the word.
**Write** the word.
**Check** the spelling.

### Elena

**Changing Final _y_ to _i_**

army + es = arm**ies**
dirty + er = dirt**ier**
scary + est = scar**iest**
happy + ness = happi**ness**

### Spelling Words

1. liberties
2. victories
3. countries
4. spied
5. enemies
6. armies
7. scariest
8. dirtier
9. happiness
10. abilities
11. pitied
12. ladies
13. busier
14. duties
15. lilies
16. worthiness
17. tiniest
18. emptiness
19. replies
20. dizziness

### Challenge Words

1. unified
2. levied
3. colonies
4. loveliest
5. strategies

**My Study List**
Add your own spelling words on the back. ➡

---

### Black Cowboy, Wild Horses

**Final /n/ or /ən/, /chər/, /zhər/**

/n/ or /ən/ ➡ capt**ain**
/chər/ ➡ cul**ture**
/zhər/ ➡ trea**sure**

### Spelling Words

1. mountain
2. treasure
3. culture
4. fountain
5. creature
6. captain
7. future
8. adventure
9. moisture
10. surgeon
11. lecture
12. curtain
13. pasture
14. measure
15. vulture
16. feature
17. furniture
18. pleasure
19. mixture
20. luncheon

### Challenge Words

1. departure
2. leisure
3. architecture
4. texture
5. villain

**My Study List**
Add your own spelling words on the back. ➡

---

### Pioneer Girl

**Unstressed Syllables**

voy | age /**voi**´ ĭj/
na | tive /**nā**´ tĭv/
no | tice /**nō**´ tĭs/
dis | tance /**dĭs**´ təns/
for | bid /fər **bĭd**´/
de | stroy /dĭ **stroi**´/

### Spelling Words

1. dozen
2. voyage
3. forbid
4. native
5. language
6. destroy
7. notice
8. distance
9. carrot
10. knowledge
11. captive
12. spinach
13. solid
14. justice
15. ashamed
16. program
17. message
18. respond
19. service
20. relative

### Challenge Words

1. adapt
2. discourage
3. cooperative
4. apprentice
5. somber

**My Study List**
Add your own spelling words on the back. ➡

## Take-Home Word List

Name _____

 **My Study List**

1. _____
2. _____
3. _____
4. _____
5. _____
6. _____
7. _____
8. _____
9. _____
10. _____

### Review Words

1. marriage
2. harvest
3. allow
4. package
5. middle

### How to Study a Word

**Look** at the word.
**Say** the word.
**Think** about the word.
**Write** the word.
**Check** the spelling.

## Take-Home Word List

Name _____

 **My Study List**

1. _____
2. _____
3. _____
4. _____
5. _____
6. _____
7. _____
8. _____
9. _____
10. _____

### Review Words

1. nature
2. picture
3. capture
4. certain

### How to Study a Word

**Look** at the word.
**Say** the word.
**Think** about the word.
**Write** the word.
**Check** the spelling.

## Take-Home Word List

Name _____

 **My Study List**

1. _____
2. _____
3. _____
4. _____
5. _____
6. _____
7. _____
8. _____
9. _____
10. _____

### Review Words

1. cities
2. easier
3. families
4. studied
5. angriest

### How to Study a Word

**Look** at the word.
**Say** the word.
**Think** about the word.
**Write** the word.
**Check** the spelling.

### Animal Encounters
### Reading-Writing
### Workshop

**Look for familiar spelling patterns in these words to help you remember their spellings.**

### Spelling Words

1. heard
2. your
3. you're
4. field
5. buy
6. friend
7. guess
8. cousin
9. build
10. family
11. can't
12. cannot
13. didn't
14. haven't
15. don't

### Challenge Words

1. truly
2. benefited
3. height
4. believe
5. received

**My Study List**
Add your own spelling words on the back. ➡

### Grizzly Bear Family Book

**More Words with Prefixes**

**com**pare **con**vince
**ex**cite **en**force
**pre**serve **pro**pose

### Spelling Words

1. propose
2. convince
3. concern
4. enforce
5. compare
6. excuse
7. conduct
8. preserve
9. contain
10. excite
11. extend
12. prefix
13. engage
14. pronoun
15. consist
16. enclose
17. consent
18. proverb
19. complete
20. exchange

### Challenge Words

1. enactment
2. procedure
3. confront
4. preamble
5. concise

**My Study List**
Add your own spelling words on the back. ➡

### One Land, Many Trails
### Spelling Review

### Spelling Words

1. unable
2. correction
3. native
4. distance
5. spinach
6. vulture
7. curtain
8. dirtier
9. spied
10. treasure
11. discover
12. inspect
13. tension
14. language
15. respond
16. voyage
17. pleasure
18. countries
19. happiness
20. furniture
21. promotion
22. react
23. solid
24. notice
25. destroy
26. mountain
27. adventure
28. busier
29. pitied
30. scariest

### See the back for
### Challenge Words.

**My Study List**
Add your own spelling words on the back. ➡

## Take-Home Word List

Name _____

 **My Study List**

1. _____
2. _____
3. _____
4. _____
5. _____
6. _____
7. _____
8. _____
9. _____
10. _____

### Challenge Words

1. except          6. architecture
2. apprentice    7. colonies
3. loveliest       8. unified
4. strategies     9. villain
5. inquiry        10. discourage

### How to Study a Word

**Look** at the word.
**Say** the word.
**Think** about the word.
**Write** the word.
**Check** the spelling.

## Take-Home Word List

Name _____

**My Study List**

1. _____
2. _____
3. _____
4. _____
5. _____
6. _____
7. _____
8. _____
9. _____
10. _____

### Review Words

1. compose
2. exact
3. enjoy
4. common
5. expert

### How to Study a Word

**Look** at the word.
**Say** the word.
**Think** about the word.
**Write** the word.
**Check** the spelling.

## Take-Home Word List

Name _____

**My Study List**

1. _____
2. _____
3. _____
4. _____
5. _____
6. _____
7. _____
8. _____
9. _____
10. _____

### How to Study a Word

**Look** at the word.
**Say** the word.
**Think** about the word.
**Write** the word.
**Check** the spelling.

### Animal Encounters
### Spelling Review

#### Spelling Words

| | |
|---|---|
| 1. excite | 16. preserve |
| 2. concern | 17. dangerous |
| 3. imagine | 18. vacation |
| 4. continue | 19. terrible |
| 5. enforce | 20. accident |
| 6. propose | 21. complete |
| 7. condition | 22. regular |
| 8. resident | 23. potato |
| 9. possible | 24. laughable |
| 10. fashionable | 25. remarkable |
| 11. consist | 26. proverb |
| 12. prefix | 27. natural |
| 13. sensitive | 28. emotion |
| 14. suitable | 29. merchant |
| 15. vacant | 30. enclose |

### See the back for Challenge Words.

### My Side of the Mountain

**Words with -ent, -ant; -able, -ible**

| /ənt/ | ➡ | student, merchant |
|---|---|---|
| /ə bəl/ | ➡ | suitable, possible |

#### Spelling Words

| | |
|---|---|
| 1. fashionable | 11. absent |
| 2. comfortable | 12. vacant |
| 3. different | 13. servant |
| 4. suitable | 14. valuable |
| 5. merchant | 15. accident |
| 6. profitable | 16. horrible |
| 7. student | 17. honorable |
| 8. possible | 18. reasonable |
| 9. resident | 19. remarkable |
| 10. terrible | 20. laughable |

#### Challenge Words

| | |
|---|---|
| 1. excellent | 4. durable |
| 2. prominent | 5. reversible |
| 3. extravagant | |

### The Golden Lion Tamarin Comes Home

**Three-Syllable Words**

va l ca l tion ➡
/vā kā′ shən/

ed l u l cate ➡
/ĕj′ ə kāt′/

dan l ger l ous ➡
/dān′ jər əs/

e l mo l tion ➡
/ĭ mō′ shən/

#### Spelling Words

| | |
|---|---|
| 1. dangerous | 11. potato |
| 2. history | 12. natural |
| 3. vacation | 13. sensitive |
| 4. popular | 14. energy |
| 5. favorite | 15. emotion |
| 6. memory | 16. period |
| 7. personal | 17. property |
| 8. educate | 18. condition |
| 9. regular | 19. imagine |
| 10. continue | 20. attention |

#### Challenge Words

| | |
|---|---|
| 1. juvenile | 4. amateur |
| 2. astonish | 5. obvious |
| 3. ovation | |

**My Study List**
Add your own spelling words on the back. ➡

**My Study List**
Add your own spelling words on the back. ➡

**My Study List**
Add your own spelling words on the back. ➡

| Take-Home Word List | Take-Home Word List | Take-Home Word List |
|---|---|---|

Name _____ | Name _____ | Name _____

 **My Study List**

1. _____
2. _____
3. _____
4. _____
5. _____
6. _____
7. _____
8. _____
9. _____
10. _____

### Review Words

1. together
2. beautiful
3. library
4. hospital
5. another

 **My Study List**

1. _____
2. _____
3. _____
4. _____
5. _____
6. _____
7. _____
8. _____
9. _____
10. _____

### Review Words

1. current
2. important
3. moment
4. silent
5. parent

 **My Study List**

1. _____
2. _____
3. _____
4. _____
5. _____
6. _____
7. _____
8. _____
9. _____
10. _____

### Challenge Words

1. confront    6. enactment
2. preamble    7. juvenile
3. astonish    8. amateur
4. excellent    9. extravagant
5. reversible   10. durable

### How to Study a Word

**Look** at the word.
**Say** the word.
**Think** about the word.
**Write** the word.
**Check** the spelling.

### How to Study a Word

**Look** at the word.
**Say** the word.
**Think** about the word.
**Write** the word.
**Check** the spelling.

### How to Study a Word

**Look** at the word.
**Say** the word.
**Think** about the word.
**Write** the word.
**Check** the spelling.

# Problem Words

| Words | Rules | Examples |
|-------|-------|----------|
| bad<br><br><br>badly | *Bad* is an adjective. It can be used after linking verbs like *look* and *feel.*<br>*Badly* is an adverb. | This was a <u>bad</u> day.<br>I feel <u>bad</u>.<br><br>I play <u>badly</u>. |
| borrow<br>lend | *Borrow* means "to take."<br>*Lend* means "to give." | You may <u>borrow</u> my pen.<br>I will <u>lend</u> it to you for the day. |
| can<br><br>may | *Can* means "to be able to do something."<br>*May* means "to be allowed or permitted." | Nellie <u>can</u> read quickly.<br><br>May I borrow your book? |
| good<br>well | *Good* is an adjective.<br>*Well* is usually an adverb. It is an adjective only when it refers to health. | The weather looks <u>good</u>.<br>She sings <u>well</u>.<br>Do you feel <u>well</u>? |
| in<br>into | *In* means "located within."<br>*Into* means "movement from the outside to the inside." | Your lunch is <u>in</u> that bag.<br>He jumped <u>into</u> the pool. |
| its<br>it's | *Its* is a possessive pronoun.<br>*It's* is a contraction of *it is.* | The dog wagged <u>its</u> tail.<br><u>It's</u> cold today. |
| let<br>leave | *Let* means "to permit or allow."<br>*Leave* means "to go away from" or "to let remain in place." | Please <u>let</u> me go swimming.<br>I will <u>leave</u> soon.<br><u>Leave</u> it on my desk. |
| lie<br>lay | *Lie* means "to rest or recline."<br>*Lay* means "to put or place something." | The dog <u>lies</u> in its bed.<br>Please <u>lay</u> the books there. |

# Problem Words continued

| Words | Rules | Examples |
|-------|-------|----------|
| sit<br><br>set | *Sit* means "to rest in one place."<br>*Set* means "to place or put." | Please <u>sit</u> in this chair.<br><br><u>Set</u> the vase on the table. |
| teach<br><br>learn | *Teach* means "to give instruction."<br>*Learn* means "to receive instruction." | He <u>teaches</u> us how to dance.<br><br>I <u>learned</u> about history. |
| their<br>there<br><br>they're | *Their* is a possessive pronoun.<br>*There* is an adverb. It may also begin a sentence.<br>*They're* is a contraction of *they are*. | <u>Their</u> coats are on the bed.<br>Is Carlos <u>there</u>?<br><u>There</u> is my book.<br><u>They're</u> going to the store. |
| two<br>to<br>too | *Two* is a number.<br>*To* means "in the direction of."<br>*Too* means "more than enough" and "also." | I bought <u>two</u> shirts.<br>A squirrel ran <u>to</u> the tree.<br>May we go <u>too</u>? |
| whose<br>who's | *Whose* is a possessive pronoun.<br>*Who's* is a contraction for *who is*. | <u>Whose</u> tickets are these?<br><u>Who's</u> that woman? |
| your<br>you're | *Your* is a possessive pronoun.<br>*You're* is a contraction for *you are*. | Are these <u>your</u> glasses?<br><u>You're</u> late again! |

**Read each question below. Then check your paper. Correct any mistakes you find. After you have corrected them, put a check mark in the box next to the question.**

- [ ] 1. Did I spell all the words correctly?
- [ ] 2. Did I indent each paragraph?
- [ ] 3. Does each sentence state a complete thought?
- [ ] 4. Are there any run-on sentences or fragments?
- [ ] 5. Did I begin each sentence with a capital letter?
- [ ] 6. Did I capitalize all proper nouns?
- [ ] 7. Did I end each sentence with the correct end mark?
- [ ] 8. Did I use commas, apostrophes, and quotation marks correctly?

**Are there other problem areas you should watch for? Make your own proofreading checklist.**

- [ ] _____
- [ ] _____
- [ ] _____
- [ ] _____
- [ ] _____
- [ ] _____
- [ ] _____

# Proofreading Marks

| Mark | Explanation | Examples |
|------|-------------|----------|
| ¶ | Begin a new paragraph. Indent the paragraph. | ¶The space shuttle landed safely after its five-day voyage. It glided to a smooth, perfect halt. |
| ∧ | Add letters, words, or sentences. | My friend eats lunch with me evry day. |
| ∧ (comma) | Add a comma. | Carlton my Siamese cat has a mind of his own. |
| ⟨⟨ ⟩⟩ | Add quotation marks. | Where do you want us to put the piano? asked the gasping movers. |
| ⊙ | Add a period. | Don't forget to put a period at the end of every statement⊙ |
| ℘ | Take out words, sentences, and punctuation marks. Correct spelling. | We looked at and admired the model airaplanes. |
| / | Change a capital letter to a small letter. | We are studying about the Louisiana Purchase in History class. |
| ≡ | Change a small letter to a capital letter. | The Nile river in africa is the longest river in the world. |
| ∼ | Reverse letters or words. | To complete the task successfully, you must follow carefully the steps. |